THE POWERS OF DIGNITY

THE POWERS
OF DIGNITY

≈

The Black Political Philosophy

of Frederick Douglass

NICK BROMELL

DUKE UNIVERSITY PRESS   *Durham and London*   2021

© 2021 Duke University Press
All rights reserved
Printed in the United States of America on
acid-free paper ∞
Designed by Matthew Tauch
Typeset in Quadraat Pro by Copperline Book Services

Library of Congress Cataloging-in-Publication Data
Names: Bromell, Nicholas Knowles, author.
Title: The powers of dignity : the black political philosophy
of Frederick Douglass / Nick Bromell.
Description: Durham : Duke University Press, 2021. |
Includes bibliographical references and index.
Identifiers: LCCN 2020024547 (print)
LCCN 2020024548 (ebook)
ISBN 9781478010227 (hardcover)
ISBN 9781478011262 (paperback)
ISBN 9781478012801 (ebook)
Subjects: LCSH: Douglass, Frederick, 1818–1895—Political
and social views. | Douglass, Frederick, 1818–1895—
Philosophy. | African American abolitionists. | Antislavery
movements—United States—History—19th century. |
United States—Race relations—History—19th century.
Classification: LCC E449.D75 B766 2021 (print) |
LCC E449.D75 (ebook) | DDC 973.8092—dc23
LC record available at https://lccn.loc.gov/2020024547
LC ebook record available at https://lccn.loc.gov/2020024548

Cover art: Photographer unknown, *Frederick Douglass
in His Study at Cedar Hill*, ca. 1890. Paper, 19.6 x 24.5 cm.
FRDO3886, U.S. National Park Service, Frederick
Douglass National Historic Site, Washington, D.C.

IN MEMORY OF JOHN LEWIS

AND TO ALL READERS OF FREDERICK DOUGLASS

PAST, PRESENT, AND TO COME

From this little bit of experience—slave experience—I have
elaborated quite a lengthy chapter of political philosophy,
applicable to the American people.

FREDERICK DOUGLASS,
"Sources of Danger to the Republic" (1867)

≈

Confronted with the master's outrageous effort to deny him all
dignity, the slave even more than the master came to know and
to desire passionately this very attribute. For dignity, like love, is
one of those human qualities that are most intensely felt and
understood when they are absent—or unrequited.

ORLANDO PATTERSON, *Slavery and Social Death:
A Comparative Study* (1982)

≈

For people of color have always theorized—but in forms quite
different from the Western form of abstract logic. And I am
inclined to say that our theorizing (and I intentionally use the
verb rather than the noun) is often in narrative forms, in the
stories we create, in riddles and proverbs, in the play with
language, since dynamic rather than fixed ideas seem more
to our liking. How else have we managed to survive with such
spiritedness the assault on our bodies, social institutions,
countries, our very humanity?

BARBARA CHRISTIAN, "The Race for Theory" (1987)

≈

CONTENTS

ACKNOWLEDGMENTS

This book draws upon an impressive body of earlier scholarship. Like all who study Frederick Douglass, I am deeply indebted to Benjamin Quarles, Philip S. Foner, John W. Blassingame, and John R. McKivigan for their pioneering work in editing and making available Douglass's voluminous writings. And like all who study Black American political thought, I am deeply indebted to Leonard Harris's pioneering collection, *Philosophy Born of Struggle*. As well, I have leaned heavily on intellectual histories of Douglass's thought by Waldo E. Martin Jr. and David Blight, and on biographies of Douglass by Blight, Benjamin Quarles, William McFeely, and Dickson J. Preston.

Over the past thirty years, the field of nineteenth-century African American literary studies has produced an extraordinary corpus of scholarship on Douglass and many other Black American writers of that time. Like all who work in this field today, I owe everything to those who created it, especially (in my case) Houston Baker, Henry Louis Gates Jr., and Robert Stepto; these scholars emphasized, in both word and deed, the importance of approaching Black cultural production through what Gates called a "black hermeneutic" instead of assuming that the interpretive methods and interests developed through the study of white artists would suffice. With respect to Douglass's autobiographies specifically, I have learned most from work by William A. Andrews, Eric J. Sundquist, Robert S. Levine, and John Stauffer. Their example has guided me to give historical texture to a book that addresses questions raised primarily in the field of political theory, and their scholarship continuously reminds us that Douglass's writings are not a transparent window into his thought, but rather his complex engagement with his historical moment, a self-representation that mounts a continuing, adaptive, and disruptive intervention in that period's field of representations.

Not surprisingly, Douglass's political thought has received its most intensive examination in the fields of philosophy and political theory. Peter C. Myers and Nick Buccola have argued that it closely resembles John Locke's natural rights liberalism, and Robert Gooding-Williams has suggested that it can be helpfully illuminated using Phillip Pettit's conception of freedom as nondomination. Philosopher Bernard Boxill was the first to perceive and explore—in richly various ways—Douglass's abiding interest in human dignity, and Frank Kirkland has made a strong case for the ways Douglass's ethical thinking is Kantian in spirit. I have learned a great deal from these and other scholars who have studied Douglass's political thought, and my own work draws often upon theirs. My aim, however, has been somewhat different. I do not try to determine where Douglass stands in the multiple traditions of Black, continental, and American political thought. Instead, I try to get to the bottom of what he meant when he claimed to have elaborated a political philosophy from his experience of enslavement. This path of inquiry was first opened up by Angela Y. Davis, and subsequently, it has been further illumined by Neil Roberts. Philosopher George Yancy has insisted for decades that Douglass was a *Black* thinker, shaped by the distinctive historical experience of Black Americans. I am grateful to these scholars for showing the way.

I would also like to thank the John Simon Guggenheim Foundation and the Charles Warren Center at Harvard University for fellowships that enabled me to bring this book to completion. Led by Brandon Terry and Kirsten Weld, the seminar at the Warren Center helped me bring depth and precision to my still inchoate thoughts about Douglass's political thought. This is also the place to acknowledge the individuals who wrote generous letters supporting my applications for those fellowships: they know who they are, and I thank them, deeply. Thanks, too, to Lewis Gordon, Jane Gordon, and their colleagues at the University of Connecticut for giving me a chance to share my work there, and to Neil Roberts for inviting me to participate in a superb and very helpful seminar he convened at Williams College in the spring of 2019. I am very thankful also for all that I have learned from the uniquely congenial group of scholars who, with the supportive participation of George Shulman and Cristina Beltrán, convene the Democratic Vistas Seminar annually at New York University.

Early versions of parts of this book have appeared in a number of journals and edited collections: the *American Scholar*, *American Literary History*, *Political Theory*, *Critical Philosophy of Race*, and *A Political Companion to Frederick Douglass*. I am grateful to their publishers and their editors for encouraging my work and allowing some of it to reappear, though usually in quite different form, in this volume. Here I want to single out in particular Gordon Hutner, editor of *American Literary History*, for his extraordinarily astute and generous help in making my political theory interests more legible to the field of literary studies.

Over the years, I have had many opportunities to think about Douglass with students. I am especially grateful to a number of graduate students with whom I have been lucky to work closely on Douglass and on African American political thought, including Marissa Carrere, Samantha Davis, Sean Gordon, Casey Hayman, Maria Ishikawa, Daniel Joslyn, Leslie Leonard, Russell Nurick, and Nirmala Iswari Vasigaren. For their continuing and generous support, I am grateful also to the Department of English at the University of Massachusetts, Amherst and its chair, Randall Knoper, and to Julie Hayes, dean of the College of the Humanities and Fine Arts.

Finally, I send my thanks to the many friends, relatives, and colleagues who have read portions of and talked with me about this project during the many years I have been working on it. Your kindness has sustained me. I want to thank also my teachers, especially Narayan Liebenson, George Mumford, and Matthew Hepburn, for guiding me step-by-step along the way. Above all, my immediate family, with its recent additions of my daughter-in-law Claire Chester and my granddaughter Celine Sahara, has reminded me again and again that what matters most in life is love. I hope that their spirit is in this book.

"The Thing Looked Absurd"

The Black in Douglass's Political Philosophy

On April 20, 1847, Frederick Douglass returned to the United States from an eighteen-month abolitionist speaking tour in Britain. He had fled there in 1845 fearing that his master Thomas Auld might send agents into New England to recapture him after the publication of his best-selling *Narrative of the Life of Frederick Douglass, an American Slave*, which had made his whereabouts widely known. Now, at the age of twenty-nine, he was legally a free man because his English supporters had purchased him from Auld and then formally freed him. Now, he was also a celebrated international figure who had addressed enormous crowds in Ireland, Scotland, and England. And now, he had ambitious new plans for himself: he aimed to found and edit a newspaper addressed primarily to free Black readers living in the North. Revisiting his decision to found the *North Star* in *My Bondage and My Freedom* (his second version of his autobiography, published in 1855), he explained his primary motive: he had believed that "a tolerably well conducted press, in the hands of persons of the despised race, by . . . *making them acquainted with their own latent powers* [and] by enkindling among them the hope that for them there is a future . . . would prove a most powerful means of removing prejudice, and of awakening an interest in them."[1] Somewhat to his surprise, however, when he arrived in Boston and shared his plan with colleagues in William Lloyd Garrison's Massachusetts Anti-Slavery Society, they were skeptical. "My American friends looked at me with astonishment!" Douglass recalls. "'A wood-sawyer' offering himself up to the public as an editor! A slave, brought up in the very depths of ignorance, assuming to instruct the highly civilized people of the north in the principles of liberty, justice, and humanity! The thing looked absurd" (390).

To his "American friends," Douglass's plan to become a public philosopher engaged with the political challenges facing both free Black and white Americans seemed "absurd"—and in a sense it was. It preposterously reversed a worldview that had come to feel natural to them: they assumed that only free persons can know what freedom is; that only those who think freely know what thought is; that only those who take for granted that they are subjects gazing on a world of objects know what knowledge is. Reading Douglass's recollections of his friends' reactions to his plan reminds us that, as philosopher Charles Mills has observed: "Insofar as . . . persons are conceived of as having their personhood uncontested, insofar as their culture and cognition are unhesitatingly respected, insofar as their moral prescriptions take for granted an already achieved citizenship and a history of freedom—insofar, that is, as race is not an issue for them, then they are already tacitly positioned as white persons, culturally and cognitively European, racially privileged members of the West."[2] Did Douglass aim to expose the unconscious workings of this white logic in his friends when, ironically mimicking their reaction, he described his ambitions as "absurd"? I think so.

What is certain is that when he founded the *North Star*, he aimed both to encourage his Black readers to be more conscious of their "latent powers" *and* to "instruct" all the American people in the "principles" of their democracy. What linked these two objectives? The short answer, as we shall see, was *white racism*. The longer answer, as I hope to show, was the distinctive political philosophy he had begun to work out as a response to racism. As he would claim himself some twenty years later: "From this little bit of experience—slave experience—I have elaborated quite a lengthy chapter of political philosophy, applicable to the American people."[3] In the book that follows, I have tried to bring into view this particular "chapter" of Douglass's political thought—that is, the part of it that originated in his experience of enslavement, that he honed through his labors as a Black public intellectual, and that he used to promote Black political solidarity, to contest white racism, and to transform the nation's understanding of democracy and democratic citizenship.

The Centrality of Human Powers

It is already well known that Douglass was a political thinker. Seeking to describe and explain his political thought, most scholars have argued that it belongs in one or more of the traditions of political thought he would have encountered after escaping enslavement. Historian Philip Foner, for one, has argued that Douglass and other Black intellectuals of his time identified strongly with "the republican traditions of the eighteenth century, particularly as expressed in the Declaration of Independence and the Constitution."[4] Robert Gooding-Williams has also placed Douglass in the tradition of republican political thought, whereas Peter C. Myers and Nick Buccola have marshaled an impressive quantity of evidence to argue that Douglass is best understood as a natural rights liberal. More recently, literary scholar Maurice Lee has persuasively demonstrated Douglass's indebtedness to Scottish Common Sense philosophers, while Douglas Jones has made a very strong case for Ralph Waldo Emerson's influence on him.[5] All of these readings of Douglass's political thought are historically informed and cogently argued; indeed, their findings—if taken as a partial and not a comprehensive account of his thought—are virtually incontrovertible.[6] However, my own focus is on the aspects of Douglass's political philosophy that he traced back to his "slave experience."[7] This dimension *cannot* be assimilated to these traditions but, rather, evades, supplements, or challenges them. And just here a less familiar Douglass becomes visible.

This Douglass did not begin his philosophical thinking, as philosopher George Yancy emphasizes, "with the abstract Cartesian 'I think,' but with a rich description of subjectivity whose historicity was linked to the Middle Passage and shaped by a racist discursive vortex."[8] A close look at that "rich description" reveals that the key word in his political lexicon is "powers," and that an attunement to power is what most markedly distinguishes his "chapter" of political philosophy from the prevailing currents of political theorizing in his time. This should not be surprising. "The slave has all his life been learning the power of his master" (352), he observed in *My Bondage and My Freedom*, and he had that power of oppressors in mind when he declared, so famously, that "power concedes nothing without a demand. It never did, and it never will."[9] What the master's power aimed for, Douglass had come to believe, was the utter submission of the enslaved through the destruction or appropriation of their own powers. As he pointed out in an 1847 speech he delivered in England: "The slave had no power to alter his relation—no assent or dissent to give in the matter—no voice in his own destiny. His mind, as a mental, moral, and responsible being, was blotted out from existence; he was cut off from his race; dragged down from the high elevation where God had placed him—'a little lower than the angels'—and ranked with the beasts of the field. All his powers were in the hands of another."[10]

Yet this speech somewhat overstates the case and misrepresents the totality of his thought, for Douglass more frequently asserted that the resilient powers of the enslaved never could be entirely "blotted out from existence." As he insisted in an 1851 speech: "Dark as is the lot of the slave yet he knows he is not a beast, but is as truly a man as his master. Nothing can make the slave think that he is a beast; he feels the instincts of manhood within him at all times, and consequently there is a perpetual war going on between the master and slave, and to keep the slave down the whip and fetters are absolutely necessary."[11] From his personal experience of this "war" between master and slave, Douglass elaborated a political philosophy that had *power* at its core—the power of the slave master as he sought to disempower the enslaved, and the powers of the enslaved as they struggled to resist. These powers of the enslaved were not granted by law or custom. Rather, as he would argue, they were lodged in the very *being* of the enslaved as human beings. Indeed, Douglass came to believe that these powers constitute the very humanness of all humans and make possible their development of their human worth, or human dignity. And so, as we shall see, while he used the conventional language of natural rights philosophy to assert that "the great truth of man's right to liberty entered into the very idea of man's creation," he interjected his own distinctive philosophy when he added that "man's right to liberty is written upon all the powers and faculties of man."[12] We cannot understand Douglass's thinking about Black politics, democracy, and citizenship until we see how his concern with power permeates all of these.

Angela Y. Davis was the first to point out that Douglass's work offers a radical analysis of the concept of freedom, one that reveals that while "the slave is actually conscious of the fact that freedom is not a fact, . . . is not a given, but rather something to be fought for, . . . [t]he slave master . . . experiences his freedom as inalienable and thus as a fact: he is not aware that he too has been enslaved by his own system."[13] Political theorist Neil Roberts has further explored Douglass's distinctive political philosophy by arguing that he developed a notion of "comparative freedom," one that is cognizant of freedom's contingency and limitations.[14] Building on these profound insights, I would suggest further that Douglass sometimes aimed to show his white readers that their freedom, too—not just the freedom of the slave master and the enslaved—was far less absolute and given than they supposed. The problem was not just that they were "enslaved by their own system" (though that was sometimes the case), but that their freedom was not a settled question and never would be. Like Black Americans, then, they must be prepared to wage an endless struggle to establish and maintain it, for themselves individually and for all other citizens. In short, Douglass's theory of democratic citizenship insists that freedom is never secure for anyone. Because those with more power will inevitably seek to limit or even destroy it, we always have a "duty to perform"—that of exercising our powers and thereby preserving our freedom and our democracy. Along with many other antebellum Black writers, as literary historian Derrick Spires has shown, Douglass believed that "citizenship . . . is not a thing determined by who one is but rather by what one does."[15]

White Racism, Black Politics, and the Need for a New Public Philosophy

By the early 1850s if not sooner, Douglass had concluded that in order to defeat both the slavery system and the anti-Black racism that was its "foundation," both Black and white Americans would have to radically revise their understanding of democracy and democratic citizenship.[16] As political theorist Juliet Hooker has argued, he "was committed to working toward the refoundation of the U.S. polity on more egalitarian terms; he envisioned its radical transformation based on an expansive notion of multiraciality that would decenter whiteness."[17] Such a refoundation was necessary because the nation's public philosophy was manifestly unable to remedy three intertwined, mutually reinforcing problems: it did not explain why Black Americans (or any Americans, for that matter) were entitled to full membership in a democratic polity; it did not provide a convincing account of why individual citizens join together to form a political community in the first place; and it did not encourage citizens to take action against injustice either on their own behalf or in defense of other citizens.[18]

All these shortcomings can be seen within the Declaration's famous assertion that "all men are created equal, endowed by their Creator with certain inalienable Rights," including the rights to life, liberty, and the pursuit of happiness.[19] First, it offers no substantive conception of "man" beyond the assertion that he is "endowed" with rights. Such vagueness works well until some members of a nation are deemed not to be men; then, when they claim their rights, they are put in the position of first having to establish that they are men—but what is a "man"? The nation's public philosophy did not say—and still does not say— probably because Thomas Jefferson and the other founders, all of them white, could simply take their status as humans for granted. And that complacence, as Charles Mills observes, is the very essence of white privilege. Similarly, the Declaration does not explain or even hint why any humans are worthy of the rights with which they are endowed. What is it about man, as a species of being, that makes plausible the belief that every man is entitled to certain rights? Without an answer to that question made explicit in the nation's public philosophy, all new claimants to those rights lacked—and still lack—an adequate philosophical basis on which to establish that they, too, are worthy of them.

The Declaration's second shortcoming is that it offers no broad, affective basis on which citizens might build and sustain a political community. In answer to the question of what binds individuals into a democratic polity, natural rights liberalism names only "self-interest." But the pursuit of individual self-interest, or "happiness," cannot provide the feelings of mutual belonging and solidarity required to create and sustain a self-governing community. Consequently, citizens may be disposed to turn to supplementary sources of political and social solidarity, such as nationalism, race, and gender. This is arguably the case today, and it was certainly true in the antebellum period, when native-born white men claimed increasingly that they were the only legitimate possessors of democratic political rights in the United States. Finally, the third flaw in the nation's public philosophy was that it imagined citizenship as a status, and the citizen as a passive holder of rights. Although the belief that democratic rights are "endowed," not won, provides a broad theoretical basis for universal democratic citizenship, it implies that these rights are real and secure until a tyrant tries to take them away. But Douglass and many other Black political thinkers of his time saw that such a view of citizenship and rights tends to make citizens quiescent in the face of more subtle forms of oppression and indifferent, or even resistant, to the arguments made by new claimants to democratic rights.

Perceiving all these shortcomings in the nation's understanding of democracy and citizenship, Douglass believed that as a Black activist intellectual he would have to do more than assail and defeat the slavery system; he would also have to develop and promote a radically new interpretation of America's public philosophy. For this reason, his well-known turn to political abolitionism in the early 1850s marks not just his recognition that abolitionists should employ political means to overthrow slavery. It reflects as well his intuition—rapidly becoming a conviction—that abolitionists would have to devise a new political philosophy, one that could fight more effectively against the menace of anti-Black racism.[20] He knew, of course, that such a philosophy would have to draw often and enthusiastically upon Americans' traditional public philosophy—a hybrid of natural-rights liberalism, republicanism, and Scottish philosophy. This was, after all, the only political lexicon that most Americans understood and endorsed, and he would have to speak their language. But he realized, too, that he would have to supplement that language, or inflect it, so as to render it more competent to redress the failings of a racist slaveholding polity.[21] Where might he—and Americans—find such a transformative supplement? The answer already lay at hand: for it was his experience of enslavement, and his perspective as a raced other, that had first spurred him to perceive the flaws not just in the nation's comportment but in the public philosophy through which it imagined and constructed its political subjects and community. These origins in his experience are precisely what makes Douglass's "chapter" of political philosophy a Black political philosophy, even though he thought it "applicable" not just to Black political struggle but to the entire U.S. polity.[22]

Early in his career, and increasingly as he committed himself to philosophizing, Douglass saw that he would have to do much more than present his political ideas for public inspection and adoption. Because he spoke to white audiences as a person of African descent, and one whose political insights emerged in large part from Black experience, he could not even be heard by many of them; indeed, he could not be seen by many as a being who could legitimately address them, and so he was frequently put in the absurd position of having to establish his credentials as a fully human person before he could begin his actual discourse. As well, because he knew firsthand the brutalities of the Southern bondage system, and because he insisted that virtually all white citizens of the United States benefited from that system, he was the bearer of bad news that most white Americans did not want to hear. Most were just as invested in white innocence as the readers whom James Baldwin aimed to disabuse in the 1960s. Consequently, every time Douglass spoke or wrote, he did so knowing that the language he had at his disposal might work against expressing what was most radical and unsettling in his thought. This is why his thinking is frequently marked by seeming contradiction, inconsistency, indeterminacy, and paradox. Instead of viewing these qualities suspiciously as mistakes, however, we should welcome and investigate them as clues. They are indications of the energy of his intellectual aspirations, and they mark the seams along which those aspirations collided with the world—physical, linguistic, conceptual—into which he was thrown.

In order to communicate his philosophy to his audiences (Black and white), Douglass had to craft a distinctive rhetorical style. But "style" can be a misleading term here unless we understand that it did more than just ornament his thinking, or package it. At a deeper level, his style also *structured* his thinking. Its key elements were irony, awareness of what we now call "standpoint," a rhetorical move I will call "reversal" or "chiasmus," and a visceral antipathy to categorical divisions of all kinds. One of his favorite techniques, combining standpoint awareness, irony, and chiasmus, was to reverse the field of vision, so that the object seen becomes the subject who sees. In his incisive 1881 essay on color prejudice, for example, he recalls: "A good but simple-minded Abolitionist said to me that he was not ashamed to walk with me down Broadway arm-in arm, in open daylight, and evidently thought he was saying something that must be very pleasing to my self importance, but it occurred to me, at the moment, that this man does not dream of any reason why I might be ashamed to walk arm-in-arm with him through Broadway in open daylight."[23] The structure of this anecdote is itself a chiasmic reversal: it pivots on his phrase "but it occurred to me" and then proceeds to show how the world looks through the opposite end of the telescope. To the mind of one who had experienced both enslavement and freedom, and who could move fluidly from one standpoint to another, how "simple-minded" were all those Americans who did not know that they saw things from a particular standpoint—and how in need of "instruction" in the "principles of liberty, justice, and humanity."

This Douglass—a self-consciously Black political philosopher concerned with both the problems of Black politics and the need to transform the racist white American polity—will seem both familiar and strange to many of my readers. Consider, for example, the light he sheds on the slavery system and the experience of enslavement. On the one hand, he confirms much that is already established: that the slavery system sought to dehumanize the enslaved, not just deprive them of freedom; that it both denied and recognized the humanity of its slaves; that individual slaveholders both enjoyed personal relationships with the enslaved and used those relationships as instruments of their own power and domination; and that the enslaved resisted their enslavement in countless small ways, and also in more frequent acts of overt and defiant rebellion than the historical record has readily admitted. At the same time, my account of Douglass's distinctive political philosophy reveals also that the experience of enslavement fostered a commonsense adoption of what we now call "standpoint epistemology"; it also promoted the development of a disposition that held all persons to be inextricably interconnected, so that no matter how much a slaveholder might strive to distance himself from the beings he had enslaved, he could not do so without distancing himself also from his own human nature. The more we attend to these aspects of Douglass's thought, the more clearly we will see that he was a far more feminist thinker, both by his day's standards and ours, than we have perceived heretofore.

Douglass's writings suggest further that while the enslaved perceived how profoundly the slavery system's culture and ideology shaped the world they lived in, they did not therefore conclude that *everything* is a cultural construct; instead, as his famous description of their singing indicates, they held both these realms in tension with one another. As we shall see, all of these dispositions—so at odds with the prevailing temperament Douglass found in the North when he escaped to freedom—critically shaped the intellect that would later claim to have elaborated a chapter of political philosophy from his experience of enslavement.[24] But they also contributed to the challenges he faced later when he tried to convey that philosophy to his audiences. Those challenges rise again to confront anyone who attempts to convey that philosophy today. Thus, even as I employ words like "Black" and "feminist" in this summary account of Douglass's thought, I must emphasize that these terms do no more than gesture toward its contours. Like the labels "republican," "liberal," "nationalist," and "assimilationist," they describe it only imperfectly. To name how his political thought both evokes and evades these and other such categories, I have turned to yet another familiar term: "fugitive." Douglass's political thought is indeed a *fugitive* mode of political thinking—but, here again, not always in the senses of that term most prevalent today.[25]

For a second preview of the ways my account of Douglass's political philosophy will be both familiar and strange, consider also how the words "humanity" and "dignity" have been used as descriptors of his thought. Historian David Blight, for example, has observed that "for black Americans, the [Civil] war took on the deepest possible meaning: it was both an end and a new beginning of a long struggle to achieve freedom and dignity out of oppression."[26] Political scientist Michael Dawson, who identifies Douglass as a "black radical egalitarian liberal," posits that Black liberals "argue for the . . . recognition of the humanity and dignity of all individuals within a political community."[27] Orlando Patterson writes, "Confronted with the master's outrageous effort to deny him all dignity, the slave even more than the master came to know and to desire passionately this very attribute."[28] Waldo Martin refers often to Douglass's "egalitarian humanism" and observes that Douglass "understood his people's need for dignity and self-respect."[29] Literary historian Douglas Jones observes that "Douglass . . . broadens the political significance of American Transcendentalism, beckoning us to 'throw off sleep' and 'awaken' to the ways in which racial difference shrouds our perception of the other's dignity and divinity."[30] As all these examples suggest, we have long been accustomed to suppose that Douglass's political thought valued humanity and dignity. But have we often enough paused to ask what Douglass *meant* when he spoke of "humanity" and "dignity?" For that matter, have we often enough asked what *we* mean by them? Many of my readers will be familiar with Douglass's famous claim, in *My Bondage and My Freedom*, that "a man without force is without the essential dignity of humanity" (286). They might also know his claim that "next to the dignity of being a free man, is the dignity of striving to be free"; and they might even be aware of his frequent references to the "unity and dignity of the human family."[31] But as I hope this book will show, we have not yet sufficiently investigated and unpacked the meaning of these formulations, much less followed the path that Douglass's deep interest in dignity and humanity indicates.[32] Yet these two concerns, along with his abiding preoccupation with power, constitute the core of the political philosophy he elaborated from his experience of enslavement.

I came to Douglass's political philosophy as a literary historian steeped in the interests and methods of nineteenth-century U.S. literary and cultural studies who had swerved into and become fascinated by the field of political theory. Not surprisingly, I have come to feel that a synthesis of both these disciplines is required in order to do some justice to the complexity of Douglass's thought and its rhetorical sophistication. Yet, as Stanley Fish pointed out decades ago, interdisciplinarity is so very hard to do. No single book can meet the expectations of multiple disciplines. My colleagues in U.S. and African American literary studies will probably want more history and less philosophy than I offer here, whereas my friends in the fields of political theory and Black political thought will perhaps ask for less history and more engagement with the traditions of political philosophy. I recall vividly the afternoon when I was explaining to a friend who is a renowned scholar what Douglass meant by "dignity" and how it resembled but also differed from Kant's understanding of the word. After listening patiently, he replied with a look of perplexity: "So is that the kind of thing political theorists talk about at their conferences?" Yes, sometimes it is.

Finally, it's worth emphasizing that my subject here is the *distinctive* chapter of political philosophy Douglass elaborated from his experience of enslavement, not the whole of his political thought, much less a complete intellectual biography of him. This means that in the following pages, some topics that interest both disciplines will receive little if any attention. For example, the transnational dimensions of Douglass's political thinking have been variously explored by scholars in both fields, including (among many others) Paul Giles, Paul Gilroy, Robert Levine, Juliet Hooker, Christopher Hanlon, Ifeoma Nwanko, Millery Polyné, Cody Marrs, and Fionnghuala Sweeney. Yet this rich topic falls beyond my scope: although Douglass certainly drew on the cosmopolitan and transnational perspective that he acquired during his first trip to Britain and later travel to Haiti, and although he increasingly positioned U.S. democracy in a global and hemispheric context, his "chapter of political philosophy" was fundamentally a response to anti-Black racism *within* the United States. This is why, with characteristic attunement to standpoint location, he claimed that it was "applicable to the American people."

Outline of Chapters

This book begins by showing that Douglass started self-consciously to philosophize when he became fully aware of the contingent nature and malignant functions of white racism, founded the *North Star* to combat it, and then plunged into the debates within the Black community about what was often termed "the condition and destiny" of Blacks in the United States. Douglass's engagement with these topics, while already productively explored by other scholars, looks significantly different when we see how strongly it was shaped by his emergent, power-oriented political thinking.

The book's second chapter shows how his political thinking deepened into a political philosophy as he sought to counter racist assertions that Blacks were not actually human, a task that required him to develop a more robust yet flexible conception of "the human" than liberalism, republicanism, and Scottish philosophy could offer. "For Douglass," as Robert Gooding-Williams has argued, "eradicating the institution of slavery require[d] a revolutionary refounding of the American polity, and hence a transformation of the norms of citizenship."[33] Such a refounding and transformation would require a new public philosophy of democracy, and this is what his own political thought proposed to offer. It is rooted in his proposition that humans are beings composed of several distinctive human powers, and that our conscious exercise of these is what accords us a worth, or dignity, one that merits respect from others and serves as the "foundation" of our natural rights.

Chapter 3 argues that the distinctiveness of Douglass's political thought resides (and must be found) not just in its substance, or in its propositions, but in its manner, or style—what I call his *fugitive rhetoric*. As Douglass aimed to give voice to what his experience of radical

unfreedom had shown him, he also had to meet the rhetorical challenges posed by his otherness as a former slave and by his racial subject position as a Black man speaking to skeptical, if not hostile, white
audiences. Consequently, he did not just have thoughts that differed
substantively from the thoughts of many persons who composed his
audiences; he often thought in a different *way*, using what he called a
different "method." As we shall see, his unusual mode of thinking is
what James McCune Smith took pains to explain to readers in his introduction to *My Bondage and My Freedom*.

The book's fourth and fifth chapters return to Douglass's participation in the debates that roiled the antebellum Black public sphere. Chapter 4 focuses on his positions on the wisdom of Black emigration schemes
and the legitimacy of violence as a weapon against slavery. Chapter 5 examines Douglass's famous change of mind regarding the constitutionality of slavery. In all of these instances, we find that topics that have
been analyzed and debated by many historians appear in a different light
when we approach them as expressions of Douglass's political philosophy, not just as a sequence of pragmatic political decisions prompted
by contemporaneous political events. We discover in particular that
what looked like "inconsistency" to many of his contemporaries—
and to many Douglass scholars since then—was in fact a consistent expression of what he called his "method" of thinking, one that held binary
"opposites" in tension rather than opting to choose between them.

Chapter 6 offers a reading of *My Bondage and My Freedom* as Douglass's retrospective investigation and representation of the origins of
his political thought. Because he believed that his political philosophy
had originated in his experience of enslavement, this second autobiography's more detailed account of his enslavement is, in part, a meditation on how that experience had yielded the insights he later elaborated
philosophically. His investigation focuses on two key issues. First, what
could he learn from his own experience about the act, or process, of
political awakening—what French theorist Jacques Rancière has called
"political subjectivization"?[34] What triggers the moment in which a
person becomes an *active* political subject? Second, and closely related,
Douglass consults his own experience to learn more about the nature
of resistance: From what inner resources do oppressed persons draw in
order to resist their oppression? What forms does their resistance take?
The answers to these questions were critical to his efforts to awaken

Americans to take action against the evils of slavery and racism, and to his efforts to spur the free Black community to more active citizenship and more assertive resistance to racism.

Chapter 7 examines Douglass's responses to the end of the Civil War; the passage of the Thirteenth, Fourteenth, and Fifteenth Amendments; and the collapse of Reconstruction. In this new political environment, in which the formerly enslaved had been granted male suffrage and a significant measure of civil rights, he faced the discouraging fact that "the malignant spirit" of white racism was still abroad in the land. His speeches and writings in this period, commonly addressing themselves to either Black or white audiences, urged both to adopt certain dispositions and strategies of citizenship in their struggle against racism. Nothing less than "the soul of the nation" was at stake, he believed.[35] Again drawing on his experience of enslavement, Douglass understood racism to be a distinctive form of oppression, one that attacks not just the formal rights but also the human dignity of its targets. For this reason, he believed more strongly than ever that the struggle against racism must include a public philosophy with a robust conception of human nature, an explicit commitment to human dignity, and a vision of citizenship that recognizes human vulnerability and encourages collaborative practices of mutual respect.

This book's concluding chapter proposes that Douglass's fugitive political philosophy will always appear somewhat "strange, mysterious, indescribable," and suggests that the radical strangeness of Douglass's thought will enable it to offer an ongoing critical perspective on all versions of political philosophy that have originated within conditions of comparative freedom. I conclude, for this reason, that we should strive to honor Douglass's fugitivity rather than absorb his political thought fully into any tradition of Black or democratic political philosophy— including even those that have been described as "fugitive."

Douglass's Political Thought and the Afterlife of Slavery

Slavery has been formally abolished in the United States, but the racism that was both its cause and its effect persists, continuing to constrain and wound most if not all dark-skinned persons living in the United States today. Now, as in Douglass's time, the United States needs to develop a different public philosophy of its democracy, one that articulates the value of the human and the citizen more concretely and vividly than does liberalism, less narrowly and exclusively than does republicanism, and without recourse to notions of community based on kinship, race, religion, or the nation-state. Douglass's theory of the human and the citizen offers one intriguing version of such a revision. As well, in our time as in Douglass's—perhaps *more* than in Douglass's—most Americans have a passive relation to their citizenship, rights, and government. The widespread belief that democratic citizenship is primarily about rights that we "possess" still discourages many from actualizing their rights by *acting* as citizens. The equally tenacious belief that citizenship is a status that is conferred still disposes many to suppose that citizenship can be fully attained and achieved when it is merely documented by the legal apparatus of the state. Douglass's power-centered conception of the human and the citizen, his linkage of freedom with responsibility, and his belief that democratic citizenship requires a democratic disposition all point the way toward a more dynamic, citizen-driven democracy.

For most of his life, Douglass steadfastly opposed the idea of Black American emigration to another place or country. He was also a firm believer in a multiracial, "composite" democracy that welcomed all races and ethnicities and privileged none. He cautiously avowed his belief in the "preponderance" of good over evil in the aggregate of human beings, and it was on this faith that he staked his loyalty to democracy and his belief that the majority of white citizens—perhaps just a bare majority—would be able to disburden themselves of the privilege and the prison of their racism.[36]

Would he have retained these beliefs had he lived through half a century of Jim Crow, then witnessed the rise of the prison-industrial complex, the mass incarceration of Blacks, and the twenty-first-century rebirth of unashamed white nationalism in the United States and across Europe? Or would he have become a pessimist? These are unanswerable questions, and I don't believe that the answers to them really matter anyway. After all, no intellectual or cultural legacy of the past is likely to be fully adequate to the problems of the present. In using it, we must be selective. And creative. This was one of Douglass's own beliefs: "We have to do with the past only as we can make it useful to the present and the future."[37] In the last analysis, then, it is not for this or any other book to decide whether his political thought is useful today. Its usefulness can be discovered and proved—as Douglass repeatedly insisted—only if and when it is put into action.

Indeed, because Douglass undertook all his political thinking with specific political objectives in mind, his political theory is more a praxis-oriented guide to citizenship-as-struggle than a speculative account of the political. It does not deal with what democracy ideally should *be*, but with what citizens both Black and white ideally should *do*. It is under no illusion that an ideal polity can be brought into being and sustained through history; yet it also believes that democratic citizens *need* ideals to motivate and sustain their struggle for greater justice. While it urges citizens to understand themselves to be situated actors in a historically contingent world, it also insists that they hold themselves accountable to principles that are true "on all occasions, in all places."[38] It understands full well that democracy is a necessarily incomplete project achieved only when citizens collaboratively make headway against repeated and never-ending impositions of injustice by those who wield inordinate power. It warns that even fully enfranchised citizens who take all their rights for granted should recognize that their freedom is far from absolute or secure. It resists habits and traditions of thought that force choices instead of opening paths to new possibilities. It takes "democracy" and "citizenship" to be verbs, not nouns, and it urges citizens to make "a leap in the dark" and act in unavoidably risky and compromised ways to bring democracy—and themselves—into being (413).

CHAPTER ONE

"To Become a Colored Man"

Proposing Black Powers to the Black Public Sphere

"*There's roguery here somewhere!*" This accusation, delivered by the most famous abolitionist in America, stunned the activists gathered at the annual meeting of the American Anti-Slavery Society (AAS) in Syracuse, New York, in May 1851.[1] Everyone present knew exactly what William Lloyd Garrison was referring to: the recent announcement by his protégé Frederick Douglass that he no longer concurred with his mentor Garrison's interpretation of the Constitution, and that he had adopted instead that of Garrison's wealthy rival and adversary, Gerrit Smith. Because of its intrinsic historical interest and narrative drama, Douglass's break from Garrison has been cast as a defining moment in his career—which it certainly was. But Douglass's relationships with Garrison and Smith, and more broadly his work as an abolitionist of either stripe, have tended to overshadow other dimensions of his career in the 1850s.

Fortunately, a number of recent studies have focused instead on his increasing involvement at that time in the debates and discussions that animated the antebellum Black public sphere. While affirming that his relations and his ultimate break with Garrison were indeed crucial moments in his career, these scholars have argued that the Black public sphere was the matrix "out of which Douglass's ideas and writings emerged."[2] Moreover, as literary scholar Carla Peterson argued some time ago, antebellum Black writing not only consisted of the slave narratives prioritized by abolitionism with its emphasis on *individual*

Black lives, but also included a much wider discourse concerned with Black *group* experience: "Nineteenth-century African-American literary production—both spoken and written—had its origins not only in the white abolitionist movements that underwrote the publication of slave narratives but also in the national institutions of the black elite that addressed a specifically black audience."[3] Derrick R. Spires has observed more recently that these institutions and the debates they fostered also influenced public discourse about citizenship and democracy.[4] Guided by this scholarship, I will try to show here that along with his experience of enslavement, Douglass's work as an activist intellectual participating in the debates of the free Black community is what formed him to be a distinctively Black political philosopher. This is what James Mc-Cune Smith was trying to convey when he wrote with some bemusement to Gerrit Smith in July 1848: "You will be surprised to hear me say, that only since his Editorial career has he seen to become a colored man! I have read his paper very carefully and find phase after phase develop itself as regularly as in one newly born amongst us."[5]

Douglass strove to be a leader of the Black community—perhaps to be *the* leader of it. And this ambition certainly shaped his political calculations and his political thinking after 1848.[6] Yet, his deepened engagement with Black politics also had another kind of influence on his political philosophy. Because the antebellum Black public sphere was concerned with a wider range of issues than the abolitionist movement, Douglass's work within it encouraged him to stretch his thinking horizontally and thereby to realize fully that he was developing not just a strategy for abolitionism concerned to destroy the slavery system, but a broader political philosophy concerned with both Black politics and democracy—above all with the need to promote Black activism and solidarity while also fighting white racism.[7] As Douglass proceeded, step by step, into a deeper examination of Black life and politics, and of the racism these had to contend with, he elaborated with increasing self-consciousness his "chapter of political philosophy, applicable to the American people."

To retrace that journey in this chapter, we begin by examining two historical origins of his earliest reflections on the nature of anti-Black racism, both of which prompted him to conclude that it was an attack on Black dignity specifically.[8] One was his discovery in Britain that white racism is not a natural phenomenon that arises from a natural antipathy between races, but rather a constructed cultural force—he called it "republican negro hate"—with a function specific to that form of governance. Its purpose was to bind a dispersed, divided, and increasingly deracinated polity into a *white* republic whose members could use skin color to distinguish between those who belonged to the polity and those who did not. A second origin of his thinking about racism was his participation in Black debates over which kinds of labor could confer dignity on Black Americans and which kinds would have the opposite effect. White racism, he became convinced, strove to segregate the labor market for two reasons: to allow white workers to monopolize the more remunerative kinds of employment, but also to deprive Blacks of the ability to make the traditional republican claim that their labor conferred dignity upon them. This second, political purpose had material consequences at least as grave as the first, economic ones. Blocked from opportunities to cultivate and exhibit their dignity, and thereby to receive others' recognition of it, Black Americans (or so Douglass thought) had begun to doubt their own self-worth and fitness for citizenship. Such doubt, or "despondency" as he called it, sapped them of the energy and the will he believed were required in order to *demand* one's political rights, not just appeal for them.

"Republican Negro Hate" and the Dignity of Labor

As is well known, when Douglass sailed for England three years before founding the *North Star*, he still lent credence to the belief—widely held in the United States—that Blacks and whites had a natural antipathy toward one another, and that this biological repugnance was the animating force behind whites' anti-Blackness. Noted colonizationist Robert Goodloe Harper, for example, had asserted that Blacks were "condemned to a hopeless state of inferiority and degradation by their color, which is an indelible mark of their origin and former condition, and establishes an impossible barrier between them and whites."[9] As soon as Douglass arrived in Britain, however, he discovered that this was not the case. As he reported in a letter home to William Lloyd Garrison: "The instant that I stepped upon the shore and looked into the faces of the crowd around me, I saw in every man a recognition of my manhood, and an absence, a perfect absence, of everything like that disgusting hate with which we are pursued in this country."[10] Indeed, anti-Black racism appeared to be a singularly American attitude: "The truth is, the people here know nothing of the republican Negro hate prevalent in our glorious land. They measure and esteem men according to their moral and intellectual worth, and not according to the color of their skin."[11]

This discovery that "Negro hate" was "republican" prompted Douglass to reflect on the political function anti-Black racism performed in the *republic* of the United States. He already knew that in the South it served to enforce and justify the slavery system. What, then, was its purpose in the free North? From his experience of enslavement, he had gained a valuable clue: he had observed that in appropriating and exploiting the bodies of the enslaved, the slavery system felt compelled also to subjugate their minds and extinguish their sense of what he called their "manhood," or "humanity." Because "the human being—the slave—was out of his place as a beast of burden, . . . it required even harsher treatment to keep him in his condition. You must bore out his intellectual eye—blind him to his humanity—for the slaveowner knows that while there is a spark of the divinity in his soul, he cannot reckon upon keeping him a slave, and accordingly it must be blotted out."[12] After his return from Britain to the United States, Douglass became convinced that anti-Black racism served a similar function there: to degrade and dispirit nominally free Black Americans so they would not insist upon and exercise their full political rights. But why did so many white Americans in the North feel the need to wage this campaign of color prejudice? What purpose did it serve?

Douglass began to find his way toward some answers when in 1848 he joined a particular debate within the Black community. It concerned the nature of the kinds of work Black Americans should perform, and whether such work affirmed their dignity or, on the contrary, degraded them in their own and others' estimation. Historians have since agreed that this question arose in the first place because the broadening reach of market capitalism and the division of labor promoted by the rising factory system were rapidly transforming the work many Americans performed. The independent yeoman farmers cherished by Thomas Jefferson were in decline; so, too, were independent artisans and the apprenticeship system. Now, wage labor was becoming the norm rather than the exception.

One consequence of these developments, as historian David Roediger has shown, was that white workers began experiencing unprecedented dependence on their employers and deepening fears of powerlessness. Wage labor threatened to turn them into mere "hirelings"—or, worse, into virtual slaves. Many of them responded by reviving and embracing the traditional republican principle that free labor confers "dignity," and with it a set of rights that affirm and protect that dignity. This belief required them also to strenuously distinguish their own "free" wage labor from the slave labor performed by the majority of Black Americans. In short, as Roediger argues, many American workers in this period "were becoming *white workers* who identified their freedom and dignity in work as being suited to those who were 'not slaves' and by association 'not blacks.'"[13] These white workers sought to protect their own threatened dignity by enforcing a distinction between themselves and Black workers, and between dignified and degrading forms of labor. Increasingly, therefore, nominally free Blacks were shut out of most wage labor jobs and restricted to work associated with servitude and deemed degrading by white workers, such as being a barber, a bootblack, or a personal servant.

Within this context, Black activists found themselves in a difficult position. They wanted to lay equal claim to the republican principle that labor confers dignity, but how could they assert the dignity of Black labor when almost the only labor Blacks were permitted to perform was deemed to be degrading and beneath the dignity of whites? Should they encourage their fellow Black citizens to perform such labor anyway, and to find such dignity in it as they might? Or should they urge them to spurn such labor and beat a path—somehow—to labor that whites recognized as respectable enough to entitle a person to citizenship in a republic?

This debate broke out at the 1848 National Convention of Colored Freemen, held in Toledo, Ohio, and Douglass played a pivotal role in it. On one side of the issue stood the advocates of a resolution, placed before the convention, urging it to declare that "the occupation of domestics and servants among our people is degrading to us as a class, and we deem it our bounded duty to discountenance such pursuits."[14] As Derek Spires has astutely argued, some of those who supported the resolution did so because they worried that observers of the convention "(both black and white) would take any equivocation from the convention as capitulative," that is, as an admission that free Blacks were not "prepared for economic citizenship."[15] Douglass shared these worries. On the other side of the debate stood those who regarded such a proposal as completely out of touch with reality, since it would place most free Blacks in the impossible position of having to forgo almost any available work in order to avoid performing so-called degrading work. Douglass was sympathetic with this view also.

Eventually, he stepped into this debate and played what Spires aptly calls an example of his "mediating practice" and his "dialogical approach."[16] Instead of siding with either the backers or the opponents of the resolution, he proposed an alternative that he hoped would satisfy those on both sides of the debate. As the official report of the convention recounts: "He thought that as far as speakers intimated that any useful labor was degrading, they were wrong. . . . He had been a chimney-sweep. . . . He had been a wood-sawyer. . . . He said: let us say [that] what is necessary to be done, is honorable to do; and let us leave situations in which we are considered [by whites] as degraded, as soon as necessity ceases."[17]

While Douglass's participation in this debate would have strengthened his surmise that racism strove to undermine Black "humanity" or "manhood," it also encouraged him to use another word for these: *dignity*. And this word opened up a productive path for his analysis of white racism. Douglass, like many of his contemporaries, assumed that to some degree human dignity was inherent in humanness itself. Yet, again like many of his contemporaries, he also perceived that a person's feeling of having dignity usually depended on certain favorable circumstances: a person had to be able to *do* things that made him or her conscious of having dignity (e.g., perform a certain kind of labor); and he or she had to display that dignity in public, where others could see and affirm it. Douglass observed, then, that although dignity seems to be woven into human nature, it is also something one possesses to the degree that one is *conscious* of having it; and one's own consciousness of having it depends in part on making others conscious of it. Others' recognition of it then flows back and confirms one's belief in having it, but conversely their refusal to recognize it has the opposite effect of weakening one's confidence in one's dignity.[18] The function of all forms of racial segregation, as he would argue in a later speech, was to interrupt and destroy this intersubjective dynamic, thereby undermining Blacks' "faith in" themselves and persuading them of their "natural inferiority."[19] The deeper motive behind this effort was precisely that of the slaveholders who sought to "blind" the slave to his own "humanity." It was to sap free Blacks' confidence in their fitness for citizenship and in what Hannah Arendt would have called their "right to have rights."[20] In this way, it sought to extinguish the very possibility of their resistance to social degradation, economic exploitation, and political oppression. The reason why so many whites in the North participated in this effort, actively and passively, was in part economic: they wished to monopolize the labor market, especially its higher paying jobs. But Douglass's reflections on the intersubjective nature of dignity led him toward another thought as well: that many whites, inwardly and perhaps unconsciously worried by the precarity of their own dignity in a republic, sought to identify it with whiteness—that is, with an attribute of their being that was natural, fixed, and permanent rather than cultural, vulnerable, and in need of continuous reaffirmation.

"The Philosophy of Reform"

Having developed this analysis of whites' anti-Black racism as an attack on Black dignity specifically, what did Douglass believe the nominally free Black community in the North must *do* to combat it? In a speech delivered in August 1847, after he had returned from England but before he had published the first issue of the North Star, he declared to a largely Black audience, "The colored people . . . have been too prone to kiss the hand which smote them. . . . They must maintain self-respect, if they would be respected; they must demand their own rights, if they would obtain them."[21] Sometimes derided as mere "uplift" ideology, arguments like this were actually an expression of Douglass's emergent political philosophy. In recommending self-respect to his audience, he was advancing his conviction that self-respect is what drives one to *demand* respect from others, a demand that also lays claim to certain political rights. As Peter C. Myers was the first to observe, for Douglass "human rights and dignity are grounded less in the dormant possession than in the efficacious exercise of our distinctive faculties and powers."[22] But Douglass was well aware, too, that maintaining self-respect depended, in part, on receiving from others the respect that such manifestation of self-respect deserved. When that respect was withheld, as it was by so many whites, Black Americans had to demand it.

In an 1849 editorial urging the formation of an all-Black political organization, the National League, Douglass argued that to mobilize their power, free Blacks would have to adopt what he called "the philosophy of reform": "The injuries which we mutually suffer—the contempt in which we are held—the wrongs which we endure, together with a sense of our own dignity as men, must, eventually lead us to combine. It will one day, become obvious to all, that the evils that afflict us all require the united strength of all for their removal. At present we as a people, do not see or feel this. We have not yet learned the philosophy of reform." In almost despairing tones, he explained: "There are many among us . . . who have not the most remote conception of the means by which . . . change is effected. Of the action of mind upon mind they are wholly ignorant." What, precisely, were the "means" he had in mind? The phrases "a sense of our dignity as men" and "the action of mind upon mind" suggest an answer.[23] Taken together, they indicate that a consciousness ("sense") of one's dignity is an indispensable motive for the claiming of one's political rights, and that an individual's or group's sense of having dignity requires it to act upon other minds. That is, one must be conscious of one's dignity *and* make others conscious of it also. Dignity was fundamentally *relational* in nature. The question he and his Black readers and audiences faced, then, was how to respond to whites' *refusal* to grant them the "recognition" of Black "manhood" that Englishmen (Douglass averred) so readily bestowed.

One course of action Douglass recommended was that Black Americans commit more deeply to generating self-respect for and among themselves. This is why most of Douglass's elevation discourse advocated Black empowerment through self-respect and self-assertion, not just Black conformity to white middle-class norms. Later in this speech, for example, Douglass again links self-respect to political activism, this time indicating that self-respect emerges when one exercises one's innate *abilities*: "If the colored man will put forth his abilities, respect himself, imitate the white man in enterprise and virtue, but reject his vices, a better day will soon dawn upon the land, and man be known as man, and not be subjected to those unholy tests only fit for a heathen age."[24] Today, the phrase "imitate the white man" is jarring (and it was to some in his day, too, I suspect). But while Douglass did indeed urge his Black audience to "imitate the white man," he was not recommending that they become *like* the white man, as the phrase "reject his vices" makes clear. Imitating the white man meant, for Douglass, adopting specific respect-building practices observable among whites: a conscious manifestation ("putting forth") of one's "abilities" that would command the respect of others ("a man will be known as a man"), which would return to strengthen that sense of self-respect. Later in the speech, Douglass asserted: "Colored men and women"—note the "and women"—"should aspire to the highest intelligence and remember that knowledge is power. They should earn money, and be prudent in expenditures, curtailing their amusements, contribute rather to the education of themselves and children in all those pursuits calculated to elevate them in the opinion of an observing community" (115). Again, Douglass's recommendation of thrift, prudence, and seriousness, along with his underscoring the importance of "the opinion of the observing [white] community," could mislead us into concluding that he was simply espousing Black adoption of white middle-class norms and values. But when we read this sentence in the context of the speech as a whole, and when we take note of his claim that "knowledge is power," it becomes clear that white norms and values are of interest to Douglass not in themselves but as a means of promoting Black empowerment and political activism.[25]

In the first six months of his editorship of the *North Star*, Douglass wrote and published a series of editorials on this theme. In the first of these, which appeared in the *North Star*'s inaugural issue, he solemnly pledged to work as strenuously for the rights of Blacks in the North as for abolition of slavery in the South. The *North Star*, he promised, "while it shall boldly advocate for emancipation for our enslaved brethren, . . . will omit no opportunity to gain for the nominally free, complete enfranchisement"; but he also warned that, "while advocating your rights, the *North Star* will strive to throw light upon your duties; while it will not fail to make known your virtues, it will not shun to discover your faults."[26] In "What Are the Colored People Doing for Themselves?" he made good on this warning: "Our white friends can and are earnestly removing the barriers to our improvement, . . . but the main work must be commenced, carried on, and concluded by ourselves. . . . If we are careless and unconcerned about our own rights and interests, it is not within all the powers of all the earth combined to raise us from our present degraded condition."[27]

Two weeks later, in his 1848 West Indian Emancipation Address, Douglass advanced his recommendation of self-empowerment more indirectly, by holding up the recent revolutions in Europe as evidence of his theory. As a number of historians have shown, these revolutions were of great interest to Douglass and his American contemporaries. To Douglass's mind, as literary historian Cody Marrs writes, "the sudden and seemingly miraculous overthrowing of kings in France, Italy, and Hungary was more or less coextensive with the American Revolution of 1776, with the British abolition of slavery in 1833, and with past and future slave rebellions throughout the Western Hemisphere. What Douglass took from these revolutions was accordingly not merely a newfound cosmopolitanism but a restructured understanding of transformation itself."[28] The experience in which such transformation began was, in Douglass's view, an individual's or a group's discovery of its powers and, with these, what we have seen him call "a sense of our own dignity as men." These discoveries would in turn catalyze free Blacks' consciousness of their rights and strengthen their will to demand them.

Facing an audience of between fifteen hundred and three thousand persons in Rochester's Washington Square, many of them African Americans, Douglass began with a strong affirmation of the American Anti-Slavery Society's principle of nonviolence. "The day we have met to commemorate," he declared, "is marked by no deeds of violence, associated with no scenes of slaughter, and excites no malignant feelings. Peace, joy, and liberty shed a halo of unfading and untarnished glory around this annual festival."[29] Then he turned abruptly to the recent bloody revolutions in Europe:

> These [revolutions] though unfortunately associated with great and crying evils—evils which you and I and all of us must deeply deplore, are nevertheless interesting to the lovers of freedom and progress. They show that all sense of manhood and moral life, has not departed from the oppressed and plundered masses. They prove, that there yet remains *an energy when supported with the will* that can roll back the combined and encroaching powers of tyranny and injustice. To teach this lesson, the movements abroad are important. . . . The great mass of the Blouses behind the barricade of the Faubourgs, evidently felt themselves fighting in the righteousness of equal rights. Wrong in head, but right in heart; brave men in a bad cause.[30]

A tremor of apprehension must have rippled through the Garrisonians in the audience as Douglass expressed this interest in violent revolutions. He almost certainly meant to imply that his millions of brethren in bondage were themselves just such a "great mass of the oppressed," and that the European revolutions therefore augured the possibility of a bloody insurrection launched by the enslaved on American soil. As well, he was drawn to these revolutions because they spoke to the broader question of why and when the oppressed sometimes do resist and revolt against their oppression—either violently or nonviolently. Such revolutions "prove," as he put it, "that there yet remains an energy when supported with the will" that can revolt against oppressors. This "energy," he suggested, lies in a potentiated state within all of the oppressed; only when "supported with the will," however, does it flow forth with such force that it can "roll back" the "powers of tyranny and injustice." To whites and slaveholders his point was implied, but clear. Some in attendance would have known that he had made it even more emphatically in an April editorial in the *North Star*; there, he had cautioned slaveholders "to learn anew, that human nature is still human nature, and that the time may not be distant when an illustration of the fact may be afforded nearer home than Paris."[31] Douglass's message to Blacks in his audience was also unmistakable: that their energies, or the "latent powers" that constituted their "human nature," could overturn the injustices of white prejudice. If any were skeptical, Douglass pointed to the revolutions in 1848 as a "lesson" that "proved" his point.

"Asserting Their Rights as American Citizens"

To bring further into view the degree to which Douglass (and his allies within the free Black community) inflected the discourse of Black elevation by emphasizing power, self-empowerment, and the assertion of dignity, it might be helpful to glance briefly at what I would argue is a more representative example of it. Meeting in 1843, Michigan's Colored Convention—like most colored conventions—issued two formal statements, one addressed to Blacks, the other addressed to whites. The address to Michigan's free Black Americans begins with a seemingly abject admission of Black deficit and the need for Black elevation: "With our crippled minds we see the season of reflection has come. Therefore let us exert ourselves—let us cultivate our minds."[32] Yet, within a few sentences, the tone shifts: "Let us arouse ourselves from our lethargy, and by an appeal to the liberal minded and generous hearted, we will retrieve that which has been kept from us by the unjust. Let the palladium of Liberty be sounded, let the voices of our parents, wives, and children be united with our own, and with one united and vigorous effort, raise ourselves from the state of disgraceful despondency into which we are plunged" (190). As these sentences suggest, the report was at least as concerned with Black morale as with Black education and self-cultivation. And with their first-person plural adjurations, "let *us* arouse *ourselves* from *our* lethargy [and] raise *ourselves* from the state of disgraceful despondency into which *we* are plunged," the writers of the report did not distance themselves from Black conditions, but rather admitted their own immersion in the gloom that gripped the state's free Black community. In short, while the report could be criticized as the expression of a self-satisfied Black elite hectoring a Black underclass to embrace white, middle-class values, it can also be read as the cry of a community rallying itself from the brink of despair. Most notably for our purpose here, however, the address made no mention of the words "power" and "dignity," nor did it urge the Black citizens of Michigan to act more forcefully to demand, not just appeal for, their rights. Its whole tone was decidedly moderate.

The same convention's address to whites—the "Address to the Citizens of the State of Michigan"—also unfolds in complex registers. Most plainly, it is an appeal, and as such it acknowledges explicitly the superior power of those to whom it speaks and the relative powerlessness of those who have sent it. Careful not to offend, it accuses whites of no crimes or misdeeds, but instead asks only for justifications of their exclusionary policies, which are, as it patiently explains, in gross violation of the principles of the Declaration of Independence: "We solemnly appeal to you for a just reason, why we should be deprived of our free born rights, which are guaranteed to us as native born Americans" (191). Invoking natural rights philosophy, Black martial valor in the wars of independence and 1812, contemporary Black achievement ("a spirit of intelligence pervades our entire population" [193], and a distinguished historical legacy ("we are informed by the writings of Herodotus, Pindar, Aeschylus, and many other ancient historians, that Egypt and Ethiopia held the most conspicuous places among the nations of the earth" [193]," the address nevertheless concludes on the note of appeal with which it began: "Therefore, Fellow Citizens—the Colored Citizens of this State, through us, their representatives, respectfully and earnestly ask at your hands, the speedy adoption of such plans, and the formation of such measures as may secure to them their Equal Political Rights" (194).

Again, while it would be easy to dismiss this address as an expression of subservient appeal for acceptance by whites, such a summary judgment would overlook too much: the rigor with which the features of the address were deliberated in advance by the convention, the care with which it was researched and composed, and the energy of its declamatory style. We should note also that all of these sat side by side with the bitter foreknowledge that nothing was likely to come of it. As the authors pointed out: "We have year after year petitioned our State Legislature for the redress of grievances, and we have received from time to time but little or no attention" (192). What may be most remarkable about this convention address, then, is not the positions it takes on issues like elevation and assimilation, but the gestures it makes: the first is a self-exhortation in the face of existential crisis, the second is a refusal—in the face of a long history of white rebuff and inattention—to descend into silent acquiescence and "despondence."[33] Yet, for all its complexity, this convention's refusal is cautiously phrased, far from assertive, and not at all demanding. It contains no hint that respectability means *power*.

Let us turn now to "The Claims of Our Common Cause," the public address to whites issued by the Colored Convention held in Rochester, New York, in July 1853, which Douglass coauthored with four other Black activists.[34] It establishes a different tone at the outset, emphatically insisting that Black Americans are Americans and fellow citizens. A subservient respectfulness is scornfully disdained: "We are Americans, and as Americans we would speak to Americans. We address you not as aliens nor as exiles, humbly asking to be permitted to dwell among you in peace; but we address you as American citizens asserting their rights on their own native soil."[35] After presenting a list of sixteen demands (each introduced with the phrase "We ask that"), the authors add a list of the steps they have resolved to take in order to secure these demands. And here, for the first time, we find Douglass using the phrase—"natural faculties and powers"—that would soon become the cornerstone of his conceptions of human nature, human dignity, and human rights: "Whereas the colored people of the United States have too long been retarded and impeded in the development and improvement of their natural faculties and powers . . . ; and whereas, the proud Anglo-Saxon can need no arbitrary protection from open and equal competition with any variety of the human family; and whereas laws have been enacted limiting the aspirations of colored men, as against white men—we respectfully submit that such laws are unjust . . . and . . . ought to be repealed" (256–57).

The central purpose of this address now appears: it is to name and to rebut the notion that citizenship and national identity belong properly to whites only. The bulk of the case the authors make is historical, demonstrating that in New York's constitutional convention of 1821, a number of highly distinguished representatives and jurists opposed "a proposition to prefix the word 'white' to male citizens" (259). First, however, the authors adroitly combine Douglass's analysis of the intersubjective nature of racism with a flattering portrait of the American character to argue that it is racism itself—not Blackness—that is truly un-American:

> The genuine American, brave and independent himself, will respect bravery and independence in others. He spurns servility and meanness, whether they be manifested by nations or by individuals. We submit, therefore, that there is neither necessity for *nor disposition on our part to assume*, a tone of excessive humility. While we would be respectful, we must address you as men, as citizens, as brothers, as dwellers in a common country. . . . To be still more explicit: we would, first of all, be understood to range ourselves no lower among our fellow citizens than is implied in the high appellation of "citizen." (258; emphasis added)

After presenting a "mass of testimony" that "the word '*white*' was unknown to the framers of the New York state Constitution" and "is a modern word, brought into use by modern legislators," the authors again advance Douglass's analysis of racism as an intersubjective dynamic, one that depends on some citizens refusing to recognize and understand other citizens: "As a people, we feel ourselves to be not only deeply injured, but grossly misunderstood. Our white fellow-countrymen do not know us. They are strangers to our character, ignorant of our capacity, oblivious of our history and progress, and are misinformed as to the principles and ideas that guide us as a people" (266). The authors conclude the address with an even deeper psychological theory about the workings of white racism: that it perpetuates itself through the circular dynamics of a guilty conscience. "Men are apt to hate most those whom they have injured most" (268). These dynamics of intersubjective entanglement persuaded Douglass (and his fellow coauthors, presumably) that the most effective way for Black men and women to combat racism was to break that self-perpetuating cycle by stoutly resisting submission in all its forms. Of course, such resistance was much more easily urged than undertaken.[36]

About this time, in his May 1853 address "A Nation in the Midst of a Nation," delivered to the American and Foreign Anti-Slavery Society, Douglass brought together all these strands of his analysis of white racism, Black dignity, and Black politics. His argument in this speech is that the slavery system had devised a "comprehensive" strategy with three main components. "Sir, it is evident that there is in this country a purely Slavery party—a party which exists for no other earthly purpose but to promote the interests of Slavery. The presence of this Party is felt everywhere in the Republic. . . . [It] has determined upon a fixed, definite, and comprehensive policy toward the whole colored population of the United States."[37] The "key stone" (430) was the Fugitive Slave Act, which was intended not just to legalize slavery throughout the United States but "to discourage, downhearten, and drive the free colored people out of the country" (431). A second part of that policy was the colonization movement: "The expatriation of free colored people from the United States, is a very desirable one to our enemies—and we read, in the vigorous efforts making to accomplish it, an acknowledgment of our manhood, and the danger arising to Slavery out of our presence" (437). And a third part was the fomenting of anti-Black racism. The slave power sought to degrade and discourage free Blacks both by enacting specific anti-Black policies and by promoting anti-Black "social influences": "Let me now call attention to the social influences which are operating and co-operating with the Slavery party of the country. . . . We see here the black man attacked in his vital interests—prejudice and hate are excited against him—enmity is stirred up between him and other laborers. . . . Every hour sees us elbowed out of some employment to make room for perhaps some newly arrived immigrants" (433).

Five years later, in a May 1858 speech protesting segregation on New York City's Sixth Avenue train line, Douglass went one step further: he now figured anti-Black racism not just as the creation of the slavery system but also as its "foundation" and "cause." "I see, in the exclusion of the colored man from the Sixth Avenue rail cars, the cruel and malignant spirit of caste, which is at the foundation, and is the cause, as well as the effect of our American slave system." The purpose of this malignant spirit, he proposed, was to crush the civil, social, and political power of Blacks by rendering them incapable of feeling self-respect: "The grand explanation of our tardiness, our spiritlessness, and our destitution as a people, may . . . be found in the fact that whatever may be the talents, worth, or wealth of a colored man in this country, he is civilly, socially and politically crushed down far beneath the lowest and most degraded white man in the country." He concluded, in short, that the underlying intention of white racism was to destroy Black Americans' "faith in" themselves: "One of the most saddening results of the circumstances of our people is, that they tend to destroy our own faith in ourselves. Having seen ourselves oppressed, despised, and hated for so many long and bitter years, we come to think at last that degradation is our doom. Instead of attributing our condition to the injustice and oppression which have been heaped upon us, we sink down into the belief that we are the victims of our natural inferiority."[38]

By the early 1850s, then, Douglass had begun to develop compelling arguments that he hoped would persuade many nominally free Blacks to become more conscious of and then to exercise their "latent powers"; only thus could they feel and project "a sense of" their dignity, and only such consciousness of their dignity would dispose them to demand and assert their rights, not humbly appeal for them. But Douglass also knew that white racism was at bottom a white problem, so he would also have to develop compelling arguments addressed to whites. In formulating arguments that Black Americans were entitled to full democratic citizenship, he would have to use the conventional lexicon of the nation's public philosophy, or its shared understanding of its basic principles. But he also saw that the nation's public philosophy was insufficient. After all, white Americans ritualistically invoked the values enshrined in the Declaration of Independence and the Preamble to the Constitution, but their racist beliefs and practices were seemingly untouched by these. Indeed, as historian Joanne Pope Melish has shown, even "the language of abolition" was inadequate: it "preserved and indeed strengthened assumptions about the ultimate availability, dependency, and instrumentality of 'free' persons of color as a class."[39] This is why, "absurd" as it might seem to his abolitionist "friends," Douglass believed that he would have to instruct "the highly civilized people of the north in the principles of liberty, justice, and humanity!" Such instruction would require him not only to expose their hypocritical violation of their principles, but also to persuade them that some *other* principles— including above all the principles of dignity and "humanity"—were foundational to the project of their democracy.

"American Prejudice against Color"

In a well-known passage in *My Bondage and My Freedom*, Douglass explains that his work as editor of the *North Star* had led him into a deeper analysis of the political philosophy of democracy, or as he puts it, "the origins, nature, rights, powers, and duties of civil government, and the relations which human beings sustain to it" (392). This course of study "conducted" him, he writes, "to the conclusion that the constitution of the United States" (392) did not in fact legitimate the slavery system but rather served as a powerful basis on which to argue for its illegality. However, this conclusion was not the only fruit of his study. As the words "relations which human beings sustain to it" hint, Douglass was interested in the nature and constitution of the polity itself, in the ways human beings living in the United States (some of them citizens, some not) *related* to their system of laws and to one another.

Perhaps because Douglass was thinking about race as he read political philosophy, not just the constitutionality of slavery, he now moves abruptly to this topic: "I will now ask the kind reader to go back a little in my story, while I bring up a thread left behind for convenience sake, but which, small as it is, cannot be properly omitted altogether; and that thread is American prejudice against color" (392–93). If we are alert to Douglass's relish for irony, we will see that he intends to convey that American racism was decidedly *not* a "small" matter in his view. As with his phrase "the thing looked absurd," he was mocking his white readers even as he instructed them. And if we attend to the associative logic that led him from his reflections on slavery's constitutionality to this "small" matter of American color prejudice, we can surmise that he undertook his reading in political philosophy in order to address this issue, too.

Before proceeding with an account of Douglass's instruction to "the highly civilized people of the north" (390), we must pause for a brief review of U.S. public philosophy in the antebellum years in order to understand why it could not provide a convincing basis on which individual citizens could or should join together to form a political community, and why it did not explain why Black Americans were entitled to be part of that community.[40] As historian Kimberly K. Smith has pointed out, "when we look back at the turbulent beginnings of mass politics in America, we find a number of different conceptions of democracy in play."[41] The two dominant conceptions, forming the two main strands of the nation's public philosophy at that time, were Lockean natural rights liberalism and what has been called "Atlantic" republicanism. We are all familiar with the Declaration's assertion that "all men are created equal, endowed by their creator with certain inalienable rights," including the rights to life, liberty, and the pursuit of happiness. This was the radical message of Locke's political philosophy, a principle that Douglass repeatedly affirmed and famously described as the "ringbolt to the nation's destiny."[42] But as I have noted already in the introduction to this book, this powerful statement does not state *what* men are that makes us *deserving of* the rights with which we are endowed.[43] Nor does it offer a broad, affective basis on which citizens might build a political community. For a time, to be sure, republicanism helped remedy this second weakness. Republicanism maintains that citizens must cultivate and possess particular virtues, or character traits, in order to deserve citizenship and succeed in the demanding work of preserving a self-governing republic. These virtues include prudence, independence, bravery, and love for the republic itself. By committing themselves to valuing and reproducing these particular virtues in their children, citizens also form a polity in which liberalism's "self-interest" is constrained by a political community's fidelity to shared civic values and obligations. However, republicanism's more substantive conception of the citizen as an aggregate of required virtues also has a distinct drawback: it is exclusive, since not everyone does or can possess those virtues. In the late eighteenth century, most of the founders thought it self-evident that only wealthy persons could be independent, and that only educated persons could have foresight. Insofar as women were by definition subordinate to and dependent on men, they could not possess most of the core republican virtues that would have entitled them to citizenship. Neither liberalism nor republicanism, therefore, offered a dependable basis on which Black Americans could assert their rights.

In her perceptive analysis of the evolution of notions of citizenship in the early republic, literary historian Dana D. Nelson suggests that "we look in a different direction from political philosophy's debates over liberalism and republicanism, or the Federalists' economic advantages and political machinations, and turn our attention instead to the way that the proponents of the Constitution, most famously 'Publius,' hold out a reformulated ideal of 'manhood.'" Nelson goes on to show that what was "new in this reorganization of manhood [was] its appeal to and nationalization of whiteness. . . . This incorporation promised to manage the potentially divisive effects of interpersonal, interclass, and interregional masculine competition by relocating them in a symbolically fraternal, reassuringly 'common' manhood."[44] If Nelson is correct, then the connection Roediger establishes between white working-class feelings of powerlessness and the emergence of a racialized white citizenry dates back to the late eighteenth century.

In any case, these weaknesses in American democracy, and in a public understanding of democracy, were apparent to a number of observers. When French political philosopher Alexis de Tocqueville visited the United States in the late 1830s, he famously remarked on a new phenomenon he called "individualism," which he defined as a "sentiment that disposes each citizen to withdraw to one side with his family and his friends, so that after having created a little society for his own use, he willingly abandons society at large to itself."[45] In the long run, he warned, this tendency born of American democracy's commitment to equality threatened to destroy the democracy itself, since self-isolating individuals cannot sustain a democratic polity if they choose to avoid the responsibilities of mutual self-government. Writing a few decades later, Walt Whitman shared these misgivings. He affirmed that "the idea of the singleness of man, individualism," was indeed the essence of U.S. democracy, but he cautioned that "the mass or lump character" of the polity, "for imperative reasons, is ever to be carefully weighted, borne in mind, and provided for. Only from it, and from its proper regulation and potency, comes the other, comes the chance of Individualism."[46]

These conceptual weaknesses in the public philosophy of U.S. democracy also had visible, material consequences. By the time Douglass became an abolitionist in 1841, a number of states had held constitutional conventions that lowered or abolished property qualifications and gave full voting rights to most white men over the age of eighteen.[47] However, as Roediger has shown, the newly enfranchised working class turned the virtue-composed citizen of republicanism against Black Americans, arguing that because so many were poor and lacked the "independence" indispensable to republican citizenship, they should be driven from the polity:

> That blacks were largely noncitizens will surprise few, but it is important to emphasize the extent to which they were seen as *anticitizens*, enemies rather than members of the social compact. . . . The more powerless they became, the greater their supposed potential to be used by the rich to make the freemen unfree. Thus, it was necessary to watch for the smallest signs of power among blacks, and, since blacks were defenseless, it was easy to act on perceived threats.[48]

In sum, at the very time Douglass escaped to the North and the comparative freedom it offered, increasing numbers of white Americans were turning to race and visible racial differences to identify who properly belonged to the polity and who did not. As Douglass and his co-authors of "The Claims of Our Common Cause" had observed, "the word *white . . .* is a modern word." This period of expanding "Jacksonian democracy" also saw a bloody renewal of efforts to purge Native Americans from the all-white polity, the rise of a strong anti-immigration movement, and a general increase in xenophobic nationalism and calls for an American "empire." Lacking a more democratic basis on which to form bonds of political and social solidarity, white Americans were using the substitutes of race, gender, sectionalism, and nationalism to bind increasingly individualistic and competitive white male citizens together in a political community, one in which they could know and recognize one another as an "us." This was the citizenry that the abolitionists, including Douglass, had to persuade to abolish slavery. This was the citizenry—as Douglass saw clearly after his first trip to England—that had to be induced somehow to repudiate its affiliation with whiteness.

Of course, Douglass never took the time to make a case for these weaknesses of antebellum U.S. public philosophy in precisely the manner I have just done. Still a young man, and recently escaped from slavery, he felt their impacts much more than he identified or analyzed them. But he certainly was aware that, as historian Rogers M. Smith writes, "U.S. citizenship laws" in his day "expressed illiberal, undemocratic ascriptive myths of U.S. civic identity, along with various types of liberal and republican ones."[49] At the very least, he would have seen that whites' anti-Black racism was intensifying in the United States, and that the nation's quasi-official public philosophy seemed unable to contend with it.

It seems likely, too, that Douglass would have posed to himself the questions William Goodell asked in his *Views of American Constitutional Law*, which Douglass almost certainly read sometime between December 1848 and May 1851. (Goodell's was surely one of the works he read as he studied "the origins, nature, rights, powers, and duties of civil government, and the relations which human beings sustain to it.") Goodell writes: "Is there, after all, anything in the social nature of man, in the relations of man to man, in the duties growing out of these relations (duties, therefore, imposed upon man by the Author of his being) which lay a foundation (as they create a moral necessity) for such a science as that of civil government, a science as fixed and determinate, in the nature of things, as any of the other demonstrative sciences, based upon 'self-evident truths'?" In these references to "the social nature of man" and "self-evident truths," we hear a blend of natural rights liberalism and Scottish philosophy, along with a strong note of the Christian absolutism embraced by many abolitionists. Goodell goes on to observe that, to be practically effective, this "science of civil government" must be easily grasped and embraced by the polity as a whole. "Unless there can be such a science of legislation and of law, which mankind can be taught, can understand, and can apply, then civil government becomes a cheat, and legislation becomes a farce, and jurisprudence becomes an usurpation." In short, the "science" Goodell called for was what I and political theorists today would call a "public philosophy," a shared understanding of democracy Americans can appeal to in times of civil discord. Like Goodell, Douglass believed that the philosophy of democracy most antebellum Americans ascribed to could not meet the linked challenges posed by an aggressive slavery system, the fraying bonds of a democratic polity, and the rising appeal of anti-Black racism.[50] His task, then, would be to meet those challenges in two ways: by urging free Blacks to adopt a more power-oriented understanding of democratic citizenship, and by writing a new chapter of antiracist political philosophy applicable to the white majority of the American people.

CHAPTER TWO

"A Chapter of Political Philosophy Applicable to the American People"

Human Nature, Human Dignity, Human Rights

In the late 1840s and early 1850s, as we shall now see, Douglass perceived that the path to such an antiracist understanding of democracy had to begin with a more robust conception of the citizen as a human being. In an 1848 speech to the American Anti-Slavery Society, Douglass observed that the United States lacked a sufficiently elaborated conception of humanity, or of the "men" whom its public philosophy claimed are created equal and endowed with human rights: "Sir, we have in this country, no adequate idea of humanity yet; the nation does not feel that these [blacks] are men; it cannot see through the dark skin and curly hair of the black man, anything like humanity, or that has claims to human rights."[1] The fault, he makes clear, lies not in some deficiency among persons of African descent, but in the American popular understanding of what we would now call "the human." The need for a more adequate idea was also made urgent by the rise of what has been called the "American school" of ethnology, which asserted the nonhuman or subhuman status of persons of African descent. As literary scholar Cristin Ellis elegantly summarizes, in the three decades prior to the Civil War "a wide variety of proslavery arguments would circulate, but none were more effectively calculated to deny Black equality while preserving the democratizing impulse of the era than those that asserted the innate, biological inferiority of Black humanity. . . . What had begun as a debate over whether the enslavement of humans is morally acceptable increasingly became a debate over whether Black humans were, biologically speaking, fully human to begin with."[2]

Yet, Douglass knew from the outset that undertaking such work would put him in the absurd position of having to argue for his own humanness, and he bridled at that prospect. "Must I undertake to prove that the slave is a man?" he scornfully demanded in his famous 1852 speech, "What to the Slave Is the Fourth of July." "That point is conceded already," he continued. "No one doubts it." And he proceeded to demonstrate that the "slaveholders themselves acknowledge" the slave's humanity in their many laws that held them responsible for their "crimes": "What is this but the acknowledgment that the slave is a moral, intellectual, and responsible being. The manhood of the slave is conceded" (433).[3] Perhaps in order to evade the insult of having to argue for his own humanity and that of other Blacks, Douglass began to focus not so much on the meaning of the words "slave" or "Negro," but on the "idea" of man.[4] That is, instead of directly seeking to persuade whites that Blacks properly belonged in the category of the human, he would examine and transform the category of the human itself. Between 1848 and 1855, he returned many times to this challenge of working out a more "adequate idea of humanity" than whites possessed and the nation's prevailing public philosophy had to offer.[5] In making this effort, he drew upon the thinking about power, action, and dignity we saw him developing in the last chapter, but he also deepened this thinking and placed it on a broader philosophical foundation.

Douglass's emphasis on the human as "a moral, intellectual, and responsible being" in this and many other speeches suggests that he may have received some assistance from a book titled The Constitution of Man, Considered in Relation to External Objects, by the noted phrenologist George Combe. First published in Scotland in 1828, the book was a sensational success, selling some 350,000 copies worldwide between 1828 and 1900. Although permeated with a human physiology we would regard as unscientific today, the book's message is that man is a part of nature and subject to natural laws just like every other creature in nature. The book is also plainly racist. Along with a number of physiologists in his time, Combe believed that different races were marked by important physiological differences, and he asserted that "the brains of the New Hollanders, Caribs, and other savage tribes, are distinguished by great deficiencies in the moral and intellectual organs."[6] Nonetheless, Frederick Douglass remarks in *Life and Times of Frederick Douglass* that while traveling in Scotland from 1845–47, he "had a very intense desire gratified—and that was to see and converse with George Combe, the eminent mental philosopher and author of 'Combe's Constitution of Man,' a book which had been placed in my hands a few years before, . . . [and] the reading of which had relieved my path of many shadows" (685).

In what ways, then, had Combe's racist book shed light on matters that concerned him? The answer, I believe, is that he found Combe's theory of the human to be remarkably helpful, for it is one in which human powers and human self-recognition play a determining role. Combe writes, for example, that "man, when civilized and illuminated by knowledge, . . . discovers in the objects and occurrences around him, a scheme beautifully arranged for the gratification of his whole powers, animal, moral, and intellectual; he recognizes in himself the intelligent and accountable subject of an all-bountiful Creator, and in joy and gladness desires to study the Creator's works." Combe writes further that the Creator has left man "to find out for himself the method of placing his faculties in harmony among themselves, and in accordance with the external world . . . history exhibits the human race only in a state of progress toward the full development of their powers." And he makes clear that, by "harmony of the faculties," he means that these limit and regulate one another.[7] All of these ideas, as we have already begun to see, came to the forefront in Douglass's political thought after 1848.[8]

In the previous chapter, I noted his use of the phrase "natural faculties and powers" in his 1853 Colored Convention proposal.[9] That wording appeared also two years earlier, in his 1851 speech "God's Law Outlawed," where he began to put his reflections on the human, with its powers, dignity, and rights, into recognizably theoretical form. Not surprisingly, since he had to address his audiences using the political lexicon to which they were already committed, he opened with a conventional liberal invocation of freedom. "The great truth of man's right to liberty entered into the very idea of man's creation. It was born with us; and no laws, constitutions, compacts, agreements, or combinations can ever abrogate or destroy it."[10] From sentences like these (and there are many in Douglass's work), a number of scholars have reasonably inferred that, in the words of one, his life "was a persistent quest for freedom," and, in the words of another, "in the life and work of Frederick

Douglass, freedom was always the guiding light."[11] But let us read a bit further into this speech. "Man's right to liberty," he continues, "is written upon all the *powers and faculties* of man."[12] These words suggest that freedom was not quite as foundational to Douglass's political thought as we have assumed, since the metaphor they turn on conveys that certain human powers and faculties come *first*, and that the right to freedom is written on them *afterward*. Indeed, the metaphor implies that we can only read our rights *out* of those powers, as an inference from them. And this helps explain also why he was so concerned to have the Black readers of the *North Star* become more "acquainted with their latent powers."

Three years after delivering "God's Law Outlawed" in 1851, he repeated himself almost verbatim in a January 1854 speech: "the great truth of man's right to liberty is written on all the *powers and faculties* of the human soul."[13] Six months later, in his important lecture "The Claims of the Negro Ethnologically Considered," he again referred to human faculties and powers. His aim in this lecture was to refute the assertions advanced by Samuel Morton, Josiah Knott, George Glidden, and other members of the American school of ethnology that persons of African descent were not descended from an ancestor shared with whites and therefore were not human in the same sense—indeed, were subhuman or not human at all.

Douglass begins his lecture by acknowledging the difficulty of his own positioning and listing the rhetorical options among which he must choose: "There are three ways to answer this denial. One is by ridicule; a second is by denunciation; and a third is by argument. I hardly know under which of these modes my answer to-day will fall." Douglass's point is that the very claim that Blacks are not human puts him in the ludicrous position of having to stand before an audience and prove that he himself is a man. Nonetheless, he will do so, and before this audience of scholars, and with this particular purpose, he will choose argument as his method. "To know whether [a] negro is a man," he begins, "it must first be known what constitutes a man." And what constitutes a man, he claims, is certain faculties and powers: "Man is distinguished from all other animals, by the possession of certain definite *faculties and powers*, as well as by physical organization and proportions."[14]

In this lecture, then, Douglass expands his claims for human powers: now they are the basis not just of our political rights but of our very humanness. But how does a conception of the human as an assemblage of faculties and powers produce the idea that humans also have certain rights? As we have seen, he had begun implicitly forging such a linkage in a number of editorials and speeches, but he did not do so explicitly until he penned an 1866 editorial on women's suffrage. Here we read: "If woman is admitted to be a moral and intellectual being, possessing a sense of good and evil, and a power of choice between them, her case is already half gained. Our natural powers are the foundation of our natural rights; and it is a consciousness of powers which suggests the exercise of rights. Man can only exercise the powers he possesses, and he can only conceive of rights in the presence of powers."[15] In this later speech, Douglass makes clear that, in his view, our "natural powers" are not just what make us human; they are also "the foundation of our natural rights." Leaving unanswered for the moment the question of *why* this is so, he warns that if we do not become conscious of our powers, we will not be moved to exercise the rights that derive from them, for "it is *consciousness* of powers that suggests the *exercise* of rights." He continues: "Power is the highest object of human respect. Wisdom, virtue, and all great moral qualities command respect only as powers. Knowledge and wealth are nought but powers. . . . We despise the weak and respect the strong. Such is human nature."[16] These harsh sentences begin to explain why our powers are the foundation of our rights.[17] "Wisdom, virtue, and all [other] great moral qualities" are but the expressions of our powers, so that when people "respect" these qualities they are in fact responding to their felt sense of our powers. In other words, while our moral qualities may be worthy in themselves, they command the respect of others only when others *feel* them and have to respond to them as powers. This train of thought hints, then, that because our powers produce our "great moral qualities," they produce not just a biological being we denominate as "man" or "human," but a being with worth or value. This hint becomes explicit when Douglass goes on to assert that our exercise of our powers produces our "natural dignity":

> But whatever may be thought as to the consequences of allowing women to vote, it is plain that women themselves are divested of a large measure of their natural dignity by their exclusion from such participation in Government. . . . To deny woman her vote is to abridge her natural and social power, and to deprive her of a certain

measure of respect. . . . Woman herself loses in her own estimation [of herself] by her enforced exclusion from the elective franchise just as slaves doubted their own fitness for freedom, from the fact of being looked down upon as fit only for slaves.[18]

Douglass argues, in short, that the denial of suffrage excludes women from "participation in government" and thereby prevents many from becoming *conscious* of their natural powers. This exclusion also injures their natural dignity because it arises from their ability to exercise their natural powers. When women are denied the opportunity to exercise these powers (as when they are excluded from participation in government), they are "deprived of . . . respect" and also lose in their "own estimation."

Thus, two ideas are braided together here. The first is that our exercise of our distinctive human powers not only expresses our humanity but also produces self-respect, or what Douglass now calls "natural dignity." This is why he asserts that "our natural powers are the foundation" of our rights: we have rights because we have a human worth, or dignity, that we feel deserves informal acknowledgment and formal protection. Douglass's second idea is one we have already noted: that our consciousness of our powers and rights depends, in some measure, on others conveying to us, through acts of respectful acknowledgment, that they, too, are conscious of and recognize our powers and rights. (As Douglass observed in an 1870 speech delivered in Washington, DC: "You know all men derive their impressions of their abilities and possibilities in some measure from the opinions of those who stand about them.")[19] Thus, while our rights derive from our innate powers, and to that degree are inherent in our very humanity, they also rest in the hands of others, who may or may not allow us to become conscious of our powers, achieve our dignity, and exercise our rights.

It is worth emphasizing that both of these ideas are elaborations of insights he had gained from his experience of enslavement. Douglass's conception of natural dignity as produced by our powers, yet also dependent on recognition and affirmation by others, stems directly from observations of the slaveholders' strategy and the resistance of the enslaved to it.[20] He had declared in an 1851 speech, as we have seen: "Dark as is the lot of the slave, yet he knows he is not a beast, but as truly a man as his master. Nothing can make the slave think that he is a beast; he feels the instinct of manhood within him at all times."[21] This "instinct of manhood," I would suggest, is the enslaved person's not quite fully conscious sense of his own humanity and his worth. A more complete and confident sense of self-worth would be produced by his "putting forth" his natural faculties and powers, but the slaveholder has denied and appropriated these. The enslaved person, "as a mental, moral, and responsible being," was "blotted out from existence . . . and ranked with the beasts of the fields [because] all his powers were in the hands of another."[22]

Observing the workings of anti-Black racism in the North, Douglass concluded that it employed precisely the same strategy: it deprived free Blacks of opportunities to exercise and become conscious of their powers, and it sought thereby to render them less likely to have faith in themselves and their own dignity; lacking such faith, they would not demand recognition of their dignity and rights from whites. "One of the most saddening results of the circumstances of our people is, that they tend to destroy our own faith in ourselves. . . . Instead of attributing our condition to the injustice and oppression which have been heaped upon us, we sink down into the belief that we are the victims of our natural inferiority."[23]

Philosopher Bernard Boxill was the first scholar of Douglass's political and moral philosophy to see how important a role power, dignity, and recognition play in it. In his 1991 essay on "Douglass against the Emigrationists," he carefully tracks Douglass's use of these words to conclude that "Douglass felt that fellow citizens and nationals should respect each other," and that Douglass believed that "power was a condition of 'honor' or 'dignity.'"[24] Boxill explains further that Douglass believed that "moral conviction and a willingness to risk one's life for one's rights may give one dignity" (41), and that such dignity deserved the respect of one's fellow citizens "who respect each other in the sense that they respect each other's moral standing" (36). My own argument closely resembles Boxill's, but it also differs in small but crucial ways. Boxill's Douglass sees "power" as flowing from "moral conviction," and he identifies "dignity" as a moral conviction so strong that it is willing to risk death in order to secure rights.[25] The Douglass I have been limning sees "moral power" as one of humankind's species characteristics; that power produces moral convictions and other "signs" of itself, and these in turn give us and others reason to believe that we have dignity.

Our dignity becomes, in turn, the basis of our claim to have rights, for the whole purpose of our rights is to protect our ability to exercise and manifest our dignity-conferring powers.

One reason these small differences are crucial is that they will address a problem Boxill astutely identifies: "while moral conviction and a willingness to risk one's life for one's rights may give one dignity, it is generally not enough to move others to acknowledge that dignity" (41). Accordingly, Boxill searches Douglass's political thought to find additional resources a person can use to compel or entice such acknowledgment, and he finds two. One that *compels* acknowledgment is "the ability and nerve to cause trouble," but Boxill points out that this is unsatisfactory, since we can be feared by others without their acknowledging our dignity. A resource that can *entice* or encourage acknowledgment of others' dignity is "moral suasion." As Boxill writes: "Sometimes, often with our connivance, our feelings enable us to ignore that we are acting for transparently bad reasons. Moral suasion involves techniques for manipulating these feelings and for redirecting our attention to the obvious errors that we contrive not to see" (42). But surely such techniques, to be effective, require appeal to a shared morality. What is that shared morality? Douglass's answer, as we shall now see, is that our moral powers, which are inherent in our very humanness, express the moral laws of the universe and establish "the laws of [our] own being."[26] Those laws *demand* that we respect others and affirm their dignity if they give us signs of it. If we disobey those laws, we forfeit our own claim to human status; we degrade ourselves. This was the philosophical basis on which Douglass developed his techniques and arguments of moral suasion.

"The Laws of [Our] Own Being" and the Limits of Our Freedom

As I have been describing it so far, Douglass's theory of human powers is strongly supportive of human agency and with it human freedom. He views human powers as, quite literally, empowering. But there is another side to his political theory: its commitment to a sense of moral responsibility, or duty. He believed that rather than simply empowering us (in the conventional sense of that word), our moral power—our ability to know what is right and to distinguish that from what is wrong—sharply curtails our freedom and demands our complete submission to its dictates.[27]

Douglass developed his thinking about moral power along two complementary lines. In one, he regards it as being somewhat more agentic, and thus more like our other powers. Seen in this light, the power of knowing right from wrong is what makes us capable of being *responsible* persons, persons who can hold themselves accountable for their actions instead of requiring the authority of positive law or divine commandments to do so. This aspect of moral power is precisely what slaveholders and anti-Black racists were bent on withholding from persons of African descent. The second way in which he describes moral power is as a force arising within and working through our intersubjective relations with other persons. Just as dignity is produced by our own consciousness of our powers, yet at the same time dependent upon recognition by others, so too our moral power seems to straddle the line that would separate subjective and objective, autonomous and dependent, individual and collective. In Douglass's opinion, we by ourselves and all alone know what is right and what is wrong; yet it is in our relations with other persons that we find confirmation of our intuitions, both as others act in accordance with and as they violate these. For even in their violation of the dictates of our and their moral powers, they involuntarily betray an awareness, often a subconscious awareness, that they are doing wrong. Therefore, struggle though they might to deny it, humans are bound together by a shared capacity to know right from wrong, and no matter how strenuously a person tries to free himself from this moral network, his own actions betray his acknowledgment of it and thus bind him ever more tightly to it.

In Douglass's speeches and writings, these two ways of thinking about moral power are intertwined and complementary. He emphasized the first when he argued that Blacks were as fully human as whites, and he foregrounded the second when he sought to understand and critique the actions and attitudes of slaveholders and racists. Often, as we shall see throughout this book, we can discern both strands running through a single sentence, or even a single figure of speech—such as his word "bound." Douglass by no means invented his conception of moral power. In developing it, he was aided most broadly by the general cultural disposition we know of as romanticism, which sought to naturalize the supernatural and humanize the divine; we can see this impulse in the works of Emerson, Thoreau, Fuller, Whitman, and other writers of the period. Douglass was aided as well (as we have seen) by his reading of George Combe's *The Constitution of Man* in the late 1840s and (as we shall see) by his reading of Ludwig Feuerbach's *The Essence of Christianity* in 1859.[28] Yet helpful as all these influences were, I would argue that the most important source of Douglass's theory of moral power was his own "little bit of experience, slave experience."

The slavery system into which Douglass had been born insisted that he lacked the ability to discern right from wrong, but he tells us that in fact he discovered early that he did possess such power. When he was still a small child, he relates in *My Bondage and My Freedom*, he began inquiring into the origins of the slavery system. When he put his questions to some of the older children, they replied that "*God, up in the sky*" had devised it (178). But this answer "came, point blank, against all my notions of goodness" (178). Douglass clearly implies that these "notions of goodness" were innate; at least, he never tells us where he acquired them. Moreover, since they were "notions," he must have been to some degree conscious of them.[29]

In *My Bondage and My Freedom*, Douglass also recalls that his relations with others reinforced in subtle ways his early understanding of the difference between right and wrong. His relationship with his master Captain Aaron Anthony, for example, was minimal but instructive. Douglass would observe Anthony closely, and what he noticed, he tells us, "awakened" his "compassion":

> Old master very early impressed me with the idea that he was an unhappy man. Even to my child's eye, he wore a troubled, and at times, a haggard aspect. His strange movements excited my curiosity, and awakened my compassion. He seldom walked alone without murmuring to himself; and he occasionally stormed about, as if defying an army of invisible foes. . . . Most of his leisure was spent in walking, cursing, and gesticulating, like one possessed by a demon. . . . Most evidently, he was a wretched man, at war with his own soul, and with all the world around him. (172)

What is it that troubles Anthony so grievously? Why is he at "at war with his own soul"? Douglass does not say, but he certainly implies that Anthony has a guilty conscience. Anthony knows that slavery is wrong, but he can do nothing (or so he has persuaded himself) about it. Watching him and feeling "compassion" for him, the young Douglass seems to detect Anthony's inward struggle between his better and worse natures. Distant as he and Anthony are from each other on the social scale, they are nonetheless linked together by a shared moral sensibility—one that is repressed but still expressed by Anthony. His many involuntary revelations of his consciousness of wrongdoing subtly confirm, though probably at a preconscious level, young Douglass's own intuitions of right and wrong.

What Douglass leaves implied in this scene becomes much more explicit when he describes the effect that slaveholding had on his new mistress, Mrs. Hugh Auld. He recalls that when he arrived in Baltimore to live with the Auld family, she had had no prior experience of possessing a slave. At first, therefore, she saw him as a fellow human being, and as such, one whom she was bound to regard with a certain respect. Her husband soon forbids her to go on treating Douglass in this manner, but Douglass tells us that she "lacked the depravity indispensable" to the role of slave mistress she was now called upon to perform: "It was . . . necessary for her to have some training, and some hardening, in the exercise of the slaveholder's prerogative, to make her equal to forgetting my human nature and character, and to treating me as a thing destitute of a moral and intellectual nature. . . . I was human, and she, dear lady, knew and felt me to be so" (221–22). And he, no doubt, *knew* that she felt him to be so.

Alas, Mrs. Auld was eventually corrupted by "the fatal poison of irresponsible power" (216). The "noble powers of her own soul" were defeated, and the "will and power of her husband was victorious" (222). Douglass then gives a remarkably penetrating account of this psychological war in which Mrs. Auld's own moral powers were defeated by the will of her husband. Her "first step, in the wrong direction," he writes, "was the violence done to nature and to conscience, in arresting the benevolence that would have enlightened my young mind." Her second step was that, feeling guilty about having taken the first, "she must begin to justify herself to herself; and once consenting to take part in such a debate, she was riveted to her position" (223). In other words, as Mrs. Auld adopted and internalized the views of her husband, what remained of her original good nature objected—so she had to justify to herself this new course she was taking. But in that very act of consenting to such self-justification, Douglass observes, Mrs. Auld was consenting to her own self-destruction. For feeling itself under attack, the internalized voice of her husband's will vigorously defended itself, and in so doing became increasingly infuriated by the stubborn recalcitrance of her guilty conscience. Consequently, Douglass relates, whenever Mrs. Auld caught him reading a book, she rushed upon him with "utmost fury." This excess of anger, he suggests, was triggered not just by his quietly resistant actions but by the war she was waging against herself on her husband's behalf. Hence the puzzling but quite brilliant metaphor with which Douglass concludes this drama: "I have had her rush at me, with the utmost fury, and snatch from my hand such newspaper or book, with something of the wrath and consternation which a traitor might be supposed to feel on being discovered in a plot by some dangerous spy" (223). The "traitor" here is the part of herself that had betrayed her own good nature by submitting to the power of her husband and disregarding the promptings of her own moral powers. The "spy" here is precisely her original good nature, with its accusing moral power that she cannot entirely suppress. All she can do, then, is perpetuate the cycle in which her exercise of irresponsible power calls forth guilt that threatens her self-esteem; unwilling to accept this guilt, she has to punish her conscience by angrily exercising yet more irresponsible power.[30]

Another intersubjective drama in which young Douglass gets further confirmation that he and his masters share an understanding of what is right and what is wrong occurs when he and Hugh Auld negotiate about his wages. Auld had allowed Douglass to seek work on his own and to strike whatever terms he might with his employer so long as he brought all his earnings and gave them to Auld. Recounting the emergence of his early belief that he had a right to retain what he had earned through his own labor, Douglass writes:

> He [Hugh Auld] had the power to compel me to give him the fruits of my labor, and this power was his only right in the case. I became more and more dissatisfied with this state of things; and, in so becoming, I only gave proof of the *same human nature which every reader of this chapter in my life—slaveholder or non-slaveholder—is conscious of possessing.* To make a contented slave, you must make a thoughtless one. It is necessary to darken his moral and mental vision, and, as far as possible, to annihilate his power of reason. The man that takes his

earnings, must be able to convince him that he has a perfect right to do so. It must not depend upon mere force; the slave must know no Higher Law than his master's will. The whole relationship must not only demonstrate, to his mind, its necessity, but its absolute rightfulness. If there be one crevice through which a single drop can fall, it will certainly rust off the slave's chain. (337; emphasis added)

The plain thrust of this passage is that the enslaved naturally do know of a "Higher Law" superior to their master's will; and it is in their nature to be able to use their "power of reason" to perceive the falsity of their master's claims. Precisely because both the enslaved and the master are "conscious" of "possessing the same human nature" and with it the same moral and intellectual powers, the master cannot possibly persuade the enslaved of the "absolute rightfulness" of their enslavement. Indeed, merely by engaging in the intersubjective give-and-take that persuasion consists of, Auld has tacitly acknowledged Douglass's standing as another human being with the same human nature as his own. Although he could have beaten Douglass into submission, such a beating could never accomplish the work of persuasion. On the contrary, it would merely have demonstrated Auld's greater power, not the righteousness of his actions. Thus, while the slave might never dare to announce it, and the master never have the honesty to acknowledge it, both *knew* that slavery was wrong. And they often knew, though the masters often denied it, that they shared this knowledge.

These were the experiences that led Douglass to believe that our moral power *compels* us to feel that we share reciprocal moral obligations and responsibilities with all other humans. This is what he meant when he wrote, "The slave is bound to mankind, by the powerful and inextricable net-work of human brotherhood."[31] Of course, slaveholders like Aaron Anthony and Hugh Auld routinely sought to evade those bonds and escape that network. Douglass repeatedly expresses his awareness that humans can and do create cultural structures that bend them *away* from their natural inclinations. He also deduced the reverse: that cultural structures, including certain political orders, can *encourage* people to follow their natural inclinations. He had observed of Captain Anthony, for example, that if he "had been brought up in a free state, surrounded by the just restraints of free society—*restraints which are necessary to the freedom of all its members*," he "might have been as humane a man . . . as are members of society generally" (171; emphasis added). Paradoxical as it may appear, then, history for Douglass was a record of humans striving to overcome their selfishness in order to be true to their human nature. One form that such striving must take is to become conscious of and to exercise one's natural powers, including one's moral power, in order to become who one always already is: a human being.

Toward the end of his life, in an 1883 lecture titled "It Moves: The Philosophy of Reform," Douglass gave his fullest and most recognizably philosophical account of moral power and its place in his political thought. Delivered to the Bethel Literary and Historical Society in Washington, DC, his lecture poses and answers a political question that had perplexed him throughout his long life as an activist: "Whence that irresistible power that impels men to brave all the hardships and dangers involved in pioneering an unpopular cause?" he asks. In other words, what moves persons to actualize themselves as political beings? "Has it a natural or a celestial origin? Is it human or is it divine, or is it both? I have no hesitation in stating where I stand in respect of these questions. It seems to me that the true philosophy of reform is not found in the clouds, or in the stars, or anywhere outside of humanity itself" (137).

With this unequivocal assertion, Douglass links what he calls "reform" to an innately human "irresistible power." In so doing, I believe, he is making more explicit what he only had implied—or was able to formulate only roughly—in some of his earlier writings and speeches. Recall that in his 1848 speech on the revolutions in Europe, he argued that bloody as they were, they nonetheless showed that "all sense of manhood and moral life, had not departed from the oppressed and plundered masses. They prove, that there yet remains an energy when supported by the will that can roll back the combined and encroaching powers of tyranny and injustice." What he called there "an energy . . . supported by the will" has here become an irresistible human power that is impelled to seek justice.

Recall, too, that in his 1849 editorial urging the creation of an all-Black political organization, he had complained that many in the free Black community had not yet learned "the philosophy of reform." They had not learned, he claims, "the means . . . by which change is effected." In this lecture delivered decades later, Douglass elaborates on what he had meant in that speech by "a sense of our dignity as men" and by "the action of mind upon mind":

[Man] has a dignity which belongs to himself alone. He is an object, not only to himself, but to his species, and his species an object to him. Every well formed man finds no rest to his soul while any portion of his species suffers from a recognized evil. The deepest wish of a true man's heart is that good may be augmented and evil, moral and physical, be diminished, and that each generation shall be an improvement on its predecessor.[32]

A sense of our dignity as individual men and women, then, rests on a sense of species dignity that arises from our being conscious not simply of our powers, but also of ourselves, and of one another, and of our shared membership in a single species. How, then, do we attain such consciousness of ourselves *as* humans living among and dependent on others who are human also? His answer here is that we exercise no will or choice in the matter: simply by becoming self-conscious in the sense of becoming an "object" to ourselves, we also recognize that object (our self) as a *human*. In other words, we instantly and involuntarily recognize ourselves as belonging to a species of which other persons are also members. Therefore, the very notion of being a self means being a *human* self, and the very notion of being a human self means belonging to the human *species*. Self-consciousness, Douglass now asserts, is always also species-consciousness. As we have seen, he had believed in the "net-work of human brotherhood" since the early 1850s at least. But the source of this *particular* language for such a network, one that links *self*-consciousness to consciousness of being human—was almost certainly Ludwig Feuerbach's *The Essence of Christianity*, which Douglass read with German journalist Ottilie Assing in the summer of 1859. There he would have read:

But what is this essential difference between man and the brute? The most simple, general, and also the most popular answer to this question is—consciousness. . . . Consciousness in the strictest sense is present only in a being to whom his species, his essential nature, is an object of thought. . . . But only a being to whom his own species, his own nature, is an object of thought, can make the essential nature of things or beings an object of thought.[33]

Whatever the sources of his language in "It Moves" might have been, Douglass is clearly asserting here that because all persons involuntarily recognize themselves as belonging to a species, they are instinctively agitated when they see another member of that species—another human being—suffer. They also feel an instinctive impulse to end that suffering. Their self-consciousness, species consciousness, and species identification all come together to *compel* them to desire the good for others. They may resist or deny this desire, but (as we shall see) they do so at the risk of imperiling their claims to humanness and human dignity. This is because the moral law is one of "the laws of [our] own being and those of the universe":

> All reform is an effort to bring man more and more into harmony with the laws of his own being and with those of the universe. . . . If the smallest particle of matter in any part of the universe is subject to law, it seems to me that a thing so important as the moral nature of man cannot be less so. . . . I think it will be found that all genuine reform must rest on the assumption that man is a creature of absolute, inflexible law, moral and spiritual, and that his happiness and well-being can only be secured by perfect obedience to such law.[34]

Somewhat like Kant, then, Douglass stresses that what gives humans their distinctive human dignity is that they have the ability to set laws for themselves and then hold themselves accountable to those laws. Douglass's humanistic moral philosophy also resembles that of Sylvia Wynter, who suggests that we humans are "governed by the 'imagined ends' or postulates of being, truth, freedom that we lawlikely put and keep in place, without realizing that it is *we ourselves*, and not extrahuman entities, who prescribe them."[35] However, unlike both Kant and Wynter, Douglass figures our relation to this law as one of "perfect obedience" to our own species nature, and *not* as a matter of individual choice or as a sovereign subject's act of free will.[36] Douglass was well aware that many persons do disobey the laws of their own being and thereby diminish both their humanity and their dignity. His difficult thought here is that all humans are free *not* to be human. His equally difficult thought is that, when we do act in accordance with our own nature, we should *not* think of ourselves as exercising our noncontingent free will. Instead, we should choose to act as if we had no choice, as if we were "bound" to act in a way that, in our own view and by our own lights, expresses "perfect obedience" to the laws of our own being.[37]

In several ways, then, Douglass's theory of human nature, dignity, and rights, originating in his experience of enslavement, met and corrected key deficiencies in the nation's public philosophy in his lifetime (and, I would argue, in ours). First, it rooted natural rights liberalism in a richer account of human nature than its principal advocates offered. It thereby answered the question, seldom discussed by the founders, of what the nature of man is such that man is entitled to certain political rights. Second, it addressed the problem of U.S. democracy that Tocqueville and Whitman had observed, and that Douglass had discerned through his participation in debates about the dignity of Black labor: namely, that a rising spirit of competitive individualism threatened to weaken Americans' understanding of the obligations of citizenship and blind them to the importance of political solidarity and community.

Douglass's conceptual linkage of power, dignity, and rights also addressed the problems of Blacks' disenfranchisement and despondence that so troubled him as a Black political activist and organizer. It did so indirectly by trying to undermine what he surmised to be the root cause of whites' racism: their disavowed anxieties about the precarity and diminishment of their own dignity, which led them to try to establish their dignity on the basis of unalterable, fixed skin color. More directly, Douglass's theory sought to empower nominally free Blacks by replacing liberalism's comparatively quiescent conception of citizenship, in which all citizens are "endowed" with rights, with a far more activist proposition. It was that, although citizens are indeed born with the *powers* that are the foundation of their natural rights, they can secure those rights only by exercising their powers, becoming conscious of their natural dignity, and demanding that others acknowledge these also. This aspect of his political philosophy was directed mainly toward the free Black community, but he was well aware that it could and should transform the practice of democratic citizenship for all Americans. If "power concedes nothing without a struggle," both Black *and* white Americans would have to reimagine democratic citizenship as a continuous exercise of their powers in perpetual struggle against domination.

CHAPTER THREE

"One Method for Expressing Opposite Emotions"

Douglass's Fugitive Rhetoric

Suppose that, by a miracle of sorts, a stranger from a different world suddenly found himself face-to-face, and for the first time, with the particular organization of the manifold data that is this world—a distribution of the sensible that is both understood and upheld through conceptual categories such as "human," "nature," "culture," "the political," "the social," and so on. What would such a stranger *see* that the denizens of this world do not? Having stepped from some other place, where this particular schema did not obtain, he would of course perceive its contingency. He would see as well that, to those who made continual use of it to understand their world, the schema had become identical with reality itself. He would notice that even the questions the inhabitants might raise about the nature of their reality, or about their ability to know that reality, would be posed in terms generated by the very schema they had brought under interrogation. Suppose, further, that although this stranger recognized his fundamental kinship with those who inhabited this world, and wished to share with them his unique perspective on it, they did not reciprocally recognize him but instead regarded him as an inferior being and a stranger in their midst. Finally, suppose that this stranger had not just stepped into their world but *escaped* into it; and suppose that one of the perceptions he wished to share with them was that their world both depended on and was responsible for the world he had fled. In all his efforts to speak to them, however, he had to use the very conceptual categories that constituted and maintained their order of things, even though they were often inappropriate, and at times inimical, to what he saw from his perspective.[1]

This hypothetical figure took actual historical form as Frederick Douglass. And as a consequence of the predicament in which he found himself—with its misfit between his "slave experience" and the lexicon in which he perforce had to cast his political thought—we have to look for the distinctive qualities of that thought not just in its words but also in its *movement* as it struggled to work through and yet also against the prevailing public philosophy of his day. We must bear in mind that, at worst, this conventional lexicon had been deployed against him from birth in order to name him a *slave* and to justify his enslavement; at best, it had failed to adequately name and speedily eliminate the crimes of slavery and racism. For this reason, "freedom," "power," "equality," "dignity," the "state," and many other of his key words can occlude his thinking almost as much as they reveal it. If we are truly to understand him, we have to catch sight of him handling these words, turning them around, trying to make them work for his own purposes. But we also have to admit that, in the last analysis, some of his thinking will remain beyond our grasp. The problem is not just that, as William James points out, we cannot catch the movement of thought—the stream of consciousness—but only its resting points, or what James called its "substantive" as distinct from its "transitive" aspects.[2] The problem is also that so much of Douglass's thinking took place in the gap between his experience and the language at his disposal. His thinking is often a rapid movement or oscillation back and forth between the profound otherness of his former identity as an enslaved human being and the comparative legibility of his identity as a distinguished Black activist. He was driven by an almost obsessive need to close this gap, a need that (along with other motives to be sure) drove him to obsessively revise his life story, hoping each time to get some aspect or moment of it right. And there is yet another reason why the study of Douglass's political thinking must try to catch hold of its style and movement, not just its logic and its propositions. Because he was always cognizant of the absurdity of his position, and because he cherished a profound and often bitter awareness of the multiple ironies of his situation—of his being a man who had to prove he was a man—his thinking is permeated with an ironic performance of itself that defies reduction to its literal meaning.

For all these reasons, Douglass's political thought is both expressed and formed by what we may fairly call his *fugitive rhetoric*, a manner or style of thought characterized by three qualities that shaped its course: a commitment to what we now call "standpoint epistemology," a willingness to hold opposites in tension (rather than choosing one), and a predilection for reversal, or what rhetoricians call "chiasmus." All can be traced to Douglass's formative experience of enslavement, and all guide both the way he approached a problem and the mode in which he presented his reasoning to others.[3] The most important of these—perhaps even the one from which all the others derive—is a deep attunement to standpoint epistemology, the belief that all knowledge is shaped and conditioned by the knower's historical and social positioning. An objective, comprehensive, or commanding view is not available to anyone; every view we take of a matter is partial and incomplete because it is *our* view, and we have been conditioned by our circumstances. "It is impossible," writes Patricia Hill Collins in one of the earliest formulations of this idea, "to separate the structure and thematic content of thought from the historical and material conditions shaping the lives of its producers."[4]

Douglass incorporated such standpoint sensibility into virtually everything he wrote. It appears, for example, in his 1852 speech "What to the Slave Is the Fourth of July?" (the very title of which embeds standpoint theory), where he had famously declared: "I shall see this day and its popular characteristics from the slave's point of view."[5] It appears in *My Bondage and My Freedom* when he observes that "it is difficult for a freeman to enter into the feelings of such fugitives. He cannot see things in the same light with the slave, because he does not, and cannot, look from the same point of view from which the slave does" (351–52). Fifteen years later, it appears in an 1867 speech in which he announces, "I appear here no longer as a whipped, scarred slave—no longer as an advocate merely of an enslaved race, but in the high and commanding character of an American citizen."[6] And toward the end of his life, it appears in his last great speech, "Why Is the Negro Lynched?" with the blunt announcement: "I propose to give you a colored man's view of the so-called 'Negro Problem.'"[7] As these passages all indicate, Douglass did not just appreciate the inevitability of standpoint; he also repeatedly *insisted on* it to his readers and his audiences. His explicit emphasis on standpoint was a crucial dimension of the philosophical instruction he "elaborated from" his "slave experience" and gave to the free people of the North. He wished to convey by it that his white listeners, too, stood at a particular point in time and space, and that their knowledge too was perforce limited and shaped by their standpoint.

The second key feature of the style of Douglass's thought—the *way* he thought as distinct from *what* he thought—could be described as a deep reluctance to choose between the terms of a binary and an inclination instead to hold both terms or "opposites" in tension with each other. That metaphor will be serviceable, however, only if we keep in mind that in this case the tension is actually a rapid *oscillation* between two terms. Sometimes these terms are literally opposites; other times they are just distinctions hardened by habit and convention; and at other times they are differences of opinion, or opposing sides in a debate. Recall, for example, the role Douglass played in the debate over Black labor at the 1848 National Convention of Colored Freemen: there he sided *both* with those who urged free Blacks to reject degrading forms of labor *and* with those who argued that necessity compelled them to perform such labor. Recall as well that in his 1849 editorial recommending the formation of all-Black political organizations, he urged his Black readers both to "imitate the white man in enterprise and virtue" *and* "to reject his vices." In his 1848 West Indian Emancipation speech, similarly, he both deplored the recent bloody revolutions in Europe and recommended them as objects of interest to all "lovers of freedom and progress."

The third feature of Douglass's fugitive rhetoric is a particular way of using what rhetoricians call "chiasmus," along with its subtype, antimetabole. Chiasmus derives from the Greek word for "crossing," as in the letter X, and it signifies reversal—"a reversal of grammatical structures in successive phrases or clauses—but without repetition of words." A classic instance of chiasmus is Douglass's famous claim in the *Narrative*: "You have seen how a man was made a slave; you shall see how a slave was made a man" (60). Antimetabole is likewise a grammatical reversal, but one that allows repetition of words so long as the essential structure of reversal is preserved. A typical instance of antimetabole in Douglass's writings would be this sentence from *My Bondage and My Freedom*: "All suspense, however, must have an end; and the end of mine, in this instance, was at hand" (149). As we shall see, Douglass often uses this rhetorical technique, especially a version of it I will call "imperfect reversibility," to structure his arguments, underscore the precarity of human existence, and call attention to the distinction between similarity and identity of condition.

"The Constitution of the Human Mind"

Both Douglass's attunement to standpoint and his inclination to hold opposites in tension are discernible in what may be the most famous and discussed passage in all his writings—his account of enslaved persons singing as they made their way through the woods to the Great House Farm. Henry Louis Gates Jr. was the first critic to observe that Douglass's description of this singing, like many other passages in his *Narrative*, is structured by a series of binary terms with seemingly opposite meanings; when yoked, they form what Simon Gikandi describes as "a chiasmus of passion."[8] The songs express both "the highest joy" and "the deepest sadness." The thoughts of the enslaved are conveyed both by their "word[s]" and their "sound[s]," and perhaps as a consequence of this confusion, they may seem "unmeaning jargon" to many who overhear them, yet they are "full of meaning" to the enslaved themselves. This ambiguity about their meaning (or lack thereof) arises, Douglass seems to suggest, from the profoundly different standpoints of those who sing them and those who hear and seek to interpret them. For the enslaved, the songs are "full of meaning," while to free persons, they are "unmeaning jargon." But a few sentences later Douglass troubles this neat distinction between insider meaning and outsider nonsense: "I did not, when a slave, understand the deep meaning of those rude and apparently incoherent songs. I was myself within the circle; so that I neither saw nor heard as those without might see and hear" (24).[9] Now the insider is the one who fails to perceive the songs' "deep meanings," and the outsider the one who succeeds. So which of these perspectives does Douglass judge to be the more accurate and authoritative?

We might be tempted to solve this riddle by concluding that Douglass intended to underscore the importance of *both* locations and to suggest that only someone like himself, who had stood (as he had) both within and without the circle of slavery, could truly understand the songs. The problem with this solution, however, is that Douglass himself does not make this reconciling move. Moreover, such a resolution of the riddle begs the question of why Douglass would have chosen to arrive at it by way of provisional and contradictory commitments to the superior validity of each standpoint taken singly. For these reasons, we can conjecture that instead of seeking to reconcile these seemingly opposite perspectives by fusing them, Douglass wished his readers to dwell for a moment in the blur created by his movement from one to the other. He was not quite saying that we should somehow *combine* both perspectives. He was making the importantly different point that each perspective perceives some aspect of the truth that the other cannot. As he pondered the differing insights of these standpoints—"within" and "outside"—he did not choose either. Nor did he choose both. He simply refused the choice presented by this binary and chose instead to keep moving in the fraught space between its two terms, which is not at all the same as choosing one or seeking to reconcile both. That *movement* is a manifestation of what I am calling his *fugitive* rhetoric.

The revisions Douglass restlessly made to the slave-song passage in subsequent versions of his autobiography keep this fugitivity in play. They should be read, I would argue, both as expressing his commitment to standpoint and to holding opposites in tension and as an increasingly self-conscious effort to identify and name his manner of thinking.[10] The first indication of such self-consciousness and self-reference occurs in a small change he made to this passage in the 1855 *My Bondage and My Freedom*. Here is the sentence as it appears in the 1845 *Narrative*: "I have sometimes thought, that the mere hearing of those songs would do more to impress some minds with the horrible character of slavery, than the reading of whole volumes of philosophy on the subject could do" (24). Ten years later, in *My Bondage and My Freedom*, he revised "whole volumes of philosophy" to read "whole volumes of mere physical cruelties" (184). Why?

The answer is embedded in another change Douglass made in *My Bondage and My Freedom*—his inclusion of a chapter on his relations with the men and women in the American Anti-Slavery Society who had first hired him to do abolitionist work. They wished, he recalls in 1855, to "pin me down to my simple narrative" of "personal experience as a slave. 'Let us have the facts,'" they advised. "'Give us the facts,' said [John A.] Collins, 'we will take care of the philosophy'" (367). The writer of the *Narrative*, he now implies, was still under the thumb of these white abolitionist employers and mentors, so he had let them "take care of the philosophy" and restricted himself to giving graphic testimony about slavery's cruelty. Ten years later, the writer who had for seven years been "presuming to instruct the highly civilized people of the north in the principles of liberty, justice, and humanity," wished to right this wrong. Instead of disparaging the "philosophy" he himself was offering, he delivered a deft, ironic thrust at the more sensationalist depictions of slavery's "physical cruelties"—those the Garrisonians had required him to provide, including his own *Narrative*.

Other revisions Douglass made to the slave song passage suggest further that by the time he wrote *My Bondage and My Freedom*, he had become interested not just in representing the singing of the enslaved, but in understanding and sharing both the substance of his philosophy and the workings of his *own mind*—the mind of a Black philosopher who had been deeply formed by his experience of enslavement. In the *Narrative*, for example, he had simply refuted the widespread belief that the songs of the enslaved gave evidence of their contentment: "It is impossible to conceive of a greater mistake. Slaves sing most when they are most unhappy." In *My Bondage and My Freedom*, he went further and took pains to *explain* this paradox to his readers: "Such is the constitution of the human mind, that, when pressed to extremes, it often avails itself of the most opposite methods. Extremes meet in mind as in matter" (185). This added sentence indicates that he had become interested in the songs of the enslaved because they expressed what can happen to the "human mind" under extremely adverse conditions, which could be paraphrased as an interest in what happens to thinking when it comes into being within conditions like enslavement. From there, it is but a small step to the question: What is philosophy when an enslaved mind undertakes it?

In the third version of his autobiography, *Life and Times of Frederick Douglass*, he comes close to answering this question, as he revised this sentence yet again, changing it to read: "It is not inconsistent with the constitution of the human mind that it avails itself of one and the same method for expressing opposite emotions" (503). This final version of the sentence is his most precise—though densely packed—description of the distinctive manner of political philosophizing he believed he had developed within slavery. In 1845, as we have seen, Douglass was still reluctantly following John Collins's advice by sticking to the "facts" and leaving others to explain or theorize them. Nine years later, by contrast, he confidently advanced a general truth about the "constitution of the human mind": in "extreme" circumstances such as enslavement, it often uses "opposite methods." Now, in *Life and Times*, a micro-revision tweaks this last formulation by adding "not inconsistent with" and by changing the plural "most opposite methods" to a singular ("one and the same") method that can "express opposite emotions." Now it is the *emotions* that are "opposite," while the *method* of the human mind singing (or thinking) in extreme circumstances is unitary.[11]

Let us look more deeply into the two linked claims Douglass is making here: "It is not inconsistent with the constitution of the human mind that it avails itself of one and the same method for expressing opposite emotions" (503). He is asserting first that his own mind, and the mind of the enslaved singers, is not "inconsistent with" the "constitution of the human mind" more generally. In other words, while the mind of the enslaved may appear to be inconsistent to those who view it from an outsider's perspective (the perspective of a beholder who thinks of him- or herself as "free"), viewed from the perspective of the enslaved, the mind in bondage is consistent with itself and with the nature of the *human* mind. He suggests as well that the appearance of inconsistency arises from the fact that, thinking within an ontology of radical unfreedom, the enslaved mind can and does express opposites with "one and the same method," whereas conventional thinking, operating in circumstances far less "extreme" and presuming itself to be free, would deem such a method to be inconsistent. (As we shall see in chapter 5 of this book, "inconsistency" was an accusation frequently hurled at him.)

What does such a method *do* when it "expresses opposites"? We have noted already that it does not recognize an obligation to choose one term of a binary over the other. Nor, however, does it seek to combine or reconcile or synthesize them. Instead, like the songs of the enslaved, it strives to express both perspectives, even though they are "opposites," and in doing so it keeps both in play. The mind of the enslaved, which is emphatically a *human* mind, sees the world from a distinctive standpoint, one in which things deemed by free persons to be "opposites" are frequently *both* present and true, however self-contradictory that might appear.

In his immensely influential reading of the *Narrative*'s critical use of binaries, Gates argues that "Douglass's narrative has aimed to destroy the symbolic code that created the false oppositions themselves" by exposing that "the oppositions, all along, were only arbitrary, not fixed."[12] But I think we can make an even more radical claim for Douglass's thought: he both exposes and eschews the distinction between cultural and natural, arbitrary and fixed. In his conception of dignity, as we have seen, he thought in terms of both nature and culture equally: dignity is a quality inherent within us *and* it requires cultural ratification. Is this a legitimate move? Similarly, as we shall see, Douglass passionately maintained that all knowledge was conditioned by standpoint *and* that some truths held true for all standpoints. Are such "self-contradictory" claims permissible? Not according to the method of thinking we conventionally employ, which would consider such reasoning to be "absurd." But Douglass employed a different way of reasoning. It undertook the demanding work of keeping the terms of some binaries in play and in perpetual tension with each other. He developed such a method for the simple reason that the world—as he perceived it from his standpoint as an enslaved person—was composed of such seeming opposites in perpetual conflict and coexistence with each other. Only thinking that stayed in perpetual motion between the terms of a binary and refused to settle on one of them—that is, only thought that had a fugitive quality—could do justice to the world as experienced by the enslaved.

In later chapters, we will examine closely several instances of that method at work, but a brief example might be helpful here. Toward the end of his 1845–47 visit to Britain, Douglass allowed himself to be bought out of slavery by abolitionist allies whom he met there. Later, in *My Bondage and My Freedom*, he recalls that several of his "uncompromising anti-slavery friends" back in the United States had deemed this a gross "violation of anti-slavery principle": by taking this step, they argued, Douglass was tacitly affirming the slaveholder's "right of property in man" that abolitionism aimed to overturn (377). His action was, in their view, morally *inconsistent* with his antislavery principles.

By the light of one logic—the kind held by those who have never stood within the circle of enslavement—this was true. But to arrive at this judgment, Douglass's critics had to step outside of the warp and woof of his lived, embodied, situated condition as someone who was unfree; they could think only in terms of what a free and unconstrained will might, or would, or should have done in order to close the gap between theory and practice, ideal and real. They failed to see that the series of moves that enabled their judgment in the first place was itself predicated on the assumption—so characteristic, as Charles Mills observes, of the *white* mind—that one can be a contingency-free mind making moral decisions in an unconditioned vacuum. Douglass's sharp understanding of the contingency of freedom—what Neil Roberts has aptly called his understanding of freedom as always "comparative"—disposed him even this early to resist such a facile assumption.[13] But we should not suppose that he therefore collapsed the distinction between real and ideal, or that he was merely a pragmatist or a political operator who was indifferent to moral claims.

For here is how Douglass defended his decision: "Viewing it simply in the light of a ransom, or as money extorted by a robber, and my liberty more valuable than one hundred and fifty pounds sterling, I could not see . . . a violation of the laws of morality . . . in the transaction" (377). He reminds his readers and critics that although he was residing in Britain at the time, thousands of miles from his master, he was in fact still legally in the grasp of a man whom he regarded as a robber. To his critics, who were free, paying that ransom might look like a compromise of principle, but to an unfree person it was a step toward attaining the condition in which the exercise of a moral will is considered a right. Nor does Douglass stop there. He goes on to explain that, unlike a number of other fugitive slaves who had paid no ransom to secure freedom because they had chosen to continue residing in Britain, he felt that he "had a duty to perform—and that was to labor and suffer with the oppressed in my native land" (377). Let us take these words seriously. For Douglass, the value of being free was that it allowed him to perform what he took to be his duty—as a citizen, a formerly enslaved person, and a Black man. In his mind, then—a mind that had had been "pressed to extremes"—freedom and duty were entwined and inseparable.

Imperfect Reversibility

Along with his commitment to standpoint, and his unusual method of holding the terms of a binary in tension with each other, the third feature of Douglass's rhetoric that we should be alert to is chiasmus, especially a variant of it I call "imperfect reversibility." In Douglass's fugitive rhetoric, one key effect of chiasmus is to call attention to the precarity of standpoint and condition that all humans share. When Douglass wrote, "You have seen how a man was made a slave; you shall see how a slave was made a man," he was remarking not only on his own triumph but also on the reversibility embedded in the human condition: a man, *any* man, may be made a slave, and a slave, *any* slave, may make himself a man. (The generality of this precarity would have been lost if he had referred to himself and used the first-person pronoun.) All humans who take themselves to be completely "free," Douglass knew, unknowingly live in a precarious state in which their subjecthood and sense of personal sovereignty could be reversed, rendering them suddenly an object or a thing. Of course, this deep and foundational precarity is perceived more readily by those who are vulnerable than by those who are assured—many of whom maintain a stubborn "innocence," as James Baldwin puts it, that denies this truth of human existence.[14] And like Baldwin, Douglass believed that because such chiasmus is in fact shared by all humans, when it is acknowledged by them it can become a basis for human fellowship and solidarity.

Chiasmus structures an extraordinary number of Douglass's insights and arguments in other ways also. To point to just a few examples, in his well-known account in *My Bondage and My Freedom* of how he came to justify stealing food from his master Hugh Auld, Douglass summarizes his reasoning through a series of chiasmic statements: "As society has marked me out as privileged plunder, on the principle of self-preservation I am justified in plundering in turn. Since each slave belongs to all; all must, therefore, belong to each" (248). Arguing that *every* man knows in his heart that slavery is a moral evil, Douglass points out: "A man that does not recognize and approve for himself the rights and privileges contended for, in behalf of the American slave, has not yet been found. In whatever else men may differ they are alike in their apprehension of their natural and personal rights" (448).

But as this last example indicates, Douglass frequently gave a twist to chiasmus by indicating that the reversal it accomplishes is bound to be imperfect—and this twist marks the distinctively fugitive quality of his rhetoric. Thus, in explaining to his former master Thomas Auld how he came to justify his desire to escape enslavement, Douglass describes his reasoning in a series of chiasmic parallels, the effect of which is to assert both his similarity to Auld *and* their non-identity: "The morality of the act I dispose of as follows: I am myself; you are yourself; we are two distinct persons, equal persons. What you are, I am. You are a man, and so am I. God created us both, and made us separate beings. We are distinct persons, and are equally provided with faculties necessary to our individual existence" (414).

An ethics based on such reversibility with difference would honor both terms of this duality—similarity and non-identity—allowing neither term to incorporate or absorb the other. Indeed, such incorporation is precisely what the slaveholder intends when he claims that he, not the enslaved, owns the slave's body. The slaveholder thus blinds himself not only to the slave's legal and existential distinction from himself, but also to the complex ethics imperfect chiasmus, or reversibility with difference, demands. Douglass concludes by humorously admitting that in running away "secretly," he gave the appearance of knowingly doing something wrong. But then he playfully justifies himself by pointing out that this was Auld's fault, not his own: "Had I let you into the secret, you would have defeated the enterprise entirely; but for this, I should have been really glad to have made you acquainted with my intentions to leave" (414). In other words, they might have shared "the secret"—that is, been open and honest with each other about their similarity and non-identity—but Auld's material interest in possessing Douglass made this impossible.

Douglass's chiasmus is often composed of movement and intersection not simply between differences, but between opposites or irreconcilables, such as "man" and "slave." Take, for example, these sentences from a speech, reprinted in *My Bondage and My Freedom*, that we will return to many times throughout this book: "The slave is bound to mankind, by the powerful and inextricable net-work of human brotherhood. His voice is the voice of a man, and his cry is the cry of a man in distress, and man must cease to be man before he can become insensible to that cry" (450). The chiasmic second sentence accomplishes structurally what the first sentence aims to say substantively: that the man who is a slave and the man who is free are caught in a matrix in which their positions are always reversible—unless one of them chooses to exit that network and thereby "cease to be a man." This sentence carries us back to and sheds light on the slave song passage, which itself is deeply chiasmic. In that passage, the songs Douglass heard were certainly the cries of men in distress. But he tells us that many outsiders *misheard* them as songs of happiness. Their misunderstanding was caused not just by their denying their brotherhood with the enslaved, but by their inability to see that their different standpoint locations made perfect reversibility of their positions impossible.

Douglass makes a further, subtler point as well when he writes that the free man "does not and cannot, look from the same point of view from which the slave does" (351–52). He is not being inattentive here when he writes both "does not" and "cannot." Nor is he implying that the inability conveyed by "cannot" excuses the failure suggested by "does not." The reason he uses *both* verbs, as will become clearer over the course of this book, is that he believed that we should strive to see from another person's point of view even while knowing that such an effort can never fully succeed. The free man who "does not" see from the slave's point of view fails ethically because he does not even attempt to do so; the free man who tries to but does not realize that he *"cannot* see" exactly as the slave does also fails to meet Douglass's standards of ethical intersubjectivity. The point Douglass is making closely resembles political theorist Iris M. Young's argument that we must recognize that reciprocity is sometimes "asymmetrical." Taking issue with theorist Seyla Benhabib's claim that, "for a person to acknowledge others to be as valuable, morally, as herself . . . [she must understand] their positions as symmetrical and reversible," Young argues that "moral respect between people entails reciprocity in the sense that each acknowledges and takes account of the other." But in some instances, they must acknowledge also that "their relation is asymmetrical in terms of the history each has and the social position they occupy." In such cases, true moral respect would require them to perceive and work with such asymmetry when it occurs. It would oblige them to see that perfect "reversibility" is not achievable.[15]

Douglass believed that his own task was to stand at the point of chiasmic intersection between enslaved and nominally free Blacks on the one hand and free whites on the other, in order to perform a mode of translation that would negotiate such inevitable differences while also respecting them. He also knew that such translation could never fully succeed. The enslaved would always remain somewhat opaque to the free, and vice versa. So even as he claimed often to see things from the point of view of the enslaved, he just as often acknowledged the impossibility of communicating to his free audiences what slavery was really like. Yet asymmetrical reciprocity does not condemn us to absolute ignorance of the other. Indeed, imperfect reversibility opens up space for us to see and respect the disagreements that arise from the fact that different persons necessarily occupy different standpoints and therefore see things differently. Grains of difference will always block perfect reversibility and transparency, so reasoning should not aim to unify different perspectives in a single outlook.

This is why, I believe, Douglass did not resolve his earlier view of the slaves' songs into his later one, but rather kept both in play. The earlier view was that of an enslaved man, the latter that of a free man. Neither was complete; both were legitimate. But this did not mean that all perspectives on the slaves' songs were *equally* true. Some perspectives had failed to try sufficiently to see and feel from the point of view of the enslaved, and they had misunderstood their songs as songs of happiness. Douglass held up many examples of such misunderstanding in his speeches and autobiographies. In My *Bondage and My Freedom*, for example, he recalls that "the abolitionists themselves were not entirely free from" color prejudice, although "they were nobly struggling against it." In their zeal to demonstrate that they were without prejudice, however, they often betrayed their failure to step out of a white person's blinkered view of race. Douglass recounts that "when it was said to me, 'Mr. Douglass, I will walk to meeting with you; I am not afraid of a black man,' I could not help thinking—seeing nothing very frightful in my appearance—'And why should you be?'" (393). Here he gives credit to the abolitionists who had at least tried to "look from the same point of view" as a Black American, while he also gently chides them for having imagined that they had fully succeeded. And in recounting such stories, he aimed to give his white readers a more accurate translation of his Black perspective while also admitting that a perfect translation was unachievable.

The work of Maurice Merleau-Ponty, the philosopher who has given us the most thoughtful account of chiasmus, suggests that reversibility with a difference also characterizes the relation of the body to itself: in any given moment, the body can be the perceiver or the perceived, the subject or the object, but never the two at once. For this reason, Merleau-Ponty argues, we have an ineluctably chiasmic relation with ourselves, not just with others; our sense of having a unity of personal identity is an illusion, arising from our rapid oscillation back and forth between our self as subject (I touch myself) and our self as object (I am touched). What is more certain is that because I can and do move fluidly back and forth across my self as subject and my self as object, I have the potential to understand that such reversibility is built into human identity: knowing myself to be split from myself, I know also that I am fated always to be an object to others who simply cannot experience my subjecthood. Perhaps Douglass, keenly aware of his simultaneous subjecthood and objecthood, had an especially vivid sense of this instability—or fugitivity—built into individual identity per se. His "net-work of human brotherhood" includes, as we shall see, a shared sense of mutually inhabiting a world in which we are all both joined and separated, from ourselves and from one another.

Returning now to the final sentence of this passage, let us note the doubled chiasmus that structures it: "His voice is the voice of a man, and his cry is the cry of a man in distress, and man must cease to be man before he can become insensible to that cry." First, we have the slave's voice reversed into the voice of a man; then we have the words "cry-cry-man" reversed into "man-man-cry." The slave, through his voice, reverses or translates himself into his real identity as a man. Hearing that cry of a man, the listener must either heed that cry or cease to be a man himself. Thus, while chiasmus can take place as two bodies cross each other in physical struggle, as in Douglass's famous fight with Covey, it can also take place anytime two persons meet in human encounters. This means, as Douglass frequently reminds his audiences, that the tragedy inherent in the difference among standpoints is always accompanied by the comedy inherent in our *sharing* the unavoidable human dance of reversibility with difference.

Douglass wrote several accounts of this dance, emphasizing now its comic, now its tragic aspects. We have already seen his bemused recollection of "a good but simple-minded Abolitionist" who "said to me that he was not ashamed to walk with me down Broadway arm-in arm, in open daylight, and evidently thought he was saying something that must be very pleasing to my self importance, but it occurred to me, at the moment, that this man does not dream of any reason why I might be ashamed to walk arm-in-arm with him through Broadway in open daylight."[16] In an 1860 account of how Blacks and whites in America tended to relate to one another, his tone is more sober: "Consciously or unconsciously, almost every white man approaches a colored man with an air of superiority and condescension. The relation subsisting between the races at once shows itself between the individuals, and each prepares, when brought together, to soften the points of antagonism. The white man tries his hand at being Negro, and the Negro, to make himself agreeable, plays the white man. The end is, each knows the other only superficially."[17] Although some comedy infuses this scene as each party tries "to soften the points of antagonism" by translating himself into the subjectivity and standpoint of the other, tragedy gets the upper hand as each fails to acknowledge that their differences make this impossible. They are at an impasse. Instead of playing what literary scholar Lloyd Pratt calls "the game of strangerhood," and finding a measure of intimacy in their shared condition of imperfect reversibility, they wind up disavowing their differences and knowing each other "only superficially."[18]

These "opposite emotions" of the tragic and the comic are fully expressed by the "human mind" when "pressed to extremes" such as enslavement. The songs of the slaves—as Douglass heard them, anyway—quite literally gave voice to this twofold nature: "in the most boisterous rapture of sentiments, there was ever a deep tinge of melancholy" (184). "Sorrow and desolation have their songs, as well as joy and peace," he wrote, rebutting simplistic misunderstandings of the songs. Yet when he claimed in the next sentence that "slaves sing more to *make* themselves happy, than to express their happiness" (185; emphasis added), he suggests that the enslaved *evaded* this categorical distinction between sorrow and joy by using sadness to "*make* themselves happy." The sadness does not disappear in the act, however; indeed, it sustains the act and is sustained by it. So when the enslaved translated or reversed their sorrow songs into songs that could *make* them happy, they were at once acknowledging and exploiting this duality even as they refused to be caught by it. Douglass himself would seek to emulate such expressions of opposites in his writings, speeches, and political philosophizing. Perhaps this is why he kept returning to his understanding of these songs, honing it into an increasingly apt metaphor for his own distinctive way of thinking, or what Gates calls his "black hermeneutic."[19]

"We Require Respect, Not Merely Sympathy"

Two more of Douglass's modes of persuasion are worth discussing before we return to his work in the Black public sphere and see how his philosophy and rhetoric shaped the way he approached such issues as the constitutionality of slavery, the wisdom of Black emigration, the legitimacy of violence against slavery and racism, and the prospects for full Black citizenship after the Civil War. Douglass greatly admired and often sought to emulate the rhetorical techniques of some of the great orators of his day, including Wendell Phillips, William Lloyd Garrison, and Daniel O'Connell. But he used two particular rhetorical modes so often that we may fairly call them his own. One was a pervasive deployment of Romantic irony. The second was a startling willingness to insult and provoke.

Many readers have commented on Douglass's frequent use of irony, but the link between his irony and his political thought has been underexplored, perhaps a casualty of the disciplinary divide that has separated literary analyses of Douglass from accounts of his political philosophy. Douglass's irony often took the particular form known as Romantic irony, which has a complex, seemingly self-contradictory nature. On the one hand, it is critical and destructive of the object it mocks. At the same time, Romantic irony always implies an alternative to the object of its critique, but it does so only indirectly and implicitly, and with a tone that disarmingly ironizes its own pretensions to supply such an alternative. In other words, Romantic irony allows one to critique something without having to claim that one's own view of the matter is a wholly sufficient replacement for that view. It works by presenting "its perspective as restricted—as only one among many different perspectives on the unconditioned whole. . . . Being ironic is a way of consciously and intentionally bringing out the fragmentary nature of the human situation as lacking 'a view from nowhere.'"[20]

If Romantic irony is a mode of critique that eschews the universalist's "view from nowhere" and sees the limitation of every standpoint, including its own, what better mode of rhetoric for a thinker who had discovered (when still a child, as we shall see), that "the point from which a thing is viewed is of some importance" (148)? Romantic irony gave Douglass a rhetorical modality with which to criticize positions he took to be wrong (e.g., Garrisonian abolitionism) while also remaining faithful to his own perspectivalism, which by definition implied the "restricted" and fallible nature of his own view of matters. This is why he asserted that "true stability consists not in being of the same opinion now as formerly, but in a fixed principle of honesty, even urging us to the adoption or rejection of that which may *seem* to *us* to be true or false at the ever-present now."[21]

Yet it is crucial to bear in mind that Douglass also had adamantine faith in our moral powers and our ability to discern and obey the laws of our own being. Throughout his long career as an activist, he used such phrases as "truth everlasting." In 1848, when he was thirty, he had remarked that "properly speaking, there is such thing as new truth; for truth, like the God whose attribute it is, is eternal."[22] In 1881, aged sixty-three, he wrote in *Life and Times of Frederick Douglass*, "Schooled as I have been among the abolitionists of New England, I recognize that the universe is governed by laws which are unchangeable and eternal" (914). It is tempting to judge his oscillation back and forth between universalism and particularism as evidence of his intellectual inconsistency. But I believe we come closer to his view of the matter if we see it as a fugitive movement that refuses to be caught in either position because—in his view—the world itself is a site of perpetual struggle that requires one to adopt both positions.[23]

A second notable characteristic of Douglass's rhetorical style was his relish for insult. When speaking to both Black and white audiences, both before and after the Civil War, Douglass frequently insulted them in order to provoke their indignant response. As I have argued at length elsewhere, many Black Americans, "often speaking from outside or the very margins of the *demos*, suggest that indignation is a political emotion with powerful consequences for democracy and democratic citizenship. These voices repeatedly indicate that the involuntary nature of the indignation we feel whenever our dignity has been slighted or denied immediately confirms to ourselves and others that we do in fact possess dignity."[24] David Walker and Maria Stewart also berated their Black audiences to the point of insult, aiming thereby to trigger their indignation, deepen their consciousness of their dignity, and spur them to political action in defense of it.[25] As well, when Maria Stewart exhorted her Black audiences to prove their "manhood," she (like Douglass) was suggesting that Black quiescence confirmed whites' beliefs that Blacks were not truly fit for freedom. And like Douglass, she urged the assertion of Blacks' rights as a way of convincing whites that Blacks were entitled to full citizenship. She and Douglass both believed that even if Black Americans failed again and again to win their rights, by asserting them they at least deprived whites of one of their excuses for withholding them.[26]

What distinguishes Douglass's use of this technique from Stewart's and Walker's, however, is that it aimed to provoke a consciousness of Blacks' own *powers*. He believed that the assertion of rights also had a crucial *inward* effect: by expressing and actualizing Blacks' "latent powers," it made Black Americans themselves more conscious of their powers and of the dignity those powers potentially produced. Consider, for example, his remarks at a May 1849 abolitionist meeting at the Abyssinian Baptist Church in New York City, where resolutions were adopted that decried the degrading conditions white racism imposed on free Blacks. No copy of these proposals remains, nor of the preamble to them that Charles L. Remond read to the audience. It is safe to assume, however, that they were strongly worded; certainly, Douglass supported them. Nonetheless, in his closing remarks, he expresses strong dissatisfaction with them and proceeds to give them his own, distinctive inflection. He observes, first, "The preamble states a broad fact, that we are compelled to occupy a degraded position by a corrupt church. But this is a very tame statement. We are not only a proscribed people—a despised people—a contemned people—an insulted people—but an outraged people—weighed down under greater oppression than any other people."[27] In this string of adjectives—"compelled," "degraded," "despised," "contemned," "insulted," "outraged"—we see Douglass seeking to effect what he is stating: to figure degradation as insult, and to transform insult into outrage. He then takes his audience back over ground already covered by the meeting and lands once again on insult and outrage: "Everywhere we are treated as a degraded people. If we go to the church, we are despised there, and made to take an obscure place, though taxed equally with all other men; . . . we are never tried by our peers, but by our enemies. . . . We are compelled to be . . . hewers of wood and drawers of water—everywhere outraged, ill-treated, insulted" (168).

At this point, however, he abruptly reverses course: "But the worst part of all is, that we are contented under these circumstances. He was ashamed! Ashamed! Ashamed of his identity with those who were thus indifferent—with oppressed cowards!" (168). What we see here is Douglass first manifesting his indignation in *solidarity* with his audience and then, without warning, turning it against them to claim that he is also *different* from them: *he* is anything but "content," and indeed he is "ashamed" to be associated with those who are. In other words, having made plain that he was indignant at how difficult antebellum Black life was, and how strongly white racism militated against Black life and self-respect, he then used that indignation to authorize another indignation, this one aimed toward those who were "contented under these conditions." But did Douglass actually believe that any Blacks in his audience were "contented"? I doubt it. Was he truly "ashamed" of his identity with those who were "indifferent"? Perhaps. What is certain is that he employed a rhetorical strategy that provoked his audience to feel a countersurge of indignation toward *him*; he was firing them up, even if that meant making *himself* the target of their ire. He aimed to strengthen their dignity by claiming to doubt it. With the energy of their indignation aroused, Douglass continued: "Our white friends may do much for us, but we must do for ourselves. Equality and respectability can only be attained through our own exertions. We require respect—not merely sympathy. We have no right to respect if, being under the hoof of oppression, we are not manly enough to rise in our own cause, and do something to elevate ourselves from our degraded position" (168).

Douglass also employed a more conventional rhetorical strategy in order to convey dignity's importance to Black politics and democracy. Instead of insulting his listeners to provoke their indignant defense of their dignity, he would call their attention to the bonds of solidarity they must form in order to nurture and protect it. In May 1853, addressing a mixed white and Black audience at the thirteenth annual convention of the American and Foreign Anti-Slavery Society in the Broadway Tabernacle in New York City, he began by underscoring that the distinction between free Blacks and enslaved Blacks was disappearing, thanks in large part to the workings of the 1850 Fugitive Slave Act: "This people, free and slave, . . . are becoming a nation, in the midst of a nation. . . . The [free] black man is linked to his brother by indissoluble ties. The one cannot be truly free while the other is a slave. . . . We are one nation then, if not in immediate condition at least one in prospects."[28] The trope Douglass uses here to figure *Black* solidarity ("The black man is linked to his brother by indissoluble ties") was one he more often used to figure human, *cross-racial* solidarity (as when he declared, in an 1854 speech to a Canadian audience, "We need all nations bound together in one grand league of freedom, to enforce the principles of truth and justice against the stupendous evil [of slavery], before we shall be able to overthrow it").[29] Working at a deep level within the metaphor was Douglass's vision of the way human interdependence shapes and nurtures human dignity. Placed in the broader context of his customary use of the metaphor, however, his use of it on this day subtly shifts its meaning from *human* brothers to *Black* brothers being linked. The underlying logic here is that, if whites chose to deny Black dignity by disavowing the bonds that forge a common humanity with them, then Blacks would be wise to establish their own bonds of *Black* solidarity—even a Black "nation"—as an enabling context for the affirmation of Black dignity.[30]

To the whites in this particular audience, Douglass unabashedly asserted his own dignity and that of all Blacks by acknowledging at the outset, "I am a colored man, and this is a white audience" (424). As a Black man, he had "an intense and painful sense of the immense disadvantage" under which he labored to persuade them of his rights. Unlike a white man, "he is little borne up by that brotherly sympathy and generous enthusiasm" that would sustain him in his efforts. Instead, he has been excluded from the human family, his human dignity has been denied, and he feels flowing toward him from his audience "a cold, flinty-hearted, unreasoning and unreasonable prejudice against him *as a man*" (727; emphasis added). Nonetheless, he proudly proclaims his identity with his race and with their "standpoint":

> But whatever character or capacity you [whites] ascribe to us, I am not ashamed to be numbered with this race. I am not ashamed to speak here as a negro. Sir, I utterly abhor and spurn with all the contempt possible that cowardly meanness, I will not call it pride, which leads any colored man to repudiate his connection with his race. . . . I would place myself—nay, I am placed—among the victims of American oppression. I view this subject from their standpoint—and scan the moral and political horizon of the country with their hopes, their fears, and their intense solicitude. (427)

Despite such explicit statements of his self-identification with the Black community, Douglass's hectoring and at times self-righteous and

self-serving tone may have offended many of his Black readers and listeners. At times, he even seemed to call for Blacks' absorption into a
white middle-class culture, while implicitly blaming free Blacks' oppression on themselves. Indeed he walked a razor's edge. On the one
hand, he was eager to motivate free Black citizens to engage more energetically in both formal politics and extra-political agitation. On the
other hand, the language in which he cast his motivational speeches
sometimes implied that, in failing to be conscious of their powers, they
had failed to meet standards of comportment that whites had set. The
ambiguity that arose from the subtle difference between these mes-
sages in fact haunted *all* antebellum Black elevation discourse, which, as
one scholar has observed, was characterized by a "pragmatic interplay
between the conventional and the subversive."[31] Douglass's distinctive
contribution to the *subversive* aspect of this discourse was his emphasis
on Blacks' powers. In his view, there was a crucial connection between
each individual's consciousness of his or her "latent powers" as a human
being and the political empowerment of the group whose possession of
those powers had been denied or abridged by racism.

About a century later, Kwame Ture (formerly Stokely Carmichael)
and Charles Hamilton would assert in *Black Power* that "the initiative for
change will have to come from the Black community. We cannot expect
white America to begin to move forcefully unless and until Black America begins to move."[32] In his editorials of the late 1840s and early 1850s,
Douglass made essentially the same point: "Our white friends can and
are earnestly removing the barriers to our improvement, which themselves have set up; but the main work must be commenced, carried on,
and concluded by ourselves."[33] Ture and Hamilton developed their theory of Black Power to motivate African Americans to engage in a more
dynamic and realistic political struggle against white racism. Douglass
also turned to the language of "energy," "latent powers," and "faculties
and powers" in large part to motivate the antebellum Black community.
Broadly speaking, then, Douglass, Ture, and Hamilton all believed that
rights talk and freedom talk, valuable as they may be, are sometimes
not enough; they have to be supplemented, perhaps even replaced, by
power talk. Yet an important difference also distinguishes their views.
For Ture and Hamilton, the powers to be recognized and exercised were
those of a race working in a solidarity forged by race pride to overturn
white supremacist oppression. Perhaps at some cost to his subsequent

relevance to Black politics, the powers Douglass had in mind were human powers. "Man's greatness," as he declared in 1848, "consists in his ability to do, and the proper application of his powers to do things needful to be done, and not in the color of his skin."[34]

"Suppose You Yourselves Were Black"

When Douglass addressed mainly white audiences, he often used this pull-and-push mode of rhetorical address, one that invited then into an intimate feeling of human brotherhood yet also repelled them with insult and sarcasm. The nature of indignation, as we have seen, is that it appears to be natural, spontaneous, and involuntary; as such, it testifies that the dignity it defends is also innate and natural.[35] But indignation can work in another way as well. It is sometimes an expostulation that protests what it regards as a violation of norms that two persons are presumed to *share*. It testifies, then, not just to the individual dignity it defends but also to a common *human* dignity shared and involuntarily recognized by all humans. Douglass delighted in compelling his white audiences to witness, feel, and share his indignation, thereby making them *experience* their common humanity with Blacks. This is not the same thing as compelling them to sympathize with Blacks, however, for sympathy can shift easily into pity, whereas indignation tends to provoke respect.

Douglass struck his most confrontational tone when he accused American churches of supporting the slavery system; his allegations, while true, outraged many in his audiences, as he knew they would. For example, according to a reporter from the antiabolitionist *New York Sun*, in an 1848 speech he declared: "It is a notorious fact that men were sold to build churches—women were sold to pay the expenses of missionaries—and children were sold to buy Bibles. The Episcopalians, the Presbyterians, the Universalists, the Unitarians, the Methodists, are all in connexion with and abettors of slavery. The American church is a brotherhood of thieves. (Great confusion, excitement, hissing, and cheering.)" Yet just a moment later, this journalist reports, Douglass "had recourse to mimicry which he appeared to be a complete master of. He had some popular pulpit orator in his mind's eye, for nearly one half the audience laughed outrageously, while the other half started on their feet to go away." The reporter goes on to relate: "Whilst the ladies and gentlemen were moving towards the door in a very excited mood, the lecturer [Douglass] addressed them thus—Suppose you yourselves were black, and that your sisters and brothers were in slavery, subject to the brutality and the lash of the atrocious tyrant who knew no mercy. Suppose, I say, that you were free, and that your dearest and nearest relatives were in the condition that the Southern slaves are, and that the Church sanctioned such infamy, would you not feel as I do?"

By thus challenging his offended white listeners to "suppose" themselves "black" and to feel as he did, Douglass alienated them more deeply, insisting on the chiasmic interchangeability that haunts human existence. "There is no use in being offended with me," he continued; "I have a right to address you. There is no difference, except of color, between us." And then he pressed his point again by shifting from indignation to humorous sarcasm: "And as I said four years ago, I say now—I am your brother—(cheers and laughter)—yes I am, and [although] you may pass me by as you will and cut me and despise me, I'll tell everyone I meet that I am your brother. (Cheers and laughter.)"[36] All these frequent and rapid shifts of tone kept his audiences on their toes, uncertain whether the "real" Douglass was a hilarious mimic, a thundering prophet, an insulting bully, or a compassionate brother. In his refusal to settle into any one of these roles and his insistence on playing all of them, we catch another glimpse of what I have been calling the fugitivity of his rhetorical style.

In a speech delivered just a few months later, Douglass again performed his indignation in a way that he knew would be offensive to some members of his audience: "What I say may not be very pleasant to those who venerate the Constitution, but nevertheless, I must say to you that, by the support you give to that instrument, you are the enslavers of my southern brethren and sisters." He went on to unsettle these listeners even further by praising the slave insurrections led by Nat Turner and Madison Washington. Then, quoting from Bishop Meade's *Sermons to Slaves*, he mimicked and ridiculed the circumlocutions by which defenders of slavery referred to it: "peculiar institution," "patriarchal institution," "our domestic relations." As the reporter from the *Liberator* observed: "Those who have never heard Frederick Douglass's sarcastic tones, and seen his expressive countenance, can have but a poor idea of the humor of this part of his speech, or of its overwhelming effect upon the audience."[37] At a deep level, I would suggest, that "effect" was to elicit whites' involuntary identification with a Black orator. Every time they laughed with Douglass, white audiences *felt* human brotherhood with him even when he was underscoring the distance that lay between them. Again, his practice was to use and exhibit the dynamics of reversibility with difference.

One of Douglass's most triumphant public performances was simultaneously an act of physical resistance and a virtuosic display of his command of chiasmus, reversibility with difference, and indignation. He was in New York, in May 1850, participating in an antislavery meeting when a gang of rough-looking men suddenly pushed their way into the hall, determined to break the meeting up by intimidating—and, if necessary, beating—those in attendance. They were led by Isaiah Rynders, a Tamany Hall strongman known in New York as "Captain" Rynders. Seeing them jostle forward, Douglass quickly stepped up to block their way. His figure, we know, was imposing, and his expression magisterial. They came to a hesitant halt.

"Sir," declared Douglass, addressing Rynders, "at Rochester, we don't know a white man who will so far demean himself as to insult a negro." His implication was clear: that Rynders was a small-minded bully who picked on the weak and therefore had no proper conception of what constituted real human dignity. Before Rynders could react, Douglass delivered a blunt warning: "I throw out this remark in order that you may know in what light I should regard the man who would offer me an insult. The fact is, I, who have endured the whip of the slaveholder, who bear the marks of the lash upon my back, who have been driven to the slave market in the town of Easton, Talbot County, Maryland, and exposed for sale, like a brute beast, to the highest bidder—I cannot well appreciate an insult. Therefore, let no man hope to succeed in insulting me."[38]

A hush fell over the crowd. Would Rynders dare to insult Douglass? Apparently not, since after a short pause Douglass demanded to know: "Am I a man?" (238).

That question backed Rynders into a corner. If he answered, "No," he risked provoking a physical fight with Douglass, which he plainly wished to avoid; on the other hand, if he replied, "Yes," he risked making an unthinkable concession. So he tried to wriggle his way off the horns of this dilemma with a witty retort:

"You are not a black man," he replied; "you are only half a nigger."

At these words, Douglass lifted his gaze and met the eyes of his audience. "He is correct; I am, indeed, only half a negro." And then, after a perfectly timed pause, he continued: "a half-brother to Mr. Rynders" (239).

Douglass's reply triggered "roars of laughter" from the assembled crowd, both friends and enemies, and sealed his triumph. He had met Rynders with a subtle insult, then cowed him with his readiness to fight, and finally overmatched him with his quicker wit—using a phrase ("half-brother") that again exemplifies reversibility with difference: they are like enough to be brothers, but different enough to be only half-brothers. Biographical accounts of this exchange stop there. But Douglass himself did not. In a quietly dramatic shift of registers, he tried to explain something to Rynders:

> Those who ask us why we don't learn trades, or do something to make ourselves respectable, do not seem to know the difficulties under which the negro labors from day to day. . . . I say we are compelled by the circumstances of our condition at present to get our living the best way we can in honesty; and I believe, considering the narrow limits into which we are driven—excluded from all trades and avocations—it is a miracle to me that we do as well as we are—that we make as respectable an appearance as we do. (241)

In this daring appeal to Rynders's sense of fair play, Douglass implicitly calls for him to consider the matter of Black dignity from a Black point of view. Douglass admits that Blacks appear to many whites to lack dignity, but he quietly asserts that, considering their circumstances, Blacks have achieved something of a "miracle" by doing as well as they have.

Eight months later, again in New York and again addressing a mainly white audience, he more fully described the condition of Black precarity in the North:

> Would to God that I could on this occasion impart to my audience even a slight idea of the mournful condition and deep sadness of the people with whom I am identified. You are strangers to our feelings. A few of you only appreciate them. There is a bitter peculiarity in the feelings which are induced by the present state of things, which you cannot fully understand. To dread the serpent, the hyena, the tiger,

and other ferocious inhabitants of the untamed forest, is natural. From these we shrink instinctively. But to be afraid of our brother man; to dread the approach of a being with faculties and powers like our own—a being whose presence should shed over us the bright beams of social happiness and brotherly kindness—. . . adds to the pang of fear and dread, an intense mortification. Too deep, too keen and too bitter to be described.[39]

Like Douglass's appeal to the buried humanity of Isaiah Rynders, this admission of a "mournful condition and deep sadness" risked portraying the free Black community's condition as one of abjection. It also risked implying that Black Americans deserved the pity of whites, not their respect. And when Douglass suggested that the "intense mortification" felt by Blacks was "too deep, too keen, and too bitter to be described," he acknowledged yet another layer of risk: that the pain inflicted by repeated insult to one's dignity is matched by the pain of *revealing* or confessing to it. Yet he also mitigated all these dangers by insisting that both whites and Blacks possessed "the faculties and powers" that comprise the essence of human nature, and by underscoring the asymmetrical reciprocity and imperfect reversibility that characterized Black and white relations: you are "our brother man," but you are also "strangers to our feelings" who "cannot fully understand" us. In this simultaneous evocation of both human brotherhood and human estrangement, Douglass once again expressed opposite emotions with a single method.

CHAPTER FOUR

"Assault Compels Defense"

Douglass on Black Emigration and Violence

What we have been tracing, then, is Douglass's elaboration of his chapter of political philosophy, the key words of which are "powers," "consciousness," and "dignity." The logic that links these ideas begins, as we have seen, with his belief that all humans possess certain moral and intellectual powers, and that these powers constitute the very humanness, or "humanity," of humankind. They lie "latent" within us until we start to exercise them, and that exercise makes us conscious of having them; experiencing such consciousness, we begin to feel a sense of self-worth, or dignity, which we expect others to acknowledge. If they do not, we feel their refusal as an injustice.

Douglass did not present these ideas in systematic form as a treatise of political philosophy; much less did he imagine—as Locke did in his *Second Treatise of Civil Government*—the conditions and motives that might have led humans to establish the earliest forms of government. But I think we can speculatively extrapolate such a mythos of the origins and purpose of democracy from his writings. A democracy, his work suggests, is a polity that prizes human dignity. It comes into existence when a group of persons agrees to acknowledge each other's dignity, both informally, through mutually respectful comportment, and formally, through the establishment of political rights. Those rights would guarantee every citizen's ability to exercise and put forth their innate human powers, thereby becoming conscious of their dignity and manifesting it to others, who would in turn acknowledge it. In such a theory, dignity is foundational to democracy. All our freedoms—of thought, religion, movement, assembly, speech, and so on—are *means* toward the end of maintaining a political community in which all persons collaboratively produce their dignity.

Douglass's chapter of political philosophy derived, as he claimed, from his "slave experience." Enslavement had indicated to him that the ultimate aim of oppressive orders is to turn humans into objects, or "things," so as to reduce them to instruments of the dominator's will and, at the same time, to deprive them of the sense of self-worth from which, Douglass indicates, all political activity and resistance arise. The curtailment of their freedoms, the destruction of their family life, the insistence that the master's capricious will may trump all moral or legal considerations—all these and many other cruelties of the slavery system had the purpose of destroying the dignity of the enslaved. But, in Douglass's personal experience, and as he repeatedly affirmed, this effort to destroy the dignity of the enslaved could seldom fully succeed. The enslaved were determined to resist it in countless ways. And the very source of that resistance was their inextinguishable consciousness of having the powers that constitute humanness, and of possessing therefore some measure of human dignity.

This theory of dignity, rights, and democracy was applicable, Douglass believed, not just to Black Americans striving for full citizenship but to all Americans. Although his experience had showed him that the resistance of the enslaved made utter destruction of their dignity impossible, it also revealed to him that human dignity is much more vulnerable than most of his white contemporaries could imagine. He saw that every link in the logic that leads from our innate powers to our political rights is vulnerable. Although our powers are an innate aspect of our very being as humans, an oppressive order may seek to prevent us from exercising those powers. Lacking opportunities to exercise our powers, we may not become fully conscious of them; even if we do have opportunities to exercise them, systematic refusal to recognize and affirm the dignity such exercise produces may weaken it. And not being sufficiently confident in our dignity, we may hesitate to demand the political rights that have been designed, as Douglass thought, to protect it. A keen awareness of vulnerability, then, permeated Douglass's political thought.

Along with his more robust conception of the human, this attunement to vulnerability and Douglass's strong belief that freedom is always accompanied (and indeed made possible) by submission to the dictates of one's conscience are what distinguish his thought from Emerson's, which closely resembles it. "Through egalitarian moral respect," writes Jack Turner in his account of Emersonian self-reliance, "the self-reliant register their commitment to human equality and signal their transcendence of the base desire to establish their dignity through others' degradation. Conditioning one's dignity on the subjection of others is not strength but weakness, an exposure of the spiritually slavish need to dominate, and an admission of a lack of self-trust."[1] Douglass would certainly have agreed with these statements, but he would have phrased them somewhat differently. The words "equality" and "egalitarian" do not appear nearly as frequently in his work as the words "power," "dignity," and "brotherhood." Although he did affirm the idea of human and political equality, and on occasion asserted it, the idea was too abstract to do the work he thought necessary—which was to establish that Blacks were substantively of the *same human nature* as whites and to persuade whites that this very nature *compelled* them to show moral respect to their Black fellow humans. Further, Emerson's language (and Turner's gloss of it) usually posits a sovereign being who can freely choose to show moral respect and refrain from domination. Douglass, by contrast, understands the being who faces these choices as far more deeply woven into the "net-work of human brotherhood" than Emerson suggests. That deeper entwinement of individual and species identity has two effects: it makes one's affective loyalty to other humans a part of one's nature, not a free choice; and it makes one's consciousness of one's dignity, and with it one's "self-trust," far more contingent on others' affirmation, and far more vulnerable to their denial, than Emerson ever imagined.

The challenge Douglass posed to himself as an activist thinker, therefore, was twofold. On the one hand, he had to try to persuade all "despondent" Black citizens to exercise their powers, to become fully conscious of their dignity, and to unequivocally demand their rights. On the other hand, he had to persuade white Americans that the core ethical responsibility of humankind, and especially of citizens of a democracy, is to defend one's own dignity while also acknowledging and protecting the dignity of all other persons. Such acknowledgment, he argued, was a duty laid upon all humans by their own moral power, that is, by their very humanness. It was what he called a "law of our [own] being." Every person intuitively understands this law, he believed, because when one becomes conscious of being a self, one at the very same time becomes aware of being a human self. Self-consciousness and species consciousness (or what Douglass called a sense of "human brotherhood") are coformative and inseparable.

In the first chapter of this book, we saw Douglass discovering and developing this political philosophy at the time he founded the *North Star* and started devoting his energies not just to abolitionism but to the debates that engaged the free Black community. In the second chapter, we traced his effort to add an "adequate idea of humanity" to the nation's public philosophy, and in the third, we examined the ways Douglass's distinctive political thought must be found in its fugitive style and rhetoric, not just in its propositions or substance. Now we shall return to the early 1850s and see how this philosophy and rhetoric informed his positions on two questions that troubled free Blacks (and many whites) at that time: the appropriateness of emigration as a response to white racism and the legitimacy of violence as a weapon against slavery. Although Douglass's engagement with both issues has been productively discussed by many scholars, it looks very different when we trace how it was guided by the philosophy and method he had drawn from his experience of enslavement.

"We Can Plant Ourselves at the Very Portals of Slavery"

Douglass was a strong advocate of Black political organizations, and an occasional supporter of all-Black schools, but for most of his life he was a fierce opponent of schemes for Black emigration. Three considerations shaped the position he took on this issue. First, he believed that Black Americans had done at least as much as any other group to clear the land and construct the material infrastructure on which the nation arose; they were therefore at least as deserving of citizenship as many whites. Second, he regarded most voluntary Black emigration schemes as plainly impractical, so he concluded that they served only a fantasy function for Black Americans who could no longer bear the indignities heaped upon them in the United States. The third and most important reason he opposed such schemes, however, was that he believed that even Black American proposals for voluntary emigration played into the hands of the American Colonization Society and lent credibility to the general belief that persons of African descent did not properly "belong" in the United States.[2]

Douglass's views on emigration have often been contrasted with those of Martin Delany, and rightly so, as we shall see. But it is important to note the similarities in their analyses of slavery and racism before examining the nature and causes of their differences. Both men believed that, historically, oppression was a common phenomenon—perhaps even the rule of social organization, not the exception. Both believed also that oppressors frequently justified their regimes by alleging the innate inferiority of those whom they rule; and both men agreed that oppressors frequently designated the most oppressed group in a society as a class or race inferior to all others who compose that society. As Delany wrote: "It is not enough that, these people are denied of equal privileges by their rulers, but, more effectually to succeed, the equality of these classes must be denied, and their inferiority as distinct races, actually asserted." Both also saw that skin color, or "race," was the marker that rulers in the United States used: the color of whites, said Delany, "is made, by law and custom, the mark of distinction and superiority; while the color of the blacks is a badge of degradation, acknowledged by statute, organic law, and the common consent of the people." Both thinkers concurred as well that in response to such conditions, Black Americans would have to act. "Except we do," declared Delany, "it is idle to talk about rights, it is mere chattering for the sake of being seen and heard—like the slave, saying something because his 'master' has said it, and saying just what he told him to say."[3] Both men also agreed about some of the specific actions free Black Americans should take: they must educate themselves so as to be less dependent on whites; they must have "a more general bearing as useful contributors to society at large," as Delany writes; they must develop better "business habits and training"; and they must refrain from mistaking "the opportunity to dress and appear well" as the path to equality of citizenship. Finally, and to my mind most interestingly, both men believed that the particular kind of citizenship Black Americans desired was citizenship that gave them scope for action rather than just conferring on them a status. As Delany wrote to William Lloyd Garrison: "The majority of white men cannot see why colored men cannot be satisfied with their condition in Massachusetts—why they desire more than the *granted* right of citizenship. Blind selfishness on the one hand, and deep prejudice on the other, will not permit them to understand that we desire the *exercise* and *enjoyment* of those rights, as well as the name of their possession."[4]

Douglass and Delany differed, however, on two key issues. One was their understanding of the function white racism served in the United States. The other, which followed from that, was their understanding of how white Americans would perceive Blacks' voluntary emigration. Delany knew well that white racism asserted the "natural inferiority" of Blacks. And he knew also that this allegation denied—remained blind to—Blacks' intellectual and cultural achievements, as examples of which he includes, in his *The Condition, Elevation, Emigration and Destiny of the Colored People of the United States, Politically Considered* (1852), brief accounts of Phyllis Wheatley (a poet), Benjamin Banneker (a mathematician), and James Durham (a physician), all of whom were "of an unmixed extraction" (198). But Delany's summary of these persons' achievements is comparatively superficial: to him, they exemplify "various talents and acquirements in the several departments of respectability."

But what produces respectability itself? This he did not ask or try to answer. What he developed instead was a theory of what he called "inherent sovereignty." In his "Political Destiny of the Colored Race on the American Continent," a keynote address delivered to the 1854 National Emigration Convention of Colored Men, he posited that "a people, to be free, must necessarily be *their own rulers*; that is, *each individual* must, in himself, embody the essential ingredient—so to speak—of the *sovereign principle* which composes the *true basis* of his liberty." Whenever rulers had managed to monopolize the principle of inherent sovereignty, allocating it only to their own people, tribe, or followers, the only way for the oppressed to regain inherent sovereignty was through complete destruction of their current identity and complete absorption into the dominant group: "to elevate to equality the degraded subject of law and custom . . . can only be done, as in Europe, by an entire destruction of the identity of the former condition of the applicant. Even were this desirable—which we by no means admit—with the deep seated prejudices engendered by oppression, with which we have to contend, ages incalculable might reasonably be expected to roll around, before this could honorably be accomplished."[5]

Delany's phrase "which we by no means admit" reveals one reason (perhaps *the* reason) for his investment in "inherent sovereignty" and his advocacy of emigration. The idea of an *inherent* principle of self-rule that oppressors deny and destroy is close to the idea that different groups have different inherent identities. "The truth is," he continues, "we are not identical with the Anglo-Saxon or any other race or pure white type of the human family. . . . We have then inherent traits, attributes—so to speak—and native characteristics, peculiar to our race—whether pure or mixed blood—and all that is required of us is to cultivate these and develop them into their purity, to make them desirable and emulated by the rest of the world."[6] If Blacks chose to remain in the United States, he argued, whatever remained of their "inherent sovereignty" and "inherent traits" would disappear within a culture of whiteness; moreover, "ages incalculable" would have to pass for this to be accomplished "honorably"—that is, through voluntary interracial marriages rather than through white sexual coercion of Blacks. To preserve their racial sovereignty and identity, then, Black Americans would have to emigrate.[7]

Douglass, however, consistently rejected such essentialist thinking. His firm belief in a universal humanity led him to regard what he called Black "race pride" with deep suspicion, for it splintered the idea of human brotherhood on which he had founded all his hopes for the world moving past racialist thinking. He also suspected that it was merely a reflexive mirroring by Blacks of whites' racial pride. Finally, he thought Black emigrationists fundamentally misunderstood the purpose white racism served for whites.

Douglass believed, as we have seen, that dignity was in considerable measure an intersubjective, collaboratively produced phenomenon. By the same token, however, the *denial* of dignity and the disparagement of another race also expressed an intersubjective relation. Because the conditions of life in a republic undergoing rapid economic change threatened the "sense of dignity" of many white Americans, they sought to establish it on a permanent, biological foundation—that is, in their "racial" identity, or in whiteness. But this strategy required whiteness to be manifestly superior to blackness. Therefore, Douglass reasoned, if Blacks insisted on demonstrating that they too had dignity, their comportment would undermine the racial foundation of whites' sense of comparative superiority on which they tried to establish their own race-based dignity. In short, white racists *required* signs of Black complacence and docility in order to continue maintaining their disparaging beliefs about Blacks and their convictions about whites' superiority and dignity. This is precisely why, as Douglass pointed out many times, that "while we are servants, we are never offensive to whites. . . . It is not our color which makes our proximity to white men disagreeable. . . . It is, as we have said, an intense hatred of the colored man when he is distinguished for any ennobling qualities of head or heart."[8] Any such manifestation of Black distinction enraged white racists because it put the lie to their belief that whiteness alone conferred human dignity.

Opposition to white racism began, therefore, with a firm refusal to "submit" to it—in word, deed, gesture, or attitude. The very impracticality of emigration schemes, and their very function as a fantasy, made them all the more potent (though of course unintentional) collaborators in whites' own belief that, as Douglass wrote in *My Bondage and My Freedom*, "it is impossible for white people ever to look upon dark races of men, or men belonging to the African race, with other than feelings of aversion" (396). Whether wisely or naively, Douglass believed that this myth would eventually be overcome by certain irresistible facts: whites and Blacks were equal members of a universal humanity, equally possessed of human powers and faculties, equally worthy of respect, and equally deserving of political rights. Black Americans' best hope, therefore, was to stand behind these facts and keep insisting upon them, instead of drifting into and supporting the delusions of their white oppressors.

Crucially, Douglass was not against voluntary Black emigration per se. Indeed, as political theorist Juliet Hooker has shown, he defended the right to migrate as a human right.[9] His position, rather, was that Black emigration would be wise *only* if it could plainly and unambiguously express Black power and dignity. He made this clear, for example, in his speech "The Present Condition and Future Prospects of the Negro People" (1853). There, he argued that Black colonization schemes reflected the slavery system's fear of the growing *power* of a free Black community: "Here is the secret of the Colonization scheme. It is easily seen that just in proportion to the intelligence and respectability of the free colored race at the North is their power to endanger the stability of slavery. Hence the desire to get rid of us." "Getting rid of," Douglass explained, meant getting free Blacks *far away* from enslaved Blacks—all the way to Africa. Douglass quite willingly entertained the prospect of

Black emigration to a more proximate location: "There are more desirable lands open to us. We can plant ourselves at the very portals of slavery. We can hover about the Gulf of Mexico. Nearly all the isles of the Caribbean Seas bid us welcome. . . . With the Gulf of Mexico on the South, and Canada on the North, we may still keep within hearing of the wails of our enslaved people in the United States." Douglass then referred to reports from the British and Foreign Anti-Slavery Society to point out that more than twelve million persons of African descent now lived in the New World. Perhaps, he implied, free Blacks in the North of the United States could and should unite with these millions into one Black nation. Then they would pose an even more formidable threat to the slavery system than they did living in the northern parts of the nation.[10]

In sum, Douglass's position on Black emigration was perfectly consistent with itself if we see it as an expression of his political philosophy. It turned on his understanding of dignity as a quality that was produced by the natural powers inherent in individuals (and groups), but that unlike Delany's "inherent sovereignty" also required some recognition and confirmation by others—in this case, specifically, the white American majority in the U.S. polity. He maintained that an inherent individual or group identity, produced completely independently and without collaboration with and recognition from others, was unachievable and an illusion. For these reasons, he believed that all proposals for Black emigration emanating from the free Black community were obliged to consider deeply how they would be read and interpreted by whites. Black emigration made sense to him only when it was presented as an expression of Black power and as a threat to white supremacy. When motivated by pessimistic despondence, however, it could be taken for a capitulation to the principles and aims of white racism—and that, in his view would be disastrous.

Black Violence in Defense of Black Dignity

The familiar question of how Douglass viewed violence also looks different when we see his positions as an expression of the political philosophy he was elaborating from his experience of enslavement and honing through his labors as a Black activist intellectual. Influenced, perhaps, by the more recent thinking of Mohandas K. Gandhi and Martin Luther King Jr., many scholars of Douglass have tended to regard *all* "violence" as categorically different from "nonviolence," a distinction that has obscured the subtler distinction Douglass drew between aggressive violence (which he often called a manifestation or consequence of "irresponsible power") and defensive violence (which he regarded as being an expression of our "moral power").[11]

Like other aspects of his political philosophy, Douglass derived this principled distinction from his experience of enslavement and his personal observations of both kinds of violence within the slavery system. He frequently asserted that the slaveholders' violence, like the craving for absolute power it expressed, knew no bounds. It was self-perpetuating and erotic, creating the *desire* to inflict yet more violence. As Douglass insists elsewhere: "I repeat, then, that a system which gives absolute power to one man over the body and soul of another man, is in its nature aggressive, and the parent of all manner of treachery and fraud. It is never satisfied."[12] It is "never satisfied" because the slaveholder can never succeed in compelling total submission, but feels compelled to continue trying to do so. It is never satisfied because, in violating the commands of his conscience, the slaveholder is at war with himself; as that war rages within him, he seeks an outlet for his rage by redoubling his aggressions against his slaves, whom he blames for his own pain. In Douglass's graphic recollection of Captain Anthony's whipping of Esther, for example, he strongly suggests that Anthony did not simply whip her; he could not *stop* whipping her, as "her piercing cries seemed only to increase his fury" (177). Aggressive violence shrugs off all restraints, and as it corrupts the character of the person who exercises it, it renders him ever less able to use self-restraint.

Having lived in such proximity to aggressive and irresponsible power, and to its natural inclination to become ever more aggressively and irresponsibly violent, Douglass consistently regarded himself as what he called "a peace man."[13] And, having observed that the souls of many whites had been poisoned and corrupted by the violence that anti-Black racism encouraged them to feel and wield, he feared what the exercise of violence might do morally to himself, to free Blacks in the North, and to his three million brethren in bondage. However, he had also observed how effective and inspiring *defensive* violence could be, and he distinguished it from aggressive violence because he understood it to be an expression of moral power, not a violation of it.

Recall George Combe's claim that man naturally has the ability to place "his faculties in harmony among themselves," and Douglass's own assertion that "all reform is an effort to bring man more and more into harmony with the laws of his own being." Defensive violence was by its very nature self-restraining and in "harmony" with our moral powers and their ethical commands. This kind of violence he frequently applauded, as when he famously declared, in August 1852: "The slaveholders not only forfeit their right to liberty, but to life itself. We expect this great National Convention to lay down some such principle as this. . . . The only way to make the Fugitive Slave Law a dead letter is to make half a dozen or more dead kidnappers."[14] On yet another occasion, he asserted that "nothing short of physical resistance will render the colored people of the North safe from the horrible enormities which must result from the execution of the fugitive slave law; and I should rather have heard that colored men had been beaten down by the two hundred police men employed on that occasion, than that there should have been no manifestation of physical resistance to the re-enslavement of poor Long [a fugitive slave]."[15] On both these occasions (and many others), the violence Douglass endorsed was defensive violence specifically.

Douglass's representation in *My Bondage and My Freedom* of his violent struggle with the "slave-breaker" Edward Covey further confirms that he regarded only defensive violence as justified. When we view his account through the lens of his political philosophy, what we notice is the philosophical depth of his claim that his physical resistance to Covey had restored his "self-respect" (286) and "manhood" (286)—Douglass's terms, as we have seen, for what he would also call "dignity" and "natural dignity." Moreover, he took pains to explain to his readers that the violence he had exercised on that occasion was a self-restraining violence: "I was strictly on the defensive, preventing him from injuring me, rather than trying to injure him" (283). Understood by some critics to be a disingenuous sop thrown to his pacifist allies in the abolitionist movement, this sentence is actually a clear expression of the distinction Douglass consistently drew between defensive (moral) and aggressive (immoral) violence. And although he called this struggle "undignified" and admitted that a "fighting madness" had overcome him, he also presented himself as having comported himself in a cool and dignified manner: "'Are you going to resist, you scoundrel?' said he. To which, I returned a polite 'yes sir'; steadily gazing my interrogator in the eye, to meet the first approach or dawning of the blow, which I expected my answer would call forth" (283).[16]

Moreover, as philosopher Frank Kirkland has persuasively argued, Douglass indicates it was not his *life* that he was prepared to defend with violence, but his self-respect: for Douglass, as Kirkland writes, "what provides moral entitlement to self-defense and non-compliance is not self-preservation in the face of death itself, but rather the restoration of self-respect in the face of the denigrating aims of an aggressor who uses violence even to the point of death as a vehicle for his aims."[17] Political theorist Margaret Kohn has observed in a similar vein that the transformation triggered by the fight with Covey turns on Douglass's realization that he is not afraid to die in defense of his dignity: Douglass's "repeated emphasis on manhood suggests that the fight was primarily about honor and dignity."[18]

Douglass's best-known use of the word "dignity" appears in a sentence he added in *My Bondage and My Freedom* to the 1845 *Narrative*'s account of this fight: "I was a changed being after that fight. I was nothing before; I WAS A MAN NOW. It recalled to life my crushed self-respect and my self-confidence, and inspired me with a renewed determination to be A FREEMAN. A man, without force, is without the essential dignity of humanity. Human nature is so constituted, that it cannot honor a helpless man, although it can pity him; and even this it cannot do long, if the signs of power do not arise" (286). Douglass's belief that "a man, without force, is without the essential dignity of humanity" should not be mistaken for a crudely masculinist identification of dignity with physical strength. Rather, Douglass regarded dignity itself as a force insofar as it was the outward manifestation of our consciousness of our "latent powers" or "energy." Consistent with his belief in the intersubjective nature of human dignity, he argued that such powers must give "signs" of themselves in order to be seen, felt, and acknowledged by others. One such sign is a determination to resist, or a refusal to be whipped. This is why, "when a slave cannot be flogged, he is more than half free. He has a domain as broad as his own manly heart to defend, and he is really 'a power on earth'" (286). Douglass's dignity is not, like Kant's, a state autonomously produced, but rather a latent energy that becomes conscious of itself through self-actualization and then affirmation by others. And because it is dependent on recognition, recognition must be struggled for when it is not freely given.

Douglass made these points vividly when he described, in *My Bond-age and My Freedom*, the long-term effects of Nelly's violent resistance to the slave driver Sevier. Although her resistance in this case proved to be futile—Sevier succeeded in tying her to the tree and whipping her severely—she had won a more important victory, that of successfully defending her dignity, or "spirit": "He had bruised her flesh, but had left her invincible spirit undaunted" (182). Resistance, Douglass repeatedly shows, was the act of standing up for one's sense of self-worth, and this act alone, whether successful or not, made one inwardly free: "The slave who has the courage to stand up for himself against the overseer, though he may have many hard stripes at the first, becomes, in the end, a freeman, even though he sustain the formal relation of a slave" (182). Thus, external freedom for Douglass meant conditions in which one's latent human powers could fully unfold themselves, creating one's dignity and receiving the dignity-confirming respect of others. Internal freedom was the affective state produced by the sense that one's self-respect was alive and well. Struggle, or resistance to domination, was the only way to secure both of these freedoms in the face of oppression. It was thus a foundational creative activity of democracy.[19]

Defensive violence, as Douglass understood it, does not fall into a category distinct from our natural powers; it is actually a "sign" or expressive extension of these. In certain circumstances, an equally valid sign of our powers would be "agitation," such as marching in the street carrying placards demanding the right to vote. As with his belief that our rights do not really exist unless we exercise them, Douglass's philosophy here verges on ontologizing action—holding that, in the human realm at least, to *be* is to *act*. This is why, "next to the dignity of being a freeman, is the dignity of striving to be free."[20] Our dignity is to some degree natural, an expression of our inherent powers, but only our striving and struggling can give "signs" of it and thus secure it. A commitment to such struggle is what Du Bois called Douglass's ideal of "ultimate assimilation through self-assertion, and on no other terms."[21] Douglass makes this point plainly in a third text in which he refers to "the philosophy of reform": "Let me give you a word of the philosophy of reform. The whole history of the progress of human liberty shows that all concessions yet made to her august claims, have been born of earnest struggle. . . . If there is no struggle, there is no progress. . . . This struggle may be a moral one, or it may be a physical one, and it may be both moral and physical, but it must be a struggle. Power concedes nothing without a demand. It never did and it never will."[22] Familiar as these words are, they too gain depth and interest when we see them as an expression of Douglass's political philosophy. A moral struggle is the action of "mind upon mind" seeking to compel recognition of one's powers and dignity. A physical struggle is the action of a person bringing his or her bodily powers to bear against others who have refused to recognize those powers and the dignity they confer. A struggle that is both moral and physical gives signs of both kinds of powers as it seeks to assert one's dignity and secure one's rights.[23]

No work of Douglass's expresses this subtle view of the relation of violence to dignity and politics better than his novella, *The Heroic Slave* (1853). As a number of critics have argued, it plainly represents and defends Black insurrectionary violence.[24] However, it also specifies—or at least strongly implies—that such violence is legitimate only when it is exercised in self-defense and with self-restraint. The ship's (white) first mate narrates the story of an actual slave rebellion aboard the ship *Creole* to a barroom of other white sailors. Because they are so doubtful of the very possibility of Black resistance and valor, they accuse the mate and other crew members of having been cowards who failed to quell an insurrection of mere "black rascals."[25] The mate replies by describing the impressive comportment of their leader, the aptly named Madison Washington: "The fellow loomed up before me. I forgot his blackness in the dignity of his manner, and the eloquence of his speech. It seemed as if the souls of both the great dead (whose names he bore) had entered him" (49). He then relates that Washington had warned him: "'Sir, your life is in my hands. I could have killed you a dozen times over during the last half hour, and could kill you now. You call me a black murderer. I am not a murderer. God is my witness that LIBERTY, not malice, is the motive for this night's work. . . . We have done that which you applaud your fathers for doing, and if we are murderers, so were they'" (48). In the narrator's account, then, Washington's forbearance toward him and the other white sailors follows naturally from the "dignity of his manner." Viewed in the light of Douglass's political philosophy, that manner is Washington's consciousness of possessing a human worthiness that arises from his submission to his moral powers.

Douglass carefully lays the groundwork for this scene, establishing both the fact of Washington's consciousness of his dignity and the process by which such consciousness arose, in the novella's opening pages. He places him alone in the woods and has him pour out his soul in a plaintive apostrophe to the natural world around him:

> What, then, is life to me? It is aimless and worthless, and worse than worthless. Those birds, perched on yon swinging boughs, in friendly conclave, sounding forth their merry notes in seeming worship of the rising sun, though liable to the sportsman's fowling-piece, are still my superiors. They live free, though they may die slaves. . . . But what is freedom to me, or I to it? I am a slave,—born a slave, an abject slave. . . . How mean a thing am I. (5)

Washington clearly feels that in becoming an "abject slave" he has lost all human dignity; he has been reduced to a "mean . . . thing." Suddenly and mysteriously, however, the natural world around him triggers an epiphany. Washington exclaims, "But here am I, a man,—yes, a man!—with thoughts and wishes, with *powers and faculties* as far as angel's flight above" the creatures of the woods around him (5; emphasis added). He regains, in other words, a sense of his worth as it derives from his "powers and faculties." His epiphany enables him to see that he had misjudged himself when he thought, "How mean a thing am I." (In chapter 6, we will find Douglass exploring in more detail how such aesthetic experience of the natural world had furthered his own political awakening.) Now, fortified by a renewed sense of his human worth, and by memories of his display of his powers and faculties to others, he concludes: "No, no,—I wrong myself, I am no coward. Liberty I will have, or die in the attempt to gain it."[26] Thus, Washington's coming-to-consciousness of his dignity is both the catalyst of his political awakening at the beginning of the novella and the restraining influence that keeps his violence defensive and under control in subsequent scenes.

Frantz Fanon's well-known espousal of anticolonial violence offers an illuminating contrast. Fanon argued that the colonizer has "shown the way" to all violence, and that "violence . . . frees the native from his inferiority complex and from his despair and inaction; it makes him fearless and restores his self-respect."[27] By contrast, far from believing that the slave master "has shown the way" to violence, Douglass developed a theory of power that drew a sharp distinction between the slave master's "irresponsible power" and "lawless violence," on the one hand,

and the self-restrained and moral violence of a resistant slave such as himself or Madison Washington, on the other. He even suggests that self-respect is the *precondition*, not merely the product, of justifiable violence, for he clearly indicates that Madison Washington had boarded the *Creole* as a man *already* conscious of his powers and dignity: "In the short time he had been on board, he had secured the confidence of every officer. The negroes fairly worshipped him. . . . He seldom spake to any one, and when he did speak, it was with the utmost propriety" (47).[28]

In *My Bondage and My Freedom*, similarly, Douglass took care to describe himself as acting defensively when he wrestled with Covey. He also takes care to describe himself as rediscovering and reasserting his dignity. For, as we shall see in chapter 6, in that book he strongly suggests that it was thanks to his mother and grandmother that he had acquired a very early sense of his dignity. Covey later came close to beating it out if him, but he did not quite succeed. This prior consciousness of his dignity is why Douglass specified that his physical resistance to Covey did not produce his dignity ex nihilo, but rather "*rekindled* in my breast the smouldering embers of liberty," "*revived* a sense of my own manhood," "*recalled* to life my crushed self-respect," and "inspired me with a *renewed* determination to be a FREEMAN" (286; emphasis added). All these verbs emphasize that his fight with Covey restored something that was already present within him—a self-respect, or dignity, that was both the precondition of his political action *and* its product.[29]

Douglass's position on violence is, as I have argued, an expression of the fugitive political philosophy he developed out of his observations and reflections as an enslaved person. Because such fugitive thought is difficult to perceive clearly, we might bring it into sharper focus by examining exactly where and why it eludes even an excellent account of it. In his early but nuanced and still very helpful analysis of Douglass's views on violence, Leslie Goldstein argues that at first Douglass deployed a "natural rights justification" of violence against slaveholders and that after 1851 "a new element appeared." It was Douglass's belief that "the quiet submission of blacks" to their enslavement had, in Douglass's words, "well-nigh established that they were conscious of their own fitness for slavery"; by the same token, however, Douglass believed that, as Goldstein puts it, "the black man could gain not only self-respect but a measure of dignity by fighting against his enslavers."[30] In outline, this is all true. But what Goldstein misses, perhaps because he construes Douglass's first argument to be solely a Lockean "natural rights justification," is that these two "elements" were conceptually fused in Douglass's political philosophy.

As we have seen, Douglass believed that the enslaved (and any other oppressed group) were justified in using defensive violence because such violence was entirely consonant with the "laws of their own being," i.e., with their knowledge of right and wrong as revealed to them by their intellectual and moral powers. Indeed, the exercise of defensive violence was itself an expression of those powers. Because slaveholders used force to deny the enslaved opportunities to exercise those powers and claim their "natural dignity," the enslaved had no choice but to use force themselves to regain that dignity—just as Douglass had when he wrestled with Covey. And when they did so, moreover, they were exercising and "putting forth" their "latent" powers, thereby becoming more conscious of their dignity and making others more conscious of it, too. In short, a single theory joins what Goldstein's approach can see only as two distinct "elements" of Douglass's position on violence.

It is worth nothing further that Goldstein correctly observes that "Douglass himself *never* participated in the kind of aggressive violence that characterized [John] Brown."[31] Unfortunately, he does not follow that insight where it points—which is toward the importance, in Douglass's philosophy, of the distinction between aggressive and defensive violence. Likewise, he quotes Douglass's declaration that "it is one thing to assert the right of a slave to gain his freedom by force, and another thing to advocate force as the only means of abolishing slavery. We . . . assert the former but . . . deny the latter. We contend that the only well-grounded hope of the slave is in the operation of moral force."[32] But why does "the operation of moral force" confer "the right of the slave to gain his freedom by force"? Goldstein does not address this question. The answer, as I have tried to show, is that the enslaved person is acting defensively and therefore in conformity with—indeed, in obedience to—the dictates of his or her moral powers, not aggressively and in violation of them.

During the past several decades, Douglass has often been compared invidiously to Martin Delany, who is taken to have been more often and more explicitly in favor of a slave insurrection. Those who share this judgment tend to read Douglass's caution about insurrection as mere pragmatism at best, and as failure of nerve at worst. Certainly, pragmatism was an aspect of his thinking on this and all other issues; he often said as much himself. But once we see that the sharp split between violence and nonviolence that structures our own thinking was not as significant to Douglass as it has been to us, we might take note of some overlooked facts and revise our assessments.

Consider, for example his response to a letter Delany sent him from the postwar South in 1871. Evidently, Delany had been disturbed by the sight of Black men carrying guns when they attended political meetings. Douglass replied: "I cannot agree with you in denouncing colored men for going armed to political meetings in South Carolina. . . . It is a bad practice, and one which cannot be commended in a truly civilized community, but everything in this world is relative. Assault compels defense. I shall never ask the colored people to be lambs where the whites insist on being wolves, and yet no man shall outdo me in efforts to promote kindness and good will between the races. But I know there can be no peace without justice, and hence the sword."[33]

In this instance, at least, Douglass is clearly more disposed than Delany to support Blacks who exercise violence to defend their lives, their dignity, and their rights. But we should take note also of the *way* he reasons, not just of the position he takes. By advancing the seemingly contradictory claims that "assault compels defense" and "no man shall outdo me in efforts to promote kindness and good will between the races," we again find him evading or blurring a binary choice. And in his assertion that "everything in the world is relative," we again find him making a universal claim ("everything is") while at the same time asserting the importance of context and standpoint. Indeed, his use of the word "relative" is a succinct microexpression of what I have been calling the fugitive quality of his thinking, in particular its oscillation between positions conventionally regarded as incommensurable. That fugitive quality is very often present in his thinking, but usually subtly. In April 1861, for example, he declared, "So much for the moral movement against slavery. Hereafter, opposition to slavery will naturally take a new form."[34] The key word here is one we might easily overlook: "naturally." Douglass believed that a moral movement can *naturally* become a physically violent movement because it is in the very nature of morality, or of moral law, to exercise violence in defense of one's dignity and rights.

Clearly, then, Douglass's views on violence cannot be adequately described by using distinctions like that between *radical* and its presumed opposite, *reformist*. Is it radical or is it reformist to endorse violence unequivocally when it is exercised in defense of one's own or another person's or a group's dignity? Is it radical or is it reformist to think that humanness itself consists in large part of having a moral power that naturally turns to a form of violence that is defensive, not aggressive, and self-restraining, not "never satisfied"? On this issue, as on many others, Douglass's political philosophy pressures us to think outside and between the categorical distinctions we habitually rely on.

CHAPTER FIVE

"A Living Root, Not a Twig Broken Off"

Douglass's Constitutionalism and the Paradox
of Democracy's Foundations

Between 1848 and 1852, Douglass engaged energetically in another debate that agitated both the free Black and the white abolitionist communities: whether the Constitution of the United States upheld and legitimated slavery or offered a powerful basis on which to oppose it. Here, too, we will find that a topic familiar to many of his readers looks different when we examine it in the context of Douglass's developing political philosophy. As is well known, Douglass at first took the position espoused by his mentor William Lloyd Garrison and other members of the American Anti-Slavery Society (AAS): the Constitution was a compromise with slavery and an "agreement with hell." No sincere and consistent antislavery activist could work within the political framework it established, and so the work of abolishing slavery had to take place outside of formal politics and primarily through moral suasion.

For a decade, Douglass had passionately held to this view—outwardly, at least. Then, in the spring of 1851, he suddenly announced his change of opinion. At the eighteenth annual meeting of the AAS held in Syracuse, New York, he shocked the gathering by declaring that he had "arrived at the firm conviction that the Constitution, construed in the light of well-established rules of legal interpretation, might be made consistent in its details with the noble purposes in its preamble." If read according to these rules, he argued, the nation's founding document did *not* legitimate slavery but could be "wielded on behalf of emancipation."[1] By taking this step, he joined the "political abolitionists"; led by Gerrit Smith, they maintained that the abolitionist movement could and should work to overturn slavery through formal politics, including voting, running for office, and forming and joining political parties. Garrison and his followers were incensed. They demanded to know how Douglass could uphold one interpretation of the Constitution so fervently one day, and then switch to the opposite view on the next. They suspected him—not without some grounds—of being an unprincipled opportunist who sought financial support for the *North Star* from Smith, who was wealthy. Subsequently, a number of historians have come to somewhat milder versions of the same conclusion: Douglass was disturbingly inconsistent.[2]

Douglass is partly responsible for these judgments, since he implied more than once that when he had joined the AAS in 1839, he was virtually a tabula rasa upon whom Garrison's organization inscribed its views about all things pertaining to slavery and its abolition. He recalled in an 1860 speech, for example: "When I escaped from slavery, and was introduced to the Garrisonians, I adopted very many of their opinions, and defended them just as long as I deemed them true. I was young, had read but little, and naturally took some of the things on trust. Subsequent experience and reading have led me to examine for myself. This has brought me to other conclusions. When I was a child, I thought and spoke as a child."[3] Many accounts of Douglass's thinking about the Constitution have taken these words as authoritative, and the result has been a strangely threadbare conception of who Douglass was when he joined the AAS.

Douglass was anything but a "child," however, when he arrived in New Bedford, at the age of nineteen. He had been observing "the power of the master" for most of his life, and he had searched to discover the mysterious means by which whites kept himself and other Blacks enslaved and justified their enslavement. He had also witnessed numerous incidents of slave resistance, and he had noticed the effects of a culture of slavery on both masters and the enslaved. Above all, he had begun to think for himself. Seen in the light of this past, his change of opinion on slavery's constitutionality was not simply a rejection of one view and the adoption of another, but rather a mature expression of the political insights he had brought with him when he escaped his enslavement. Harriet Beecher Stowe perspicaciously discerned this deeper source of his thinking. In a letter to Garrison defending Douglass, she wrote: "I am satisfied that his change of sentiments was not a mere political one but a genuine growth of his own conviction. . . . At all events, he holds no opinion which he cannot defend, with a variety and richness of thought and expression and an aptness of illustration which shows it to be a growth from the soil of his own mind with a living root and not a twig broken off other men's thoughts and stuck down to subserve a temporary purpose."[4]

Thus, like Douglass's positions on Black elevation, emigration, and violence, his changed views on the constitutionality of slavery were an expression of the political philosophy his work as the editor of the North Star was permitting him to develop. To be sure, as many historians have noted, other factors played a role. The most crucial was the slavery system's dismaying political victory in the Compromise of 1850, which prompted Douglass to reconsider whether abolitionism should concede the political playing field to the enemy. As well, he had long resented the Garrisonians' efforts to control him, and his move to Rochester in 1848 placed him much closer to the community of political abolitionists in northern New York. His subsequent course of study in the constitutional interpretation of Lysander Smith, William Goodell, and Gerrit Smith encouraged if it did not precipitate his eventual change of mind. Yet even as we give due weight to all these influences, we should not forget that the man who reflected on these events, and who read, parsed, and evaluated these arguments, already knew his own powers and was becoming increasingly confident in the value of his distinctive perspective and nascent philosophy—forged, as he testified later, by his experience of enslavement.

In this chapter, we will see how this philosophy shaped three important facets of Douglass's thinking on slavery's constitutionality. First, it led him to reject Garrison's way of approaching the problem. Although as a young man he had emulated Garrison's tendency to think in terms of incommensurable opposites one must choose between, as he grew older he increasingly sought to "express" opposites and to hold them in tension with each other. As we have seen, this method, when combined with his commitments to standpoint epistemology and moral law, constituted the manner or mode of his thinking, which he would soon describe as a "fixed principle of honesty." Such a mode came to reject Garrison's rigid identity logic, took seriously the views held by Smith and other political abolitionists, and eventually arrived at its own conclusions. Second, the "living root" of Douglass's thinking also guided him to a somewhat paradoxical resolve that has been overlooked by most scholars: he maintained Garrison's emphasis on the framers' intentions even after he had rejected Garrison's views on slavery's constitutionality. This unwavering belief in the importance of intentionality had everything to do with Douglass's notions of standpoint knowledge and human dignity. Third, his deep belief in moral power, and in the qualified conception of freedom that it entailed, helped him justify his volte-face by enabling him to figure it not as an act of a sovereign, free will, but as obedience to a moral duty. For all these reasons, then, Douglass's change of opinion on slavery's constitutionality was not simply a sacrifice of principles to pragmatism or expediency, but an expression of both the substance and style of thought he had brought with him from his experience of slavery. This is what Stowe sought to convey to Garrison when she wrote that his new opinion was "a growth from the soil of his own mind with a living root and not a twig broken off other men's thoughts and stuck down to subserve a temporary purpose."

"A Fixed Principle of Honesty"

In *My Bondage and My Freedom*, Douglass himself ascribes his change of mind to the work he performed as the editor of the *North Star*: "But for the responsibility of conducting a public journal, and the necessity imposed upon me of meeting opposite views from [the political] abolitionists in this state, I should in all probability have remained as firm in my disunion views as any other disciple of William Lloyd Garrison" (392). To grasp why this happenstance was so crucial, it helps to keep in mind Douglass's account of his reflections on the songs of the enslaved and their meanings. Just as he had understood those songs by standing both within and outside the circle of slavery, so he arrived at his new view of slavery's constitutionality through a process of taking seemingly "opposite views" and standpoints as seriously as he took his own, neither rejecting one nor synthesizing both, but keeping them in perpetual tension with each other.

Consider how different this method was from his mentor's. Garrison was by temperament an absolutist. His reasoning emphatically founded itself on identity logic—the principle that something cannot be itself and its opposite at the same time. In an 1855 speech, for example, Garrison asked:

> When will the people of the North see that it is not possible for liberty and slavery to commingle, or for a true Union to be formed between freemen and slaveholders? Between those who oppress and the oppressed, no concord is possible. This Union—it is a lie, an imposture, and our first business is, to seek its utter overthrow. In this Union, there are three millions and a half of slaves, clanking their chains in hopeless bondage. Let the Union be accursed! Look at the awful compromises of the Constitution, by which that instrument is saturated with the blood of the slave![5]

Note how deeply Garrison assumes that opposites are incommensurable. "Liberty" and "slavery" cannot "commingle," a union cannot exist between "freemen and slaveholders," and "no concord is possible" between "those who oppress and the oppressed." Although the founders had wickedly conjoined these, he argues, their incommensurability means that the nation is no real union in truth. Abolitionists should therefore abandon all hope for the self-reforming possibilities of U.S. democracy and disavow the Constitution, with its tainted, pro-slavery provisions. All antislavery citizens must cease living a lie and separate from their fellow Americans to found the nation anew, on purer foundations. Nothing short of revolution would suffice. "I stand outside of this Government," said Garrison, "and, by the help of God, I mean to effect its overthrow. That seems to me to be the only *consistent* course to be taken."[6]

As a lecturer for the Massachusetts Anti-Slavery Society, Douglass for some time based his own arguments on these principles of identity logic: opposites may not be yoked, and reasoning must be "consistent" in the sense of choosing between opposites instead of embracing both. He continued for some time to insist on these principles even after founding the *North Star*. In an editorial dated April 5, 1850, for example, he wrote: "Liberty and Slavery—opposite as Heaven and hell—are both in the Constitution. . . . It is this radical defect in the Constitution—this war of elements, which is now rocking the land. . . . This fundamental contradiction in the Constitution is the real cause of the present storm-tossed condition of the public mind. . . . We must continue to hold, for the present, that the Constitution, being at war with itself, cannot be lived up to, . . . and that, therefore, the platform for us to occupy is outside that piece of parchment."[7]

However, even while he was publicly espousing Garrison's position using Garrison's rigid logic, Douglass began to deploy his own method of thinking in a number of the editorials and letters he wrote about slavery's constitutionality. On March 16, 1849, in one of his most important essays on this topic, "The Constitution and Slavery," he wrote to clear up a misunderstanding that had arisen because of his willingness to take seriously a view, or opinion, different than his own. In an essay (also titled "The Constitution and Slavery") that he had published in the *North Star* five weeks earlier, he had written that "'the Constitution, if strictly construed according to its reading,' is not a pro-slavery instrument." That declaration, he now admitted with characteristic understatement, "has excited some interest amongst our Anti-Slavery brethren" on both sides of the issue.[8] What he wished to do now, therefore, was to clarify that he had merely been stating a *hypothetical*: "how a document *would* appear under one construction" (362). In fact, he now emphasized, he still disagreed with such a construction. Clearly, however, such confusion would not have arisen at all if Douglass had not been using his method of respecting and occupying others' "opposite" viewpoints as a way of reaching his own opinion on a matter.

Douglass seems to have been aware that his distinctive willingness to take opposing views seriously might not be legible to his purist Garrisonian colleagues, for he went on to explain and defend it: his "only aim," he claimed, "is to know what is truth and what is duty in respect to the matter in dispute, holding ourselves perfectly free to change our opinion in any direction, and at any time which may be indicated by our immediate apprehension of truth, unbiased by the smiles or frowns of any class of abolitionists" (361). Such a method might *appear* to be inconsistent, Douglass acknowledged, but in truth it was perfectly consistent with itself and its own principles. As he explained: "We bring to the consideration of this subject no partisan feelings, nor the slightest wish to make ourselves consistent with the creed of either Anti-Slavery party. . . . The only truly consistent man is he who will, for the sake of being right today, contradict what he said wrong yesterday" (361). Such a "truly consistent" thinker understands that the view from any particular standpoint is necessarily incomplete, even while it may be the nearest approximation to truth he can yet attain. Aware also of the highly contingent nature of his own and any other person's view of the truth, such a thinker is disposed to reassess his earlier views as time and experience lead him to further reflection. What makes his new view "consistent" with the older one is that both are faithful to the demanding principle of committing fully to each standpoint under consideration while at the same time remaining aware of its incompleteness and contingency. Douglass attempted to further clarify and justify this method when he insisted that "true stability consists not of being of the same opinion now as formerly, but in a fixed principle of honesty, even urging us to the adoption or rejection of that which may seem to us true or false at the ever-present now" (361).

Several details in this intriguing statement are worth noting. The first is Douglass's careful choice of the word "seem" (not "is"): it, too, expresses a principle that follows from his standpoint epistemology. Douglass's attunement to contingency did not mean that he ruled out the possibility that certain truths could be universally true; on the contrary, he insisted often on the universality of certain truths. But his word "seem" reminds us that we can see such truths only from our standpoint, and since our standpoint is by definition limited, we must remain vigilantly aware that our view of such truths may be partial and even distorted. Nonetheless, in any given moment, we may be called on to *act*, and we can do so only on the basis of what *seems to us* to be true or false in that moment of action.

A second detail to consider is Douglass's substitution of the word "stability" for "consistency." The difference is subtle but important, as it registers a shift from the unachievable and ultimately irrelevant criteria of logic and mathematics to those of the political realm in which historical actors must try to hold a steady course even as they must sometimes change their minds. This shift acknowledges that political reasoning is unavoidably, and productively, permeated by affect and standpoint. (The very idea of standpoint implies an affective mode of knowing the world and others in it.) Yet at the same time, Douglass believed that we should preserve the value of "impartiality" in a way that neither identifies it with "reason" narrowly construed nor opposes it to sentiment and feeling.[9] We find Douglass attempting to articulate such an understanding of impartiality as involving both reason and affect in his phrase "fixed principle of honesty," which links two ideas in a startling juxtaposition: "fixed principles" (and eternal truths) are usually imagined as standing outside history and beyond human revision, but Douglass instead places them within a human disposition—that of being "honest." Once again, seeming opposites are held in tension.

As he struggled to express such difficult thinking using the conventional philosophical lexicon of his time, Douglass probably knew he was likely to be misunderstood. Perhaps for this reason, he made a final effort to explain and defend himself by contrasting his fixed principle of honesty with a hypothetical alternative. In point of fact, however, this alternative mode of thinking was no mere hypothetical; it was precisely the rigid style of thinking employed by Garrison and his followers—including himself, until he made his decisive break. As one of his few explicit accounts of his method of political thinking, this passage is worth quoting in its entirety:

> We might just here drop the pen and the subject, and assume the Constitution to be what we have briefly attempted to prove it to be. Radically and essentially pro-slavery, in fact as well as in its tendency; and regard our position to be correct beyond the possibility of an honest doubt, and treat those who differ from us as mere cavillers, bent upon making the worse appear the better reason; or we might anticipate the objections which are supposed to be valid against that position. We are, however, disposed to do neither.—We have too much respect for the men opposed to us to do the former. And have too strong a desire to have those objections put in their most favorable light, to do the latter.—We are prepared to hear all sides, and to give the arguments of our opponents a candid consideration. Where an honest expression of views is allowed, Truth has nothing to fear. (366)

Douglass begins here with the imagined but highly performative gesture of dropping his pen and, secure in the knowledge that his "position [was] correct beyond a possible doubt," withdrawing altogether from the debate over slavery's constitutionality. But he invokes this possibility only to repudiate it. Indeed, he ridicules the notion that one ever could "assume" oneself to be "correct beyond a possible doubt." For what his own political philosophy with its standpoint epistemology understands is that, while not every view of a matter is plausible, none can rightly claim to be the only correct view. Standpoint epistemology goes hand in hand with an ethics of intersubjectivity that "has too much re-spect" for those with whom one disagrees to treat them in such a dis-missive manner. Indeed, when representing their views to others, one is even obliged to put them in the best possible light. In short, Douglass is enunciating a method here that anticipates more recent thinking in political theory that has marched under the banner of democratic "de-liberation." He is concerned not just to argue for a particular position on the constitutionality of slavery, but to articulate a democratic mode of managing different, conflicting, and even opposite views of matters that might trouble a democratic polity. Two weeks later, in a letter to Gerritt Smith, he reiterated his commitment to such a mode. The North Star, he wrote, "is not a party paper and looks with grateful friendship upon all classes of abolitionists, and is not disposed to denounce as knaves those who believe that voting is a duty."[10] He also invoked his perspectival orientation when, in his critique of Smith's address pub-lished that day, he wrote, "could we see the Constitution as they [the po-litical abolitionists] do"; this phrasing suggests that he had tried to see the matter from their standpoint, but that he had not yet succeeded in doing so.[11]

Let us turn at last to the climax of these deliberations—Douglass's official explanation of his thinking in "Change of Opinion Announced," published in the North Star (and Garrison's Liberator) in May 1851. He had "arrived," he declares, "at the firm conviction that the Constitu-tion, construed in the light of well-established rules of legal interpre-tation, might be made consistent in its details with the noble purposes in its preamble" and that the Constitution could "be wielded in behalf of emancipation."[12] Here, with his usual care, he states that the found-ing document can "be made" consistent, not that it "is" consistent. He thereby suggests that the challenge facing concerned antebellum cit-izens is to make the "details" of the Constitution, by which he means the compromised historical forms in which the framers cast their new democracy, consistent with its "noble purposes and the eternal truths expressed in the Constitution's preamble." Both contingent historical "details" and eternal truths—seeming opposites—must be kept in play through a "fixed principle of honesty." As he had realized when reflect-ing on the meaning of the songs of the enslaved, the interpreting mind must sometimes use a single method to express, or hold, opposite ideas.

Intentions, Accountability, and Resistance

Attention to Douglass's distinctive method of thinking politically also sheds light on an overlooked question embedded in his shift from Garrison's view of the Constitution to Smith's: Why was he so deeply committed—both before and after his change of opinion—to the principle that we must honor the framers' intentions? In "Comments on Gerrit Smith's Address," an 1849 *North Star* editorial published two years before he announced his change of mind, he had made clear that, as far as he was concerned, the founders' intentionality was the crux of the issue:

> As to what Mr. Smith says of determining the meaning of the Constitution by its letter alone, and disregarding as utterly worthless the intentions of the framers of that instrument, it may require consideration when he gives us some fixed and settled legal rules sustaining his views on this point. Such rules may exist, but we have not yet seen them; and until we do, we shall continue to understand the Constitution not only in the light of its letter, but in view of its history, the meaning attached to it by the framers, the men who adopted it, and the circumstances in which it was adopted.[13]

Nearly two years later, and just four months before formally and unequivocally adopting Smith's position, Douglass wrote him a letter reiterating that the framers' "intentions" were still a matter of "much importance" to him. Was it "good morality" to ignore, defy, or twist them to other purposes?

> I am sick and tired of arguing on the slaveholders' side of this question, although they are doubtless right so far as the *intentions* of the framers of the Constitution are concerned. But these *intentions* you fling to the winds. Your legal rules of interpretation override all speculations as to the opinions of the Constitution makers and these *rules* may be sound, and I confess I do not know how to meet or refute them on *legal* grounds. You will now say I have conceded all that you require, and it may be so. But there is a consideration which is of much importance between us. It is this: may we avail ourselves of legal rules which enable us to defeat even the wicked *intentions* of our Constitution makers? It is this question which puzzles me more than

all the others involved in the subject. Is it *good morality* to take advantage of a legal flaw and put a meaning upon a legal instrument the very opposite of what we have good reason to believe was the *intention* of the men who framed it? Just here is the difficulty with me.[14]

Even *after* Douglass made his formal announcement of his change of mind, he continued to explain to Smith that this question of the founders' intentions had been the primary obstacle keeping him from adopting Smith's view: "The only points which prevented me from declaring at that time [two years earlier, i.e., May 1849] in favor of voting and against the disunion ground related to *the intentions* of the framers of the Constitution." His recent change of position, he insisted, did not reflect a devaluing of those intentions but rather a new understanding of where and how to locate them: "I had not made up my mind then, as I have now, that I am in reason and in conscience bound to learn the intentions of those who framed the Constitution in the Constitution itself."[15]

Much of this history is known to all scholars who have studied this phase of Douglass's life and thought. Nonetheless, we have not yet paused to ask, *Why*—while waging a war against a moral evil as gigantic as the slavery system—did Douglass feel so deeply obliged to respect "even the wicked intentions" of the founders? The reason, I suggest, lies in the philosophy he brought with him to his deliberations. First, his belief in the inevitability and validity of standpoint required him to take note of every person's intentions, for intentions are a translation of perspective from the realm of seeing and knowing into the realm of considering and doing. In other words, if I respect the legitimacy of your having your own way of seeing things even if I disagree with you, I must likewise respect the legitimacy of your intentions even if I disapprove of them. This is why one may deem a person's actual intentions to be "wicked" and at the same time continue to respect them—in the sense of taking them into account rather than summarily dismissing or disregarding them.

A second motive for Douglass's unwavering respect for others' intentionality is that, as an enslaved person, he had been exposed to slaveholders steadily striving to reduce the enslaved to beings *without* intentions, so as to make them purely the instruments of their own will. He saw, in other words, that outright dismissal of others' intentionality is a hallmark of oppression, which means conversely that respect for others' intentions must be a moral principle of those who strive for justice. An intention is not merely a passive thought; it is an inclination toward, a leaning into, a certain action. As such, it is an expression of a person's inherent human powers. To believe that the enslaved continued to have innate, natural powers was to believe, in effect, that they continued to have intentions: they *intended* to do certain things, whether or not they actually had the freedom to accomplish them. Both their dignity and their resistance, then, resided in their suppressed but inextinguishable intentionality.

A third reason that Douglass could not simply dismiss as irrelevant the founders' wicked intentions was that the very idea of moral accountability rests on the presumption of intentionality: no one is held responsible for actions they do not intend. If it becomes permissible to disregard intentions, it becomes permissible likewise to disregard accountability. Although Douglass frequently argued that slaveholders, too, were "victims" of the slaveholding culture into which they had been born, he was careful to emphasize that this cultural influence was not wholly determinative and certainly did not exonerate them. "All attempts to remove the responsibility of the slaveholder from the individual to the nation, are erroneous, fallacious, and false," he declared. "All attempts to make it exclusively an individual wrong are equally wrong—however it is more of an individual matter than a national one. The slaveholder holds his slave from *choice*."[16] His writings and speeches graphically portray individual men and women who, precisely because they encountered the intentional resistance of their slaves on a daily basis, had daily to intend the perpetuation of slavery through countless acts of discipline and cruelty.

Indeed, Douglass's firm conviction of slaveholders' individual culpability drove him to relentlessly personalize the slavery system. In 1848 he wrote a public letter to his former master, Thomas Auld, in which he identified him and held him to account. In an 1849 critique of an address written by a group of Southern senators, he emphasized that they were just forty individual men, all of them slaveholders: he called them "the forty thieves."[17] And in his 1851 "Lecture on Slavery," he declared, "I prefer to speak of the villains in connection with the villainy, and of the criminals in connection with the crime."[18] Douglass was certainly able to think in terms of systems, institutions, and structures. But he always emphasized that, in the last analysis, individual men and women benefited from and were responsible for these. For all these reasons, then, intentionality and accountability were key components of Douglass's political philosophy. No wonder that he kept asking himself, "Is it *good morality* to take advantage of a legal flaw and put a meaning upon a legal instrument the very opposite of what we have good reason to believe was the *intention* of the men who framed it?"[19]

Freedom and Moral Compulsion

The "living root" of Douglass's political philosophy also helped him navigate his change of opinion in a third way: by allowing, or perhaps even requiring, him to figure it as obedience, or submission, to the promptings of his moral powers. Recall that in his 1849 essay "The Constitution and Slavery" he had asserted: "Our only aim is to know what is truth and *what is duty* in respect to the matter in dispute, holding ourselves perfectly *free to change our opinion* in any direction, and at any time which may be indicated by our immediate apprehension of truth, unbiased by the smiles or frowns of any class of abolitionists."[20] Here he holds "duty" and "free" in tense equipoise: he is "perfectly free" to decide what is in fact his "duty." Recall, too, the wording of his retrospective account of his conversion in *My Bondage and My Freedom*: "But for the *responsibility* of conducting a public journal, and the *necessity imposed upon me* of meeting opposite views from abolitionists. . . . My new circumstances [as an editor] *compelled me* to re-think the whole subject" (392; emphasis added). Finally, consider the language of the last sentence of his formal announcement of his change of mind: "It is the first *duty* of every American, whose conscience permits so to do, to use his *political* as well as his *moral* power for its [slavery's] overthrow."[21]

Of course, Douglass was not the only thinker and activist of his time to deploy such deontological language to justify having taken certain positions. For example, at the 1848 National Convention of Colored Freemen, the authors of the proposal on labor had declared that "the occupation of domestics and servants among our people is degrading to us as a class, and *we deem it our bounded duty* to discountenance such pursuits."[22] What set Douglass apart, I would argue, are the frequency and the purposefulness with which he used such language as he developed its implications for his life and work—as when he yoked domination and liberation in the title of his second autobiography, *My Bondage and My Freedom*, and when he defined the essence of his "philosophy of reform" in his 1883 lecture "It Moves": "All genuine reform must rest on the assumption that man is a creature of absolute, inflexible law, moral and spiritual, and that his happiness and well-being can only be secured by perfect obedience to such law."[23]

Perhaps the deepest source of Douglass's use of deontological language and argument was that, as a standpoint thinker, he had an especially keen need for it. Douglass understood to the marrow of his bones that, as he wrote in *My Bondage and My Freedom*, "the point from which a thing is viewed is of some importance" (148). He understood too that as one's temporal or physical location changes, one's view of things may change as well. He knew that he never thought or changed his mind in the airless laboratory of a philosophy, and he explicitly rejected the notion that his thought was the expression of a sovereign subject's free will. Therefore, in moments of decision, he always felt the pressure of changing historical events on one side, and of his moral power's "immediate apprehension of truth" on the other. He stood in the space between these, doing his best to make the right decision, guided only by what he called his "fixed principle of honesty." This principle dictated that, since one could know only what *seemed* to be true in any moment, to offset the anarchic tendency to inconsistency implied by this view, one must always consult and *obey* one's moral powers.

Virtually every consequential decision Douglass made was, he believed, an expression of his moral powers, a submission to the laws of his own being, and a fulfillment of his responsibilities. Perhaps his most concise expression of this view appears in the chapter of *My Bondage and My Freedom* titled "New Relations and Duties." There he relates that William Freeland was the best master he ever had "until I became my own master and assumed for myself, as I had a right to do, the responsibility of my own existence and the exercise of my own powers" (301). This sense of a right to be responsible for himself and to exercise his own powers originated, he repeatedly indicates, in his experience of enslavement. In the next chapter of *My Bondage and My Freedom*, titled "The Runaway Plot," he recalls that at the beginning of the year 1836, he had mused on his discouraging future prospects. "'Notwithstanding,' thought I, 'the many resolutions and prayers I have made in behalf of freedom, I am, this first day of 1836, still a slave, still wandering in the depths of spirit-devouring thralldom. My faculties and powers of body and soul are not my own, but are the property of a fellow mortal, in no sense superior to me except that he has the physical power to compel me to be owned and controlled by him'" (303–4). What we may be seeing here is Douglass in 1855 projecting his faculties-and-powers conception of the human being back into the thoughts that had passed through his mind in 1836, when he was just eighteen years old. However, it is just as likely that in 1855 he decided that he had perceived, in glimmering form, that conception of the human and of human faculties and powers back on that New Year's morning of 1836.

In any case, these ruminations led him to make a "solemn vow" that, within the coming year, he would attempt an escape (305). This vow, he goes on, "only bound *me* to make my escape individually"; but the year he spent at Freeland's "attached" him, "as with 'hooks of steel,' to my brother slaves. The most affectionate and confiding friendship existed between us; and I felt it *my duty* to give them an opportunity to share in my virtuous determination" (305; emphasis added). As the day of their planned escape drew near, Douglass relates, they were beset with fears and doubts—he "more deeply" than any of the others because "the *responsibility* of the whole enterprise rested on my shoulders" (314; emphasis added). On the very eve of their attempt, as he sought to fortify them in their resolve, he cast their escape as their fulfillment of a pledge they had made to themselves and one another: "If after having solemnly promised to go, as they had done, they now failed to make the attempt, they would, in effect, brand themselves with cowardice, and might as well sit down, fold their arms, and acknowledge themselves as fit only to be *slaves*" (315). The underlying logic of Douglass's argument here is that, by taking responsibility for themselves and resolving to escape, his comrades had actualized the latent powers and faculties that constituted their human nature. To renege on the vows they had made would be to fail to exercise those powers, to fail to take full responsibility for themselves, and thereby to prove the slaveholders' assertions that they *lacked* the powers that would have entitled them to human status, and therefore were "fit only to be slaves." For Douglass, the path to freedom passed through duty.

He eventually came to believe that democratic citizenship requires *all* citizens to understand that their freedom, too, depends on their having such strong feelings of responsibility for themselves and for one another. They must realize that, because they are part of the inextricable "net-work" of humanity, because their individual perspective is both valid but limited, and because their freedom is never secure but always at risk, they must submit to the moral laws of their own being. Those laws will serve them as a "fixed principle of honesty" and enable them to chart a course of determined action despite their being aware of their own fallibility. Those laws will also compel them to act in defense of their own and other citizens' dignity and rights. Consequently, although citizens sometimes may be free of tyranny, they are never free of their democratic responsibilities. As Douglass declared in an 1860 Glasgow address: "I admit our responsibility for slavery while in the Union, but I deny that going out of the Union would free us from that responsibility. There now clearly is no freedom from responsibility for slavery to any American citizen short of the abolition of slavery."[24] He made essentially the same point when he told a Boston audience: "Remember [the fugitive] George Latimer in bonds *as bound with him*. . . . Now make up your minds what your duty is to George Latimer, and when you have made your minds up, prepare to do it and take the consequences."[25] And he did so in 1848, when he observed: "We are more than spectators of the scenes that pass before us. Our interests, sympathies, and destiny *compel us* to be parties to what is passing around us."[26]

Far from simply expressing a choice of pragmatism over principle, then, Douglass's change of mind about the constitutionality of slavery was thoroughly expressive of, and deeply consistent with, the principles of the political philosophy he was beginning to elaborate from his experience of enslavement. As we have seen, that philosophy rejects a predicate on which so much conventional thought in its time and ours rests: namely, that thinking is performed by the disembodied mind of a sovereign agent who is unconditioned by historical existence and location and is constrained only by the rules of logic, including the requirement that one be consistent and not self-contradictory. Douglass believed that no thinker is truly sovereign, and that no thinking is *entirely* free, both because our intellectual powers must be in harmony with the laws set by our moral power, and because all thinking is ineluctably conditioned yet enabled by one's standpoint location in time and space. However, Douglass also insisted that our reasoning and actions are accountable to principles that are eternally true. Although he sometimes did figure them as having a kind of transcendental origin and status, his tendency (especially as he grew older) was to weave them into the nature of humanity, or humanness, itself. They are the laws of our own being.[27]

Does Democracy Need Foundations?

I turn now to the way Douglass's political thought speaks to a broad and enduring question about constitutional democracy itself, one that troubled political theorists in his time and continues to do so in ours. I refer to what theorists today call the question of "foundations." Must a democracy rest upon truths that citizens regard as immutable and eternally true, such as the self-evident truths enunciated in the Declaration of Independence? Or are such truths so-conceived inimical to democracy insofar as they deprive citizens of the right to decide for themselves, through collective deliberation, what the underlying principles of their democracy are? Phrased in terms of the rights and responsibilities of citizenship, the question becomes: Should citizens forever accept the principles and institutions of their democracy as these are given to them, or may they legitimately strive to alter these as they see fit?

In the antebellum period, these questions were discussed by a number of the civics textbooks that were being written and published with the aim of educating Americans for democratic citizenship. Answers to these questions differed. In *The Political Class Book: Intended to Instruct the Higher Classes in the Origin, Nature, and Use of Political Power* (1832), Democrat William Sullivan took a strong antifoundationalist position. Anticipating more recent democratic theory by Sheldon Wolin and Benjamin Barber, he argued that no principles are fixed, and no principles should be regarded as such. Since political "authority resides, always, in those who compose the political community, . . . this community has not only the exclusive right to judge whether power, established for its benefit, is constitutionally exercised but also the absolute right to amend, and even to abolish, the existing system, and substitute any other."[28] But even as Sullivan emphasized the citizens' right "to amend and even to abolish, the existing system," including the Constitution, he acknowledged that there must be a limit to such changes, one established by the immutable and universal truths discoverable by "reason," which he defines as "that power whereby the mind comprehends truths, which are necessary and universal in their application . . . ; as that two things, each of which is equal to a third, must be equal to one another" (10). Thus, even as citizens of democracy have an absolute right to revolution, they are also obliged to use their reason to discover the immutable laws to which they must submit: "Our first duty . . . is to use the gift of reason in learning the laws which are prescribed to us" (12).

In his own civics textbook from the 1830s, Federalist Joseph Story took nearly the opposite view. He began by explicitly acknowledging the philosophical and existential challenge embedded in constitutional democracy: "A Government, which has no mode prescribed for any changes, will in the lapse of time become utterly unfit for the nation. . . . But at the same time, it is equally important to guard against too easy and frequent changes; and to secure due deliberation and caution in making them."[29] The solution Story proposed came straight from Edmund Burke. It was "to follow experience, rather than speculation and theory." Story argued: "It cannot escape notice, how exceedingly difficult it is to settle the foundations of any government upon principles, which do not admit of controversy or question. The very elements, out of which it is to be built, are susceptible of infinite modifications" (142). While giving due place to "reason" in his conception of citizenship, Story warned explicitly against "speculation," "theory," and conjecture. In his view, the principles of democratic government should definitely *not* be conceived of as abstract truths such as "two things, each of which is equal to a third, must be equal to one another." Unlike the axioms of geometry, the principles of democratic government are by definition controversial and revisable, and dangerously so. Therefore, civic education should train citizens to accept change but not to seek it. Story urged his young readers to believe that "experience" is the safest hedge against "too frequent and easy changes." "Whatever, then, has been found to work well in experience, should rarely be hazarded upon conjectural improvements. . . . To be of any value, they must become cemented with the habits, the feelings, and the pursuits of the people" (153).

For his part, Frederick Douglass held fast to both terms of the binary that structured this debate. On the one hand, he insisted on the intellectual and ethical legitimacy of changing his mind, so long as such seeming inconsistency was actually guided by a "fixed principle of honesty." And he repeatedly affirmed that democratic citizenship requires unending "struggle" against the powers that seek to undermine it, which in turn means that citizens should regard their democracy as never fully achieved and always open to revision. This view, writes Juliet Hooker, is one of the characteristics of his thought that make him a "fugitive democratic thinker": "he emphasizes the revolutionary and unsettled character of democratic politics, and asserts the right of ordinary citizens to interpret the law, such as when he exhorts his audience to read the [C]onstitution themselves."[30]

On the other hand, Douglass was also a foundationalist insofar as he believed that democracy was derived from principles to be found in a higher law that was eternal and unchanging. "Schooled as I have been among the abolitionists of New England," he writes in *Life and Times*, "I recognize that the universe is governed by laws which are unchangeable and eternal" (914). Therefore, although he certainly shares political theorist Sheldon Wolin's view that democracy is best understood as "a rebellious moment," not as "a form of government," his thinking was more dialectical than Wolin's insofar as he also maintained that certain principles and dispositions must remain "fixed."[31] Similarly, Douglass's thought is in agreement, up to a point, with political theorist Benjamin Barber's argument that "foundationalism, even where it represents an authoritative establishing of the credentials of democracy [as, e.g., in the work of the founders], tends . . . to undermine democracy, and democracy both requires and entails an immunity to its own foundations if it is to flourish." But when Barber asserts that "the free must freely choose (rechoose) their principles to make them their own," Douglass would insist that the "free" are not nearly so free to choose as they (and Barber) suppose. Only their naïve confidence in the security of their rights and their freedom, together with a delusional sense of their own sovereignty, allows them to suppose that they are. If they had ever occupied the standpoint of an enslaved person, they would instantly perceive the extreme precarity of their democracy and of the rights and protections it confers. That precarity means that human dignity and human rights require the protection not just of positive laws but of a higher law beyond the reach of history. Yet, the eternal truths of this higher law are never fully graspable by individual persons, who necessarily see them from a standpoint that has its insights and its blind spots. For this reason, free citizens who believe in the eternal truth of their right to be free must bear in mind both the historical contingency of their actual possession of freedom and the fallibility of their perceptions of the truths that vouchsafe their rights.[32]

We find Douglass's notion that freedom is always qualified both by its precarity and by our moral powers expressed most eloquently in his most famous address, "What to the Slave Is the Fourth of July?"[33] As many of its readers have noticed, he adopts in this speech the unusual and brilliant strategy of taking the standpoint of the enslaved and refusing to identify with his free audience. This rhetorical stance affords him a liminal position outside of the American polity from which he can see and critique it. "I shall see this day and its popular characteristics from the slave's point of view," he declares. "Standing, there, identified with the American bondsman, making his wrongs mine, I do not hesitate to declare, with all my soul, that the character and conduct of this nation never looked blacker to me than on this fourth of July."[34] This day of national celebration is one that he cannot share: "Your high independence only reveals the immeasurable distance between us. . . . This Fourth [of] July is yours, not mine" (368).

However, when seen in the context of Douglass's philosophy, his rhetorical strategy is more complex than has heretofore been recognized. His self-marginalization does indeed provide him with a vantage point from which to see the American polity and thereby criticize it. But this distance does not create objectivity or neutrality, since Douglass emphatically calls attention to the contingency and the value of his standpoint. But he believes, in this case, that his personal experience of enslavement has produced a knowledge that *all* Americans need in order to make their purported democracy a reality. As he insisted in *My Bondage and My Freedom*, "a slave, brought up in the very depths of ignorance" can indeed "instruct the highly civilized people of the north in the principles of liberty, justice, and humanity" (390).[35]

One sign that Douglass saw himself as giving such instruction appears in a detail that many readers emphasizing the critical payoff of his self-marginalization have missed: Douglass addresses his audience as "fellow citizens" not fewer than eight times. If he had wished to suggest only that he was in no way a communicant with his audience in this celebration of the nation's birth, he would not have employed this phrase. But he does, repeatedly, and his purpose is to bind his audience to him even as the main thrust of his rhetoric insists on "the immeasurable distance" between them. In this way, Juliet Hooker has argued, Douglass "rhetorically performs the civic in-betweenness of slaves, fugitive ex-slaves, and free African-Americans by continually aligning and disaligning himself with the United States." That continual aligning and disaligning—what I have called his "oscillation" between positions and perspectives—is another expression of the fugitivity that characterizes the style of Douglass's thinking as much as its substance.[36]

Douglass's method of holding contingency thinking and universalism in tension with each other finds its most intense expression in a metaphor he uses several times—that of a "ring-bolt." As we have seen, he believed, on the one hand, that the meaning of the Constitution is ultimately contingent on what it can "be made" to mean in response to present-day needs. But Douglass also repeatedly declared that certain principles—those embodied in the Constitution's preamble and in the Declaration of Independence—are beyond the reach of contingency; they cannot be molded by interpretation. In this speech, he asserts the force of those principles using an unusual metaphor: "The 4th of July is the first great fact in your nation's history—the very ring-bolt in the chain of your yet undeveloped destiny. . . . I have said that the Declaration of Independence is the very RING-BOLT to the chain of your nation's destiny; so, indeed, I regard it. The principles contained in that instrument are saving principles. Stand by those principles, be true to them on all occasions, in all places, against all foes, and at whatever cost" (363–64).

"Ring-bolt to the chain of your nation's destiny" is a puzzling metaphor for Douglass to have used here. "Ring-bolt" refers literally to a fixture, on a boat, to which a chain is fastened; but "chain" is a word that he and other abolitionists frequently employed as a synecdoche for enslavement. (To choose just one example among many: he writes in *My Bondage and My Freedom*: "For ten or fifteen years I had been dragging a heavy chain, with a huge block attached to it, encumbering my every motion. . . . All efforts . . . to separate myself from the hateful encumbrance, had only seemed to rivet me the more firmly to it" (350).) Why, then, would Douglass have chosen this particular image from his experience of enslavement as a metaphor for "the saving principles" of the Declaration of Independence?

The answer, I suggest, is that this figure gave him a way to express the strongly deontological understanding of freedom that he had acquired from his enslavement. Indeed, one reason why he declares in this speech that he "stands identified with the American slave" is that he believed such an understanding was an insight far more available to "the slave's point of view" than to that of a free person. A few years later, in *My Bondage and My Freedom*, he would observe of his master Captain Anthony that if he "had been brought up in a free state, surrounded by the just restraints of free society—*restraints which are necessary to the freedom of all its members*," Auld "might have been as humane a man . . . as are members of society generally" (171; emphasis added). Douglass's implicit logic here is that our principles actually fetter us because true freedom can never be absolute; it is always conditioned by our circumstances and secured by the binding nature of our principles. Democratic citizens must accommodate themselves to the paradox that the chains that bind them to their principles also secure their freedom and security. Without those principles, "the ship of state" will founder in the "heavy billows" of a national crisis. "Cling to this day—cling to it, and to its principles, with the grasp of a storm-tossed mariner to a spar at midnight" (364). Although proposed by a number of political philosophers, most notably John Locke, this seeming paradox—that freedom requires all citizens to submit to "just restraints"—would have been far more viscerally true to a man who had lived at the mercy of unrestrained slave masters than it could have been to most of the free white men and women in his audience.

Douglass maintained, then, contra Barber, that free citizens of a democracy must *not* consider themselves to be *wholly* "free to choose." This is the core paradox of democratic citizenship that Barber overlooks. The "free" are bound to their principles, though they know it not. Moreover, while Barber is correct that "in America the revolutionary spirit founded a constitution that in time came to be at odds with that spirit," Douglass's thought reveals that the conflict or inconsistency Barber names takes one form in the realm of theory and another in the realm of democratic practice (351).[37] In the realm of theory, the conflict appears to be a negative: the Constitution appears to "betray" the "spirit" that brought it into being. But in democratic practice, the conflict takes the form of an enabling challenge. It lodges a permanent instability in democracy, one that requires citizens to continually wrestle with a paradox: democracy requires them to grasp a "ringbolt" of eternal, ahistorical truths, yet also to continually debate the meaning of those truths, revising them in the light of changing historical circumstances and needs.

Instead of being dismayed by this inherent inconsistency, advocates of strong democracy should be encouraged by it, since the instability it perpetuates might allow democracy to retain at least some of its revolutionary vigor, or what Douglass in his speech on Europe's 1848 revolutions called the people's "energy."[38]

Douglass most explicitly articulated this distinctive understanding of democracy's "foundations" in an 1886 speech advocating women's suffrage. Interestingly, the speech echoes his famous "Change of Opinion Announced" published thirty-four years earlier in the North Star and uses a metaphor drawn straight from his reflections on the songs of the enslaved. "A difference of opinion," Douglass observes, "like a discord in music, sometimes gives the highest effects of harmony. . . . For myself, from what I know of the nature of the human understanding, I at once suspect the sincerity of the man or woman who never has an opinion in opposition to mine. Differing as all human minds do, in all their processes and operations, such uniform agreement is unnatural, and must be false, assumed, and dishonest. The fact is, *no family or State can rest upon any foundation less solid than truth and honesty.*"[39] As this last sentence suggests, Douglass's "fixed principle of honesty" was for him the only foundation on which a polity could safely stand. Foundations are "solid" and have "stability," he believed, only when they allow free play for differences and disagreements. They must be able to accommodate the conflicts that will inevitably arise in a democratic polity in which individual citizens with equal worth and rights occupy different standpoints and see things differently. No view can be dismissed outright; all must be considered. Therefore, while the citizens of a democracy must be guided by fixed and eternal truths, the only secure foundation of their polity is a principle of flexibility and openness to difference; only such a principle can welcome and harmonize the contingency and pluralism that any flourishing democracy rightly produces.

CHAPTER SIX

"Somebody's Child"

Awakening, Resistance, and Vulnerability in
My Bondage and My Freedom

When Douglass sat down sometime in 1853 or 1854 to write *My Bondage and My Freedom*, he had been self-identifying as a Black public intellectual for about six years. His work required him, as we have seen, to give a good deal of thought to issues other than slavery and abolitionism. As the slave states gained one political victory after another, from the Fugitive Slave Act in 1850 to the Kansas–Nebraska Act in May 1854, he had committed more and more of his time to electoral politics, which meant familiarizing himself with democracy's institutional mechanisms at both state and national levels. Debating whether Black emigration was a sound policy, he had thought long and hard about the meaning of race, about the racial makeup of the U.S. polity, about the functions of white racism, and about the prospects for Black dignity and freedom in the United States. In order to understand whether the Constitution did or did not sanction the U.S. slavery system, he had read deeply in constitutional law and in political theory more broadly. Putting his emergent political philosophy to work across this range of issues, and becoming increasingly aware that as a man who had been enslaved he had a valuable perspective to offer his free readers Black and white, he now returned to what Harriet Beecher Stowe called the "living root" of that philosophy in his experience of bondage: How, he must have wondered, had his early years prepared him to become a Black political activist and thinker? What might he learn now, through a rigorous retrospective analysis of his past, about how his experience of enslavement had shaped his political philosophy?

To date, the most comprehensive studies of this book—by William L. Andrews, Eric J. Sundquist, and Robert S. Levine—have focused on a different but related issue: how Douglass crafted My Bondage and My Freedom into a deliberately shaped representation of himself as he wished to be seen and understood by his readers in the middle of the 1850s. Andrews set the template for such interpretations when he argued, in a seminal 1987 essay, that My Bondage and My Freedom "is the first Afro-American autobiography publicly designed to argue that a black man's life story had wider significance than was usually accorded to the narratives of former slaves." The complexity of this work compared with the Narrative, according to Andrews, arose from Douglass's desire to represent himself in a particular, and perhaps somewhat contradictory, way: as both Black and "nationally significant." Andrews skillfully traced Douglass's efforts to reconcile or balance his dual commitments to Black "solidarity," on the one hand, and to "Romantic individualism," on the other. In pursuit of these aims, Douglass "designed" his book, "fashioned" its narrator, and determined to "treat" his own life in particular ways.[1]

Following in the path laid out by such readings, I too see Douglass's revisiting of his past as an active intervention in his present.[2] But instead of focusing on Douglass's fashioning of his public identity, I read it in a complementary way: as a rich, and at times philosophical account of two linked aspects of his enslavement: his political awakening and the nature of slave resistance—his own and that of the other enslaved persons whom he observed. To be sure, his deeper examination of his own awakening and resistance in My Bondage and My Freedom might merely have been an unintended consequence of his deeper scrutiny of his childhood and youth. But I believe it was more deliberate, driven by several motives. In a letter that forms part of the editor's preface to My Bondage and My Freedom, Douglass explains that one reason he is representing his life is to refute the widespread view, among whites anyway, that "the enslaved people . . . are so low in the scale of humanity, and so utterly stupid, that they are unconscious of their wrongs, and do not apprehend their rights" (106). His revised life story would demonstrate that, on the contrary, at least some of the enslaved were conscious of their wrongs and did apprehend their rights. But how did they attain such consciousness? Or were they born with it? These are the kinds of questions he now pursued by way of his reflections on his past. Moreover, as we have seen, at the time he was writing this book, Douglass was confident that he had a distinctive political philosophy, and that its origins lay in his experience of enslavement. It seems reasonable that he would have explored those origins even as he refashioned his public identity in a revised autobiography. Finally, as a Black public intellectual writing and working within the matrix of the antebellum Black public sphere, he was striving to persuade all free Black Americans to insist on their dignity and demand their rights, which meant awakening them to their possession of certain powers and mobilizing them for active resistance to white racism and the slavery system. With all these objectives before him, why not examine, learn from, and share his own experience of political awakening and resistance?

"Somebody's Child": Feeling That One Is Worthy of Respect

As many scholars have noted, the biggest single difference between the *Narrative* and *My Bondage and My Freedom* is that in the latter Douglass gives a far longer and more detailed account of his first ten years.[3] This longer account sheds illuminating light on the stages by which he became aware of the real nature of his condition, realized its injustice, and determined to resist it. This gradual process began with a stroke of good fortune: instead of being raised in the slave quarters like most enslaved children, he was sent to spend his first six or so years with his grandmother on the outskirts of the plantation. There, "living with my dear grandmother," he writes in the book's opening chapter, "I knew many things before I knew myself to be *a slave*" (143). What were these "many things"? And why did they matter?

The most important, we soon learn, was that he knew that he had a home. He recalls tenderly the feeling of "being with [his grandparents] so snugly in their own little cabin" (143). He lingers nostalgically over the details of this dwelling, fondly recalling the fascination they had for him, and concludes: this "was MY HOME—the only home I ever had; and I loved it, and all connected with it" (147). Along with the sense of security it gave him, Douglass emphasizes two other benefits of having had a home: an affection for a place, and a loving relationship with other persons. His grandmother's home gave him a space where his sensuous, embodied sense of wonder about the world could expand and flourish. This affectionate energy is an *aesthetic* capacity in the broad sense of the word, one that does not narrow its meaning to aesthetic judgment of works of art but builds on the meanings of the Greek root (bodily sensation and perception) and includes what has recently come to be called "everyday aesthetics."[4] It is the energy of *feeling* the world and then responding to it with creative appreciation. It is the faculty that changes space into place, and that turns the earth into a world and a home. Douglass closely associated this power with his youthful exuberance and irrepressible joie de vivre. It is first and foremost a power of the *body*.

Douglass tells us that he had ample opportunity to exercise this faculty when living with his grandmother; for example, the rough cabin itself appeared to his "child's eye" to be a "noble structure," and the ladder that led to the loft "was really a high invention, and possessed a sort of charm as I played with delight upon the rounds of it" (141–42). He "loved it" because he knew so intimately "its rail floor and rail bedsteads up stairs, and its clay floor down stairs" (146). When he recalls that the "old fences" and the "stumps" and the "squirrels" he had observed around the cabin were all "objects of *interest and affection*" (147; emphasis added), he is expressing his memory of a particular way he had *felt* about the home, a particular kind of affective relation he had had to things that did more than merely mark space: they built a particular kind of place, the kind one calls "home."[5]

His feelings for these objects was complemented by—and perhaps even made possible by—his love for his grandparents and the other children who lived with them in their cabin. He calls the social world they made a "joyous circle": "My grandmother! My grandmother! And the little hut, and the joyous circle under her care, but especially she, who made us sorry when she left us but for an hour and glad on her return—how could I leave her and the good old home?" (144–45). The phrasing here suggests that it was her *caring*—her attentive and protective love—that created this small and happy community. And when he recalls that the children missed her terribly when she was gone, and then rejoiced when she returned, he is simply suggesting that, like all children, they were learning about the intersubjective dynamics of love and human relationships: her love was both a natural phenomenon, like sunshine, and a precarious one that depended on her actual presence, which could come and go. Through such comings and goings, Douglass and the other children learned that the world is held together by contingent human relationships. They were learning that they depended on another person. And the mere fact that this person could be absent sometimes, or could withhold love even though present, taught them that such relationships have to be continuously created and sustained.

It has been tempting to read this account of his grandmother rather skeptically: less as a faithful record of his past than as an example of his cannily crafting a self-image that would appeal to his white readers, many of whom shared the period's sentimental veneration of the home and a mother's love. By invoking the well-worn tropes of the antebellum period's culture of sentiment, these critics have suggested, Douglass induced his white readers to cross racial lines and empathically identify with him.[6] I would suggest, however, that while Douglass certainly did write with his white readers in mind, he must also have been thinking about his African American readers. To them, as we have seen, he had been urging a program of "elevation" that signified not so much Black imitation of white, middle-class values (including domesticity), but rather Black *political mobilization* sparked by collaboratively produced Black self-respect. As Douglass wrote in one of his anti-emigration editorials, a sense of home instilled a person with *motives*: "home is the fountain head, the foundation, and main support, not only of all social virtue, but of all motives to human progress."[7] It is reasonable to suppose, I would argue, that Douglass was modeling such respect-building practices in his portrait of his grandmother, suggesting that her home and her care had provided enabling conditions for the growth of a sense of self that deserved respect—self-respect and respect from others. He implies, too, that he had benefited both from her example and from her love. Although enslaved, she had managed to achieve distinction and win respect from others (albeit with great effort and much luck). She "was held in high esteem," he writes, "far higher than is the lot of most colored persons in the slave states," and "her high reputation was full of advantage to her" (141). As critic and historian Sterling Stuckey notes: "His confidence in himself and his self-respect, despite the fierceness of opposing forces, owed much to her extraordinary example."[8]

In this longer account of his childhood, Douglass's mother, too, played a crucial role in nurturing his confidence and self-respect. He very seldom saw her, and so he admits that his feelings for her were not strong; however, the mere fact that she would travel long distances to see him, and then lie down and spend the night with him, must have conveyed to the small boy that she had strong feelings for him. As well, Douglass recalls that his mother, like his grandmother, was a woman of some distinction, one who knew her own worth and projected that sense into the world, where others took note of it. His account of her "appearance and bearing," which "are ineffaceably stamped upon my memory," emphasizes that "she was tall, and finely proportioned; of deep black, glossy complexion" (151–52), and that "she was endowed with high powers of manner as well as matter" (154). After his mother's death, he learned that she could read "and that she was the only one of all the slaves and colored people in Tuckahoe who enjoyed that advantage." Douglass wrote:

> That a "field hand" should learn to read, in any slave state, is remarkable; but the achievement of my mother, considering the place, was very extraordinary; and, in view of that fact, I am quite willing, and even happy, to attribute any love of letters I possess, and for which I have got—despite of prejudices—only too much credit, not to my admitted Anglo-Saxon paternity, but to the native genius of my sable, unprotected, and uncultivated mother—a woman, who belonged to a race whose mental endowments it is, at present, fashionable to hold in disparagement and contempt. (155–56)

This passage, too, has commonly been read in terms of Douglass's self-representational objectives: it conveys his embrace of his Black identity, his new orientation toward the Black community, and his fitness for Black leadership. We may supplement such a reading, I suggest, with one that sees Douglass also discovering and representing here the foundational conditions that made possible his eventual political awakening. If so, that representation presents a much less masculinist and individualistic Douglass, and one much more attuned to an ethics of care and interdependence, than most of his readers have heretofore noticed and acknowledged.[9]

Douglass vividly dramatizes his indebtedness to his mother in one of the most affecting scenes in all of My Bondage and My Freedom. After being separated from his grandmother and left with his master on the Lloyd plantation, he found himself for the first time inhabiting a world where no one cared for him. He was alone. To make matters worse, the most powerful woman in that world, and one whom he had every reason to expect might be such a caretaker, proved to be a tyrant who persecuted him. This Aunt Katy ran the kitchen and distributed the food with an iron hand, dispensing favors to her own children and terrorizing all the others. Douglass relates how on one particular evening, when Aunt Katy had deprived him of food all day, his mother made one of her rare appearances in his life:

> And now, dear reader, a scene occurred which was altogether worth beholding, and to me it was instructive as well as interesting. The friendless and hungry boy, in his extremest need—and when he did not dare to look for succor—found himself in the strong, protecting arms of his mother; a mother who was, at the moment (being endowed with high powers of manner as well as matter) more than a match for all his enemies. I shall never forget the indescribable expression of her countenance, when I told her that I had had no food since morning; and that Aunt Katy said she "meant to starve the life out of me." There was pity in her glance at me, and a fiery indignation at Aunt Katy at the same time; and while she . . . gave me a large ginger cake, . . . she read Aunt Katy a lecture which she never forgot. . . . That night I learned the fact, that, I was not only a child, but *somebody's* child. (154–55; emphasis added)

Although not as dramatic as the "resurrection" Douglass attributes to his victory over slave breaker Edward Covey, and not as traumatic as his witnessing his Aunt Esther's whipping, this moment is of equal importance. The "indescribable expression" on his mother's face gave the small boy a talisman he could carry for the rest of his life, for in her expression of shock, tenderness, and anger he glimpsed the depth of his *worth* to her. It was precisely this sense of his own dignity that Aunt Katy's capriciously excessive punishment threatened. As he relates at the beginning of this story: "Against this disappointment, for I was expecting that her heart would relent at last, I made an extra effort *to maintain my dignity*" (154; emphasis added). But when he saw all the other children receiving food, he "could stand it no longer. I went out behind the house, and cried like a fine fellow" (154). This injury to his self-esteem is what his mother instantly perceived when she entered the kitchen: her child was not just hungry but wounded, and she responded with "fiery indignation" (154).

This trope of "fiery indignation," as I have noted earlier, appears frequently in African American literature, and in slave narratives especially. Precisely because it is spontaneous and uncontrollable, this anger that arises to defend a person's self-esteem gives proof that a natural dignity lives irrepressibly within—bursting forth uncontrollably in response to insult to oneself or to a loved one.[10] In this moment, then, his mother's surge of anger strongly confirmed the small boy's sense that he mattered deeply to her. And if we take Douglass's words "instructive" and "learned" seriously, they indicate that her anger also imparted a crucial lesson to him. He learned that he was "somebody's child." As George Yancy has astutely observed, "The recognition that he was somebody's child militated against his simply being somebody's property."[11] Yet we can go a step further than this negative construction (not-property) to the positive implications of this moment: when he discovered that he mattered to someone, he discovered that he had worth. Despite all the slavery system's efforts to crush or deny it, he had a human worth that was, as Kant would put it, beyond all price.

It is worth pausing to note again that a somewhat overlooked Douglass is coming into view here. Because so many current assessments of him were forged in the 1970s and early 1980s, when most scholars derived their understanding of Douglass from the Narrative, he gained the reputation of being a strongly masculinist thinker who promoted the traditionally manly virtues of rugged independence and self-reliance.[12] This reputation has endured to this day. But the Narrative was not Douglass's final word on his life, his values, his political awakening, or his political philosophy. Indeed, when writing My Bondage and My Freedom, he seems to have set out to revise thoroughly the image of himself as a heroic, self-reliant individualist male that he had presented in the Narrative.[13] There, as critic Deborah McDowell pointed out long ago, he had virtually erased his grandmother, mother, and wife from his life story. There, too, he had made a spectacle of the brutal whipping of his Aunt Hester and positioned her punishment as his own entrance into the hell of enslavement.[14] But in his second autobiography, as we have seen, he makes clear that his grandmother and mother provided the crucial care he needed in order to acquire an early sense of his own self-worth. And the whipping of his aunt is now described much less graphically, and it does not appear until the book's fifth chapter.[15]

Indeed, these early chapters give an account of the origins of Douglass's attunement to interdependence that Ange-Marie Hancock Alfaro astutely perceives to be at work later in the book—in, for example, his account of his relations with "Uncle" Charles Lawson and Sandy Jenkins. In *My Bondage and My Freedom*, she argues, Douglass presents a "black male ethic of care." She suggests further that we can read Douglass's account of this ethic as his sharp dissent from prevailing assumptions that self-reliant individualism and an embrace of a "liberal democratic notion of freedom, defined . . . by the thirst and willingness to die for freedom" are the indispensable "prequalifications for liberal democratic and republican citizenship."[16] What I would add to this account is that, for Douglass, the specifically Black male ethic Alfaro describes was part of a larger ethic in which all persons and citizens should care for one another, recognize their interdependence, and collaboratively produce and affirm each other's dignity. The early pages of *My Bondage and My Freedom* describing "the many other things [he] knew" before he knew he was enslaved lovingly convey Douglass's later appreciation of the two Black women who loved and respected him. Because their very comportment showed that they mattered to themselves, they commanded his respect. And because he mattered to them, he began to respect himself.

Douglass relates in *My Bondage and My Freedom* that he was schooled in the protocols of respect by other enslaved persons on the Lloyd plantation as well:

> Strange, and even ridiculous as it may seem, among a people so uncultivated, and with so many stern trials to look in the face, there is not to be found, among any people, a more rigid enforcement of the law of respect to elders, than they maintain. I set this down as partly constitutional with my race, and partly conventional. There is no better material in the world for making a gentleman, than is furnished in the African. He shows to others, and exacts for himself, all those tokens of respect which he is compelled to manifest toward his master. (164)

There is much to infer from this passage. It suggests, first, that Douglass grew up within a still partially African culture, one that emphasized the giving and the receiving of respect. It hints also that the enslaved on the Lloyd plantation kept alive practices through which they collaboratively produced a genuine respect for one another both to compensate for the slavery system's denial of their dignity and *to offset* the respect (if it can be called that) they were "compelled" to show to their masters.

In the opening chapters of *My Bondage and My Freedom*, then, Douglass indicates that what he knew before he knew he was "a slave" included crucial knowledge about self-respect and respect gained from his family and from the Black community of the plantation. He also makes this point explicitly, as when he observes that the slavery system's "practice of separating children from their mothers" is "to reduce man to a level with the brute" by "obliterating from the mind and heart of the slave, all just ideas of the sacredness of the family, as an institution" (142). A "brute," by implication, is a being who has no sense of its own worth, or dignity, and thus no motive for resistance. It should not surprise us that slaveholders knew well that the early childhood experience of loving and being held within human relationships was powerfully constitutive of human self-respect, and that such self-respect could become a dangerous disposition to resist and rebel. This is what sociologist Orlando Patterson famously argued in *Slavery and Social Death*. Yet, as Patterson also observes, the slavery system seldom if ever succeeded in destroying the slave's sense of his or her own self-worth: "There is absolutely no evidence from the long and dismal annals of slavery to suggest that any group of slaves ever internalized the conception of degradation held by their masters. . . . Indeed, it is precisely this irrepressible yearning for dignity and recognition that is hardest to understand about the condition of slavery."[17]

Many historians have concurred, demonstrating further the degree to which the enslaved were able to maintain dignity-conferring relationships among one another. As Steven Hahn writes:

> Slavery . . . was a system of extreme personal domination in which a slave had no relationship that achieved legal sanction or recognition other than with the master, or with someone specifically designated by the master. . . . Consequently, the slaves' struggles to form relations among themselves and to give those relations customary standing in the eyes of masters and slaves alike was the most basic and the most profound of political acts in which they engaged.[18]

In his speeches, and above all in *My Bondage and My Freedom*, Douglass offers a deeper explanation of *why* these acts of forming relationships were so political: without a sense of self-worth, or dignity, one would feel the pain of one's oppression but not its injustice. And without a profound conviction of its injustice, one would not feel justified in striving to overturn or escape it. Slaveholders knew that the most effective way to render the enslaved submissive was to deprive them of the influences that instilled and nurtured their self-respect. For Douglass, therefore, the most effective way to resist the slavery system and racism was to recognize human dignity, to cultivate self-respect, and to respect the natural dignity of other humans.[19]

As I have suggested earlier, it is this emphasis on human dignity and its intersubjective, collaborative nature that distinguishes Douglass's thought from what I take to be the mainstream tradition of liberalism. Because Douglass is so often described as a "liberal," this distinction is important; but it is also subtle, so I will try to restate it here. The crux of the matter lies in how Douglass conceives of the relation between the individual and the social. He vividly describes those relations throughout *My Bondage and My Freedom*, and he gives one of his most explicit and philosophical accounts of them in an 1851 editorial, "Is Civil Government Right?" There he writes that "man is a social as well as an individual being" and "is endowed by his Creator with faculties and powers suited to his individuality and to society." Douglass asserts further that "individual isolation is unnatural, unprogressive, and against the highest interests of man." Therefore, "society is required, by the natural wants and necessities inherent in human existence."[20]

In a trenchant analysis of this editorial, political theorist Nick Buccola—who takes Douglass to be a political philosopher of liberalism—does full justice to what I have called the "tension" in Douglass's thought, a word Buccola uses, too. As well, Buccola convincingly argues that Douglass's political philosophy rests upon "a theory of human nature," one that sees it as composed of some "central dualities."[21] One of these, as Buccola writes, is "the sociality-individuality duality" (254), which is epitomized, he observes, in these sentences from "Is Civil Government Right?" Buccola then glosses these as follows: "Douglass seems to have adopted the Aristotelian idea that a self-sufficient man would have to be either beastlike or godlike. Society is, according to Douglass, natural in the sense that the survival and flourishing of individuals is best achieved through interaction with others" (256).

To borrow a phrase Douglass himself uses in this editorial, Buccola's interpretation "contains the skeleton, but the life is not there—The bones and sinews are retained, but the vital spark which should animate them is gone" (209). Perhaps inadvertently, Buccola's phrasing implies that "individuals" exist first and independently of others, and that they survive and flourish best when, as independent beings, they "interact" with one another. But Douglass's point is that, to *become* individuals, humans *require* a caring social context that mirrors back to them their own worth. Without that sense of their individuality's worth to others, their individuality would mean little to them. As we have seen, Douglass suggests that it was his feeling of being *somebody's child* that made his individuality meaningful and precious to him—and not, say, a hellish loneliness. When Douglass observes that isolation goes against "the highest interests of man," he is telling us that it disregards the preciousness of human worth that is produced through intersubjective dynamics of love and respect. And it is this complex understanding of "sociality-individuality" in relation to dignity that crucially distinguishes Douglass's political thought from the tradition of natural rights liberalism.[22] Buccola correctly observes that "Douglass's appreciation for natural sociality and individuality enabled him to avoid the extremes of radical individualism and radical communitarianism"; but he misses the fact that this "appreciation" rested in a belief that a person's individuality was itself the expression of a human nature shared with all others. Even in his lecture "Self-Made Men," which many readers take to be an unequivocal celebration of individualism, Douglass is careful to stress the importance of "inter-dependence and brotherhood" as a *condition* of individuality:

> It must in truth be said though it may not accord well with self-conscious individuality and self-conceit, that no possible native force of character, and no depth of wealth or originality, can lift a man into absolute independence of his fellow-men, and no generation of men can be independent of the preceding generation. The brotherhood and inter-dependence of mankind are guarded and defended at all points. I believe in individuality; but individuals are, like the mass, like waves to the ocean. The highest order of genius is as dependent as the lowest.[23]

"The Point from Which a Thing Is Viewed"

To get from a consciousness of one's worth to a realization of the injustice of one's condition, a second step is required: one must believe that one's own perspective on the world has as much value and validity as anyone else's. This is especially the case for severely oppressed persons who are caught up in a system of near-total domination. As Douglass frequently observed, to perpetuate itself, such a system must do more than inflict brutal punishment on resistance; it must also create an ideological order in which one's intuitive and reasoned critiques of the system are overwhelmed by its dismissal of the validity of one's perspective. To be motivated to rebel against such a system, then, one must feel that it is profoundly unjust; and to feel such injustice, one must have a sense both that one's personhood has value *and* that one's perception of things has as much validity as that of one's oppressors. One must acquire, in other words, the belief that all knowledge is dependent on a person's standpoint, that every standpoint has some validity, and therefore that no single standpoint can be universally true or absolutely authoritative.

In *My Bondage and My Freedom*, Douglass writes what is virtually a parable about his own discovery of standpoint. It took place on the very day he left his grandmother's house and, unbeknownst to himself, was being taken by her to the scene of his actual enslavement: the Lloyds' great plantation. There, he would learn for the first time what it meant to be a "slave." Not surprisingly, Douglass writes of that morning: "I remember [it] as well as if it were yesterday" (147–48). Something in the gravity of his grandmother's manner filled his soul with dread. All these years later, he could still feel the terror that flooded him after they entered the dark woods that lay between her home and the Great House Farm. In the gloomy light that filtered through the trees, shadows became monsters, and wild beasts seemed to lurk behind every stump, ready to rush out and devour him. He gripped his grandmother's hand more tightly and drew closer to her side, reminding himself that within the protective circle cast by her presence nothing could threaten or harm him. And, sure enough, as his eyes grew accustomed to the darkness, he saw that his imagined monsters were mere illusions: "The eyes were knots, washed white with rain, and the legs were broken limbs, and the ears, only ears owing to the point from which they were seen" (148). Just here, we may imagine, Douglass the writer might have paused, his quill pen hovering over the paper on which he wrote: How best to express the *meaning* of this moment to which his memory had so forcefully carried him? He dipped his pen in ink and wrote, with his signature ironic understatement: "Thus early I learned that the point from which a thing is viewed is of some importance" (148).[24]

From our vantage point today, we can see that Douglass was announcing his discovery of standpoint epistemology.[25] "It is impossible," writes Patricia Hill Collins in one of the earliest formulations of this idea, "to separate the structure and thematic content of thought from the historical and material conditions shaping the lives of its producers."[26] Consequently, there is no objectively correct perspective from which to view the world and judge others; every perspective is just that—a perspective. Within the context of *My Bondage and My Freedom* and its retracing of the origins of his political philosophy, especially his political awakening, this scene suggests that the discovery of standpoint enabled the young Douglass to believe subsequently that his observations of the slavery system were valid and had value. For example, when he writes in a later chapter, "I saw at the stable, another incident, which I will relate," and goes on to describe the elderly coachman William being flogged by Colonel Lloyd, we can infer that the small boy who witnessed this scene already had a sense, however faint, that his gaze upon the colonel was as legitimate as the colonel's gaze upon him. Likewise, when Douglass writes that his master Captain Anthony (who was rumored to be his father) "little thought that the little black urchins around him, could see . . . the very secrets of his heart" (172), he strongly implies that even as a child he *knew* that he saw things about Anthony's character to which Anthony himself was blind.

Douglass's introduction of his discovery of standpoint epistemology so early in *My Bondage and My Freedom* suggests, too, that by 1854 he was well aware that his thought arose not in a neutral space abstracted from history and political struggle, but from within what philosopher George Yancy calls "the muck and mire of *raced* embodied existence."[27] We might even surmise that Douglass constructed this discovery (rather than the whipping of his Aunt Hester) as the threshold of his entrance into slavery precisely in order to have his readers likewise enter into his recollections of enslavement through the gateway of such an epistemology. Indeed, this change of thresholds precisely reflects his shift from being a witness to being a philosopher of slavery. His commonsense observation that "the point from which a thing is viewed is of some importance" quietly establishes his authority to speak on the nature of his bondage and freedom, on domination, resistance, justice, power, and other key concepts in political philosophy. It thereby offers an implicit *philosophical* response, delivered with his hallmark irony, to John A. Collins and other abolitionist friends who had advised him, "'Give us the facts, we will take care of the philosophy'" (367). What those friends had failed to grasp was that the appearance of all "facts" changes as the point from which they are viewed shifts. Tree trunks in a forest, the slavery system, the political principles of justice and equality—all these things appear differently to persons who occupy different places in society, and in time and space. For this reason, the perspective of a formerly enslaved person on the slavery system, and his reflections on it, was at least as legitimate as the views of persons who had never experienced enslavement. As well, this scene and the conclusions Douglass draws from it implicitly justify his use of autobiography as a medium in which to write political philosophy: If thought is always embodied in a particular person, not just floating abstractly in the air, what better way than autobiography to convey the substance and development of one's philosophy?[28]

Finally, if "being black means belonging to a state that is organized in part by its ignorance of your perspective—a state that does not, that cannot, know your mind," then insistence on one's particular standpoint is in itself a powerful political statement.[29] Douglass's announcement of his standpoint discovery was a conscious effort to dispel that ignorance and make his Black mind known to a white supremacist order. This may explain why Douglass so frequently announced his particular standpoint, in so many of his speeches and editorials. To give just three examples: "I shall see this day and its popular characteristics from the slave's point of view," he declared in his famous 1852 speech "What to the Slave Is the Fourth of July?" Fifteen years later, in 1867, he called his audience's attention to his changed standpoint: "I appear here no longer as a whipped, scarred slave—no longer as an advocate merely of an enslaved race, but in the high and commanding character of an American citizen" (152). And toward the end of his life, in 1894, he began his essay "Why Is the Negro Lynched?" with the blunt announcement that "I propose to give you a colored man's view of the so-called 'Negro

Problem.' "[30] Douglass's insistence on standpoint was part of what I have called his strategy of reversal, or chiasmus: simply by announcing that he spoke and saw from a particular standpoint, he forced his audiences to acknowledge the perhaps humbling fact of their own.

The Dynamics of Political Awakening

Equipped, then, with a budding sense of his worth as a person and with a precocious awareness that the truth of things depends on standpoint, a six-year-old boy emerged from the woods clutching the hand of his grandmother and entered the domain of his actual enslavement. Given what Douglass had written by 1855 about the powers and faculties that make us worthy of rights—specifically, our intellectual and moral powers—one might expect him to begin narrating at this point his discovery that he possessed such powers. Memory or inclination, however, took him down another path first.

The day they arrived at the Great House Farm, Frederick's grandmother slipped away and left him behind. At first, Douglass relates, he felt stunned, betrayed, and grief-stricken. But he also recalls that he adapted to his new circumstances with surprising ease: "Keen as was my regret and great as was my sorrow at leaving [grandmother's cabin], I was not long in adapting to this, my new home. . . . The little tendrils of affection, so rudely and treacherously broken from around the darling objects of my grandmother's hut, gradually began to extend, and to entwine about the new objects by which I now found myself surrounded" (161). This metaphor of "little tendrils" comes straight from what critic Arthur Riss has called the "lexicon" of the sentimental culture in which Douglass lived and worked after his escape from slavery.[31] Harriet Jacobs, for example, also uses this figure when she asks: "Why does the slave ever love? Why allow the tendrils of the heart to twine around objects which may at any moment be wrenched away by the hand of violence?"[32] But the conventional nature of this expression should not prevent us from perceiving its full purpose and force. Douglass employed it, I would argue, not merely because he knew that it would appeal to the sentimental culture he addressed, but also because he wished to convey that, as a child, he had been infused with an unrestrained and irrepressible energy, like that of a growing vine. Without any effort of his will, or even any consciousness on his part, his affections—that is, his primal, erotic interest in life—had reached out and transformed his immediate surroundings, making them both familiar and precious. In *My Bondage and My Freedom*, the adult Douglass often reveals his fascination with this childhood capacity to respond to the beauty and wonder of the world despite the terrible conditions into which he had been thrown.

This interest led him to pen a remarkable and puzzling passage, one in which he seems to celebrate the "advantages" of the boyhood he had experienced as a slave:

> The slave-boy escapes many troubles which befall and vex his white brother. . . . He is never expected to act like a nice little gentleman, for he is only a rude little slave. Thus, freed from all restraint, the slave-boy can be, in his life and conduct, a genuine boy, doing whatever his boyish nature suggests. . . . His days, when the weather is warm, are spent in the pure, open air, and in the bright sunshine. . . . In a word, he is, for the most part of the first eight years of his life, a spirited, joyous, uproarious, and happy boy, upon whom troubles fall only like water on a duck's back. And such a boy, so far as I can now remember, was the boy whose life in slavery I am now narrating. (145)

Why would Douglass have written a passage that (despite its irony) so plainly risked confirming pro-slavery arguments that the enslaved were docile, contented, and even happy? The explanation is hinted in his shift to the present tense and the moment of the book's composition. When Douglass writes, "I can now remember" and "I am now narrating," he is invoking the present-tenseness and open-endedness of the book as he sat writing it. Although readers naturally receive it as a finished *product*, the writer himself experiences his work as a *process*; for the autobiographer especially, it may feel like an unfinished search for the truth and the meaning of the past. Here, perhaps more than in any of the other revisions Douglass made to the *Narrative*, he commits himself fully to an autobiographical project that exceeds the constraints of an abolitionist agenda. His project is not merely what Eric Sundquist calls a "blending of a campaign for black freedom and black rights with a telling of his own representative story," for the story it tells is not always "representative." Nor does it merely "demonstrate that Douglass was . . . qualified to interpret the meaning of his own life." Such phrasing inadvertently suggests that his own life lay there beneath his retrospective gaze, complete and formed and ready for interpretation.[33] The writing of *My Bondage and My Freedom* was certainly calculated to a degree, but it was also a struggle and a search—often a perplexed search—for the origins of his singular perspective on enslavement and the political. That quest led him to think long and hard about the importance of "the pure, open air and the bright sunshine" he had enjoyed, and of the "spirited, joyous, uproarious, and happy" disposition he had maintained despite slavery's hardships.

In this search, he might have been guided, and provoked, by Combe's book *The Constitution of Man*. Recall Combe's belief that "man, when civilized and illuminated by knowledge, . . . discovers in the objects and occurrences around him, a scheme beautifully arranged for the gratification of his whole powers, animal, moral, and intellectual; he recognizes in himself the intelligent and accountable subject of an all-bountiful Creator, and in joy and gladness desires to study the Creator's works." Combe's argument, though somewhat controversial in its time, meshed smoothly with the larger Enlightenment project of creating the modern subject. However, as literary historian Simon Gikandi has argued, that very project also aimed to exclude the enslaved from human status by denying their capacity for moral reflection and aesthetic response: "the act of enslavement was predicated on the exclusion of the slave from the moral and aesthetic realm."[34] No doubt because he wished to contest this exclusion, Douglass's account of his childhood suggests that even an enslaved man, one who is *not* "civilized and illuminated by knowledge," can nonetheless make such discoveries in the "objects and occurrences around him" and "recognize" himself to be an "intelligible and accountable subject"—that is, a human being who possesses certain powers and from those powers derives a sense of his self-worth.

Although Douglass associates his "affection" and "spirit" with his body and what he would also call the "elastic spirit of the bondsman" (422), he does not identify it with mere physical force, since it often manifested itself as stillness or attentiveness. He repeatedly recalls how the wondrous beauty of the world around him—its scenes and objects—called forth a dreamy, meditative, thoughtful response. "Down in a little valley, not far from grandmammy's cabin, stood Mr. Lee's mill. . . . It was a water mill; and I shall never be able to tell *the many things thought and felt*, while I sat on the bank and watched that mill, and the turning of its ponderous wheel" (147; emphasis added). At the Great House Farm, the bustle of work and life nurtured this meditative faculty and stimulated it to curiosity and speculation: "It was a source of much amusement to view the flowing sails and complicated rigging, as the little crafts dashed by. . . . With so many sources of interest around me, the reader may be prepared to learn that I began to think very highly of Col. L's plantation. . . . Here was a field for industry and enterprise, strongly inviting; and the reader may be assured that I entered upon it with spirit" (166).

In an especially suggestive passage, Douglass considers the role that "objects" and "things" themselves played in the growth of his reflective consciousness. Recalling the long hours he had spent gazing at the Lloyds' sloop and windmill, he writes: "The sloop and mill were wondrous things, full of thoughts and ideas. A child cannot well look at such objects without *thinking*" (161; emphasis added). This prompts one to ask: How can mere "things" be "full of thoughts and ideas"? The answer may be that these man-made objects were permeated with, and expressive of, the thoughts and ideas of the persons who had made them. If so, it might well be that as a boy who had been deemed a "thing" himself, and thus incapable of having thoughts and ideas, Douglass was unusually attuned to this permeation of "things" with thought. Likewise, as a boy who had been allowed to run "wild" for years, and who had thereby evaded a conventional education instructing him to disregard such intuitions, he remained receptive to them. In any case, he seems to have felt a sympathetic identification with these things, for he was virtually compelled by them to engage in "thinking" himself.

Douglass also remembers that he had thrilled in response to the red-winged blackbirds in the trees that surrounded Colonel Lloyd's magnificent plantation mansion. "The tops of the stately poplars were often covered with the red-winged black-birds, making all nature vocal with the joyous life and beauty of their wild, warbling notes." Somehow, despite all the "heart-rending incidents" of punishment he witnessed, he could still take pleasure in the "joyous life and beauty" of the world around him. But writing as an adult looking back on those days, he inserted a comment that deftly hints at the political implications of this boyhood pleasure: "These all belonged to me, as well as to Col. Edward Lloyd, and for a short time I greatly enjoyed them" (162–63). This remark prompts us to ask: Did he enjoy them *because* he sensed that they belonged to him as well as to his master? Or did his enjoyment of them lead him to reflect, if only preconsciously, that they also belonged to him in a sense? In short, was his enjoyment the cause or the consequence of his political reflection? Later, in a vivid and more pointed account of the Lloyd family's magnificent house, he writes: "It was a treat to my young and gradually opening mind, to behold this elaborate display of wealth, power, and vanity" (162). Are these last words expressing only his retrospective judgment? Or do they indicate that his aesthetic enjoyment of the home's grandeur triggered a preconscious political insight that the Lloyds' stately home was an expression of "wealth, power, and vanity"? Read in the context of the moments that precede it, the latter seems more probable.[35]

Douglass's investigation of the ways his aesthetic responsiveness to the natural world nurtured his "gradually opening mind" culminates in this remarkable paragraph, which I quote in full:

> As I grew older and more thoughtful, I was more and more filled with a sense of my wretchedness. The cruelty of Aunt Katy, the hunger and cold I suffered, and the terrible reports of cruelty and outrage that came to my ear, together with what I almost daily witnessed, led me, when yet but eight or nine years old, to wish I had never been born. I used to contrast my condition with the black-birds, in whose wild and sweet songs I fancied them so happy! Their apparent joy only deepened my sorrow. There are thoughtful days in the lives of children—at least there were in mine—when they grapple with all the great, primary subjects of knowledge, and reach, in a moment, conclusions which no subsequent experience can shake. I was just as well aware of the unjust, unnatural and murderous character of slavery, when nine years old, as I am now. Without any appeal to books, to laws, or to authorities of any kind, it was enough to accept God as a father, to regard slavery as a crime. (209)

Here we find again a description of a mode of reflection that is not yet conscious thought, yet which leads to an awareness that his condition is profoundly wrong. Here again, the cruelty and outrage he witnesses catalyze such thought, but here, too, they are twined with influences of a milder sort. And here again the singing blackbirds have a message to impart, but this time a different one. On earlier occasions, their music had prompted him to ask something like: *How can I, a being who thrills to* the music of these birds, be doomed to be a slave forever? Impossible! Now, however, their song provoked a complementary question: How can the very same world that arouses the happiness of these blackbirds be a place of captivity and despair for me? In short, as these songs deepened his sorrow, they also nurtured his reflections on his condition. They produced, as he puts it, "thoughtful days" when, as a mere child, he grappled "with all the great, primary subjects of knowledge" and reached, "in a moment, conclusions which no subsequent experience can shake."

What are these "great, primary subjects"? Douglass does not specify them, but we can surmise that they are the fundamental existential and moral questions every thinking person asks at some point in his or her life: Who am I? What is my purpose? Why do I feel as I do? What is the meaning of my experience? Much as his later wrestling with Covey would trigger a transformation familiar to all who have read his work, so his early melancholic reflection on these questions seems to have initiated or at least encouraged his political coming to consciousness by confirming his sense that slavery was a "crime." Although he experienced this conclusion as a suffering so intense that he often wished he had "never been born," this pain was nonetheless a necessary precondition of his later resistance to and escape from slavery. Thus, while it may be true that, as Simon Gikandi writes, "many enslaved Africans conceived and performed sorrow as the true representation of their state and drew on the reserves of their unhappiness and depression to find a language for expressing the integrity of the self against overwhelming conditions of oppression" (191), Douglass suggests that melancholy could also serve another function for them: it could kindle their resistance to enslavement— but only if it shifted registers from despondence to indignation.

"The All-Important Thing":
Aesthetic Power and Political Awakening

To understand more fully what Douglass meant by a child's apprehension of "all the great, primary subjects of knowledge," it may be helpful to look forward in time to a lecture he delivered in Boston in 1861. Titled "Pictures and Progress," both its concerns and its language resonate suggestively with these passages from My Bondage and My Freedom.[36]

Early in the lecture, Douglass offers this poetic evocation and analysis of "the divine meditations" of a "boy of ten":

On the hillside in the valley under the grateful shades of solitary oaks and elms the boy of ten all forgetful, of time or place, calls to books, or to boyish sports, looks up with silence and awe to the blue overhanging firmament and views with dreamy wonder, its ever shifting drapery, tracing in the Clouds, and in their ever changing forms and colors, the outlines of towns and cities, great ships and hostile armies of men [and] of horses, solemn Temples, and the Great Spirit of all; Break in if you please upon the prayers of monks or nuns, but I pray you, do not disturb the divine meditations of that little Child. He is unfolding to himself the Divinest of all human faculties, for such is the picture making faculty of man.[37]

Surely, we have encountered these "divine meditations" already in Douglass's recollection of "the many things thought and felt while I sat on the bank and watched that mill, and the turning of that ponderous wheel" (147), in his remembrance that "a child cannot well look at such objects without *thinking*" (161), and in his account of the "thoughtful days" of his boyhood. Later in the lecture, he gives a fuller account of this "Divinest of human faculties," which he now calls a "power": "It lies, directly in the path of what I conceive to be a key to the great mystery of life and progress. The process by which man is able to invert his own subjective consciousness, into the objective form, considered in all its range, is in truth the highest attribute of man[']s nature. All that is really peculiar to humanity—in contradistinction from all other animals[—]proceeds from this one faculty *or power*" (461; emphasis added).

Let us examine this passage carefully. First, Douglass takes this "picture-making power"—which is, I would suggest, an aspect of what I have been calling *aesthetic* power—to be the one "faculty or power" that most decisively distinguishes humans from nonhuman animals and thus most assuredly constitutes our humanity. Second, he argues that this power is the primary means through which we become self-conscious: responding aesthetically to the world is "the process by which man is able to invert his own subjective consciousness, into the objective form." Third, he goes one step further and attributes to this faculty our dawning *consciousness* not just of ourselves as *persons* but as persons of some *worth*. He writes: "The world has no sight more pleasant and hopeful, either for the child or for the race, than one of these little ones [that is, children] in rapt contemplation. . . . The process is one of *self-revelation*, a comparison of the pure forms of beauty and excellence without, with those which are within." In other words, our aesthetic powers reveal to us, probably preconsciously, that the beauty and mystery we behold in the world around us mirror the "beauty and excellence" of our own subjective nature "within" us. The fact that we can see and respond to beauty and excellence in the world, and in art, testifies to our own beauty and excellence. Thus, read as a later philosophical elaboration of these passages in *My Bondage and My Freedom*, Douglass's lecture suggests that (as he later put it) when he had mused upon objects that were "full of thoughts and ideas," he was intuiting in them the "objective form" of "his own subjective consciousness": *they* were full of thoughts because *he* was full of thoughts looking at them. He was also *feeling himself* to be full of thoughts, a feeling that nurtured his sense of his own value, or inner dignity. Likewise, his contemplation of the watermill and sloop, and of the "ever-shifting drapery" of the "blue overhanging firmament," was a process of "self-revelation" in which he was inwardly feeling the "beauty and excellence" of his own subjectivity.

Twenty years later, in the 1883 lecture "It Moves," Douglass describes the faculty that engages in this process as "strange, mysterious, and indescribable": "What is true of external nature is also true of that strange, mysterious, and indescribable, which earnestly endeavors in some degree to measure and grasp the deepest thought and to get at the soul of things; to make our subjective consciousness, objective, in thought, form and speech."[38] This phrasing—"grasp the deepest thought and . . . get at the soul of things"—brings to mind his description in *My Bondage and My Freedom* of his earliest efforts, while still a boy, to do just that: "The sloop and mill were wondrous things, full of thoughts and ideas. A child cannot well look at such objects without *thinking*" (161).

Let us return now to that book. At the beginning of its sixth chapter, Douglass writes, "The heart-rending incidents, related in the foregoing chapter, led me, thus early, to inquire into the nature and history of slavery. *Why am I a slave? Why are some people slaves, and others masters? Was there ever a time when this was not so?* These were perplexing questions which now began to claim my thoughts, and to exercise the weak powers of my mind" (178). We should notice, first, that Douglass here attributes his political awakening to the powers of his mind as it inquires into the nature and history of slavery, even though those powers are still "weak." At the same time, he also makes clear that the impulse to undertake his inquiry was triggered by the heartrending scenes he had witnessed—that is, by scenes that triggered a powerful affective reaction to the manifest immorality of whipping. Douglass then takes his inquiry to some of the older enslaved children on the plantation. When they explain to him what they have been told, that "God made white people to be masters and mistresses, and black people to be slaves," and that this arrangement was just because "God was good, and . . . He knew what was best for me, and best for everybody," he is far from satisfied: "It came, point blank, against all my notions of goodness. . . . I could not reconcile the relation of slavery with my crude notions of goodness" (178–79). So here, too, we find his powers—specifically his moral powers—playing a crucial role in his political awakening, even though his notions of right and wrong are still "crude."

Douglass turns next to some of the plantation's enslaved who were "direct from Guinea," and they tell him the plain truth of the matter: "Their fathers and mothers were stolen from Africa—forced from their homes, and compelled to serve as slaves." The effect of these words is electrifying: "The appalling darkness faded away, and I was master of the subject" (179). Here, at last, is what appears to be the definitive moment of his awakening, signaled by his metaphor of darkness fading as the light breaks in upon him. This awakening is excruciatingly painful:

This, to me, was knowledge; but it was a kind of knowledge which filled me with a burning hatred of slavery, increased my suffering, and left me without means of breaking away from my bondage. Yet it was knowledge quite worth possessing. I could not have been more than seven or eight years old, when I began to make this subject my study. It was with me in the woods and fields; along the shores of the river, and wherever my boyish wanderings led me; and though I was, at that time, quite ignorant of the existence of free states, I distinctly remember being, even then, most strongly impressed with the idea of being a free man some day. This cheering assurance was an inborn dream of my human nature—a constant menace to slavery— and one which all the powers of slavery were unable to silence or extinguish. (179)

Weak as they were, then, Douglass's boyhood moral and intellectual powers were at work when he awakened to the evil and injustice of slavery and thereby to the political reality of his condition: he and his people had been kidnapped by robbers. But what made this enslavement palpably unjust was that it violated his *self-worth*; by the time he learned from other slaves how the slavery system worked, he already knew himself to be more than a mere "brute." He had already acquired his sense of his humanity and its value from multiple sources: the love of his mother and grandmother, his discovery of perspectivalism, and his experience of becoming an object to himself as he beheld the natural world. No doubt, a great many of the enslaved did likewise, which is why they refused to submit entirely to the will of the slaveholders. Douglass tells us that this bitter but priceless knowledge of his enslavement at first "increased his sufferings." He could not get rid of it or forget it. But he also tells us that he carried it "with him" back into the natural world that had delighted and sustained him, back into the "woods and fields," and "along the shores of the river." There, in what historian Stephanie M. H. Camp has called a "rival geography" within the plantation system, a crucial reversal occurred: he discovered within himself a "cheering assurance" that he would one day be free.[39] Whence came that assurance? What led him to believe that "all the powers of slavery" would be unable to crush or hold him? How did he move from consciousness of the unjustness of his enslavement to this nascent determination to resist and escape it? Literary historian Ian Finseth has suggested that in *My Bondage and My Freedom* Douglass was deeply interested in "how a turn to nature can provide an opportunity for escape from a vicious culture, and for psychic restoration."[40] But how, precisely, does such "restoration" occur?

Douglass's implicit answer to that question is that his "boyhood wanderings" continued to encourage the free exercise of his picture-making, aesthetic powers. He himself, or at least the memory of himself that he later constructed, was that "boy" of the 1861 lecture, who "all forgetful, of time or place, . . . look[ed] up with silence and awe to the blue overhanging firmament and view[ed] with dreamy wonder, its ever shifting drapery." (Or, to use Combe's words, he "recognized in himself the intelligent and accountable subject of an all-bountiful Creator, and in joy and gladness desires to study the Creator's works.") This spontaneous exercise of his aesthetic powers was the "process by which" he had been "able to invert his own subjective consciousness, into the objective form, considered in all its range," and through which he also sensed the beauty and excellence of a sensibility that could behold such a beautiful world. Later, his recently acquired knowledge about the cause of his enslavement collided with the process of "self-revelation" as he experienced it in his solitary walks. That collision powerfully and painfully demonstrated the incommensurability of his personhood with his enslavement, and it catalyzed his determination to become free. That determination was rooted, however, in his sense of who and what he already was. The "self-revelation" made possible by his aesthetic powers gave him—or so he writes—the "cheering assurance" of his eventual freedom. Aesthetic experience revealed, as he goes on to tell us, the "inborn dream of my human nature," one which "all the powers of slavery were unable to silence or extinguish" (179).

Perhaps we can see a bit further into the meaning of Douglass's meditations on his boyhood moments of "silence," "awe," and "dreamy wonder" with the help of poet Kevin E. Quashie's argument that "quiet" has always been both a supplement to and a form of "resistance" in Black culture:

> Quiet . . . is a metaphor for the full range of one's inner life—one's desires, ambitions, hungers, vulnerabilities, fears. The inner life is not apolitical or without social value, but neither is it determined entirely by publicness. In fact, the interior—dynamic and ravishing— is a stay against the dominance of the social world: it has its own sovereignty. It is hard to see, even harder to describe, but no less potent in its ineffability. Quiet.[41]

In calling his readers' attention to these moments, Douglass was certainly making a case for the full humanity of the enslaved Black subject, laying claim to a Black interiority that was not always already "determined entirely by publicness." He was also recalling the way these moments of quietness were for him a refuge and a "stay against the dominance of the social world." In Quashie's phrase "stay against," we catch a glimpse of what we will explore more fully in a moment: a rethinking of the meaning of "resistance" that acknowledges the resistant qualities of quiet and vulnerability.[42]

Douglass was by no means the first or the only antebellum Black activist to attribute such political effects to aesthetic experience in the natural world. Ian Finseth has revealed the ways many slave narratives were engaged with nature and invoked the values embedded in the pastoral tradition. Lance Newman has argued in a similar vein that there is a "radical pastoral mode" in African American literature more broadly; its "most central trope" is "the image of nature as a sacred space wherein the hero experiences a transformative epiphany that produces militant political consciousness."[43] One especially notable Black activist to experience such a transformative epiphany was Martin Delany. In a letter published in the North Star in 1849, he gives the following account of his political energies being galvanized by "the works of nature" in the Allegheny Mountains:

> The soul may here expand in the magnitude of nature, and soar to the extent of human susceptibility. Indeed, it is only in the mountains that I can fully appreciate my existence *as a man* in America, my own native land. It is then and there my soul is lifted up, my bosom caused to swell with emotion, and I am lost in wonder at the *dignity of my own nature*. I see in the works of nature around me, the wisdom and goodness of God. I contemplate them, and conscious that he has *endowed me with faculties* to comprehend them, I perceive the likeness I bear to him. What a being is Man![44]

For Delany in 1849, then, as for Douglass later, aesthetic experience allows the self to see itself objectively and thereby to become aware of its worth, or dignity. Delany beholds the beauties of nature; doing so makes him aware of his own "faculties" of aesthetic reception; contemplation of those faculties and their divine power causes him to "be lost in wonder at the dignity of my own nature." Such awareness of his own dignity, which had been denied and violated so often by white racism, provokes in turn a surge of indignation—the "energy" that Douglass believed drives political awareness into activism. Delany seems to have believed likewise, for he continues: "What a being is Man—of how much importance!—created in the impress image of his Maker; and how debased is God, and outraged his divinity in the person of the oppressed colored people of America! The thunders of his mighty wrath must sooner or later break forth, with all of its terrible consequences and scourge this guilty nation, for the endless outrages and cruelty committed upon an innocent and unoffending people." The outrage that Delany believes God must be feeling is an externalization of the outrage that he himself *does* feel—and wants his readers of the *North Star* to feel with him.

One of those readers, of course, was Frederick Douglass. Scanning Delany's letter in the office of the *North Star* in Rochester, he would have been deeply stirred by it—not to political consciousness per se, which he had already acquired, but to a more appreciative awareness of the role aesthetic experience can play in catalyzing both self-consciousness and political action. Delany's language here—"the *dignity of my own nature*" and "*endowed with faculties*"—should remind us that Douglass did not invent the key terms of his distinctive political philosophy. Like Delany, he found them around him, but unlike Delany, he fashioned them into a philosophy.[45]

The Resistant Power of Vulnerability

Along with the dynamics of political awakening, the nature of resistance—his own, and that of the other enslaved persons whom he knew or observed—is Douglass's central political concern in *My Bondage and My Freedom*. Historians of U.S. slavery have called attention already to the multiple ways the enslaved resisted their enslavement. These included work slowdowns, breaking tools, meeting secretly to worship, meeting secretly to acquire literacy, communicating to plan and support escape attempts, actual escapes, and acts of violent resistance. As a number of scholars have shown, Douglass testifies to all of these, especially in his autobiographies. At the same time, as we shall now see, he describes another form of resistance practiced by the enslaved: it is resistance that works, paradoxically, through a directed vulnerability that makes war on the slaveholder by appealing to his humanity, to the wellsprings of his dignity, and to the "laws of his own being."

"The slave has been all his life learning the power of his master," Douglass remarks in *My Bondage and My Freedom* (352). And while that close observation of the master was motivated by fear, above all by the desire to avoid punishment, it also discerned weaknesses that the enslaved could exploit. Douglass provides a detailed account of himself making precisely such observations of his first master, Captain Aaron Anthony: "Most evidently, he was a wretched man, at war with his own soul, and with all the world around him" (172). In Douglass's view, Captain Anthony's "war within himself" arose from the continual conflict between his identity as a human and his identity as a slave master. Having often observed the painfulness of this war, Douglass later claimed that the excessive power wielded by the slave master—and by the slavery system itself—victimized the slaveholder almost as much as the enslaved.

Even a naturally kind and generous person could be corrupted by this power. In the *Narrative*, Douglass writes that when he had first met Mrs. Hugh Auld, she was kind and even maternal toward him: "But, alas! . . . The fatal poison of irresponsible power was already in her hands, and soon commenced its infernal work" (37). "Slavery," he concludes, "proved as injurious to her as to me" (40). He uses similar words in *My Bondage and My Freedom* to describe the autocratic character of Colonel Lloyd. When the colonel whipped his stableman Barney, Barney "must make no reply, no explanation: the judgment of the master must be deemed infallible, for his power is absolute and irresponsible" (194). The slaveholder's unquenchable and "irresponsible power" was always at odds, however, with his moral power, which established the laws of his own being. This is why, Douglass suggests, all but the most hardened slaveholders suffered searing pangs of self-doubt and self-reproach. This is why they were "at war with their own souls" and why they behaved as if they were "possessed by a demon." And this is why, he concludes, "there is more truth in the saying, that slavery is a greater evil to the master than to the slave, than many, who utter it, suppose. The self-executing laws of eternal justice follow close on the heels of the evil-doer here, as well as elsewhere; making escape from all its penalties impossible" (189).

Douglass observes further that this internal war between the slaveholder's human nature and his actions as a slaveholder could be exploited by the enslaved themselves, who could provoke such self-recrimination by making appeals to the master for mercy. In so doing, he suggests, they inflicted both psychological injury to the slaveholder and material damage to the slavery system. Douglass links the internal war with this external warfare when, immediately following his psychological portrait of Captain Anthony's inner torment, he describes and analyzes such an appeal: "One of the first circumstances that opened my eyes to the cruelty and wickedness of slavery and the heartlessness of my old master," he writes, "was the refusal of the latter to interpose his authority to protect and shield a young woman" (173). Milly (a cousin of Douglass) had been savagely beaten by one of the plantation overseers, and she had fled to her master to seek protection. However, Captain Anthony sternly refused to help her and instead threatened her with even more violent punishment if she did not return instantly to the overseer. Douglass offers this analysis of the politics of appeal:

> I did not, at that time, understand the philosophy of his treatment of my cousin. . . . The treatment is part of the system, rather than a part of the man. Were slaveholders to listen to complaints of this sort against the overseers, the luxury of owning a large number of slaves, would be impossible. It would do away with the office of the overseer, entirely; or, in other words, it would convert the master himself into an overseer. . . . A privilege so dangerous as that of appeal, is, therefore, strictly prohibited; and anyone exercising it, runs a fearful hazard. (174)

In a perceptive account of the rhetorical force of appeal, political theorist Melvin Rogers helps us see how the intersubjective dynamics of appeal unfold: "Appealing is a bidirectional rhetorical practice that affirms the political standing of the claimant and the one to whom the appeal is directed. . . . The action and attitude of the addresser (i.e., the appealer) does not merely function in the subjective 'I-mode,' in which mere performance by an individual brings that role into existence; rather, the cultural and linguistic norms denote the background presence of a 'we-mode' (i.e., thinking and acting in light of a shared understanding)."[46] Even in the slavery system's conditions of extreme vertical hierarchy, Douglass indicates, the enslaved and their masters shared some "cultural and linguistic norms" that composed "the background of a 'we-mode.'" It was on this basis that the enslaved made their appeals.

Whether successful or not, then, the appeals of the enslaved in themselves affirmed, if not "the political standing," then at least the moral and existential standing of the claimants making those appeals. This was so partly because, as Saidiya Hartman has argued, the slavery system traded on the personhood of the enslaved even as it relegated them to the status of subpersons or nonpersons. Indeed, as she shows, the ideology of the slavery system "depicted the slave-master relationship as typified by the bonds of affection and thereby transformed relations of violence and domination into those of affinity. This benignity depended upon a construction of the enslaved black as one easily inclined to submission, a skilled maneuverer wielding weakness masterfully and a potentially threatening insubordinate who could be disciplined only through violence."[47] Yet, just here, a question arises: If this ideology's aim in celebrating these supposed "bonds of affection" was to make "relations of violence and domination" look like "those of affinity," why did the masters repeatedly contradict and undermine this representation by also insisting that the enslaved "could be disciplined only through violence"?

The reason, I would suggest, is that the masters were never wholly in control of their "construction of the enslaved black"—precisely because, as Douglass indicates, the enslaved themselves were so adept at bending that construction to their own purposes. Douglass also went one step further to argue that this strategy was based on a truth about human nature, such that the appeals of the enslaved made an imperious call from one human person to another. This, he believed, is what made an appeal so "dangerous": it could not be voiced or heard without eliciting from the slaveholder a certain *involuntary* recognition that a fellow *human* was speaking, crying, or begging for mercy. Try as he might, the slaveholder could not refuse to hear and see the humanity of the enslaved without at the same time diminishing his own. To deny one was to deny both. And this was so because—deny it though he might—he was caught up in *relations* with the persons whom he had enslaved. As Douglass put the matter in an 1855 speech: "It is beyond the power of Slavery to annihilate affinities recognized and established by the Almighty. The slave is bound to mankind, by the powerful and inextricable net-work of human brotherhood. His voice is the voice of a man, and his cry is the cry of a man in distress, and man must cease to be man before he can become insensible to that cry."[48]

Of course, most slaveholders chose to "cease to be a man." Their frequent disavowal of their human relations with the enslaved was a constitutive feature of the slavery system. As Douglass observed much later, "Husband and wife, parent and child, guardian and ward, apprentice and master, and the relation of labor and capital were cited [by slaveholders] as involving the principle of slavery. But all analogies fail when likeness disappears. In all these cases and relations there is the principle of reciprocity, the interchange of good offices, and the equity of sharing and sharing alike is recognized." But if slaveholders were unique in their complete denial that the "principle of reciprocity" obtained between them and the persons they had enslaved, the consequence was the gradual destruction of their own humanity and dignity.[49]

Thus, when Anthony categorically refuses to entertain Milly's appeal, a call that powerfully invoked "the background presence of a 'we-mode,'" that is, their shared humanity, he was compelled to turn away from her and "cease to be a man" himself. His only alternative would have been to recognize her humanity, along with that of "the little black urchins" playing around him, but to do so would have been to expose and implicitly acknowledge the fraud of the entire slavery system. Douglass suggests, then, that a power can be exerted even by, as Hartman suggests, "forwarding the strength of weakness": it is the power of expressing one's human worth, and of making a claim on another's moral obligation to recognize this worth. It is to insist, as Stanley Cavell puts it, that "to be human is to be one of humankind, to bear an internal relation to all others."[50] One can exert this insistent and resistant force even in the act of imploring a slaveholder to be merciful. We can now understand *why* Esther's "piercing cries seemed only to increase [Aaron Anthony's] fury" (177) : her cries made plain to him that he was choosing to degrade himself as he punished her, and this naming of his inner conflict infuriated him.[51]

While there is nothing new in observing that the enslaved always retained some powers of resistance, no matter how severe their conditions, it may be challenging to accept that even a cry for mercy could be a resistant act. To grasp this difficult thought, we may need to disentangle the idea of resistance from the idea of agency, and Douglass's thinking helps us do so. Clearly, there can be no "agency" in an involuntary scream for mercy. But in this particular case, it is not the enslaved person's agency, much less her heroism, that resists, contests, and undermines the slavery system. Rather, it is her absolute vulnerability braided with her conviction that she has a worth, a worth that she involuntarily voices, and that her master is morally obligated to respect. Contrary to the familiar view that embodied pain cannot be spoken, she *does* in fact voice her pain, and her words and sounds cannot pass by unheard, no matter how resolutely the slaveholder tries to deafen (and dehumanize) himself. In doing so, she exercises her own powers to call to the moral powers of the slaveholder, requiring him to *hear*—though seldom to acknowledge—the justice of her plea.[52]

In the chapter of the *Narrative* in which Douglass describes his fight with Covey, he provides a long list of gestures of resistant obedience as he catalogs the reasons the enslaved were whipped: "Does a slave look dissatisfied? It is said, he has the devil in him, and it must be whipped out. Does he speak loudly when spoken to by his master? Then he is getting high-minded, and should be taken a button-hole lower. Does he forget to pull off his hat at the approach of a white person? Then he is wanting in reverence, and should be whipped for it" (69). Douglass's ironic mimicry of the slave master's voice and logic deftly evokes the scene at which the master speaks—to the slave, or to a white acquaintance, or to himself—in a ritual self-justification of the whipping he is about to administer, or just has. The ritualistic nature of these moments reflects how often they must have occurred, which tells us in turn that the enslaved never stopped acting in small ways that they knew would provoke the master's wrath. To be sure, the master's wrath was often triggered by an *unintended* note of resistance, or one that he merely imagined. But that just makes plainer that the master who was "seeing things" did so because he was haunted by the specter of his own powerlessness.

As poet and theorist Fred Moten puts it: "While [the slave master's] subjectivity is defined by the subject's [i.e., his own] possession of itself and its objects, it is troubled by a dispossessive force objects exert such that the subject seems to be possessed—infused, deformed—by the object it possesses."[53] What Douglass refers to as the inextinguishable powers of the enslaved is precisely such a "dispossessive force." Moten's "force" and Douglass's "powers" wage "perpetual war" against the condition of enslavement because they reside in, and emanate from, the very humanness of the enslaved—their "manhood," as Douglass frequently calls it. As we have seen, he declared in his August 1848 West Indian Emancipation speech that "all sense of manhood and moral life, has not departed from the oppressed"; and he wrote in 1855, "Nothing can make the Slave think that he is a beast; he feels the instincts of manhood within him at all times, and consequently there is a perpetual war going on between the master and slave, and to keep the slave down the whip and fetters are absolutely necessary."[54] In a late, unpublished essay, Douglass declared that "there are attributes and qualities of manhood too subtle and vital to be reached and extinguished by the power of slavery," and, "to succeed in making a man a slave, this difference between the man and the brute must be removed, or so subdued and so completely that it shall not dare to assert itself. As a man, a slave has some sense of the dignity of his manhood."[55]

The meaning of "manhood" flows implicitly through all these uses of the term and appears explicitly in the last: it is humanness that carries with it a sense of its own worth, or "dignity." The aim of the slavery system, Douglass believed, was "to buy and sell, to brand and scourge human beings with the heavy lash . . . [and thereby] to destroy their dignity as human beings."[56] But their inextinguishable dignity, prompting countless acts of resistance that were often veiled as seeming or even *actual* compliance, dispossessed the master of his assurance that he was actually in control of those whom he had enslaved. Their resistant acts were intended, often, to force him to issue commands that sought more total control and submission, but that had the reverse effect of highlighting the limits of his power by reminding him of the ultimately inextinguishable powers of the enslaved. Appeals were an expression of these powers: in begging the master for mercy, enslaved persons were indeed acknowledging their master's absolute authority over them. The effect of those appeals, however, was to force the slaveholder to make an impossible choice: between preserving his own humanity and preserving the slavery system itself.

For Douglass, then, resistance to oppression is not always an intentional or conscious act, much less is it always heroic. It may well take the form of a quiet inwardness, a stubborn reluctance, or even a cry for mercy, for what it expresses is "the instincts of manhood" within the oppressed. These preconscious instincts cannot be whipped out of a person for the reason that a person is not merely a hollow vessel containing attributes nor simply a bloodless ego but, rather, an assemblage of powers that are inherently dynamic and perpetually in a state of coming into being. All the slaveholder or oppressor can do is try to prevent a person from putting forth those powers and thereby becoming conscious of the dignity they confer and of the natural rights that dignity deserves.

In this analysis, just as resistance may or may not be agentic, so it may or may not be political. Resistance becomes *political* precisely when it is an expression of such consciousness of one's dignity. This is why, for Douglass, political awakening and political resistance were conjoined processes, or acts. Awakening naturally led to resistance, as when Douglass's inquiries into the reasons for his enslavement prompted his inner conviction, and resolve, that he would one day escape it. Once he realized that slavery was not an expression of nature or a design of God's, but a system of oppression constructed by men for their own profit, he knew somewhere in his being that he could evade or defeat it. Conversely, however, resistance could sometimes catalyze awakening, as when Douglass's combat with Covey "revived" his "sense" of his "own manhood." He writes that he "was nothing before; I WAS A MAN NOW." But as his string of verbs—"rekindled," "revived," "renewed"—indicates, this was not quite the case: he had always been a man, but it took physical resistance to Covey to revive his consciousness of this fact.

What Douglass's analysis reveals, then, is the literally pivotal role played by dignity, for dignity is a *consciousness* of self-worth that makes resistance become a *political* act—that is, an act that resists not merely the infliction of pain but what one knows to be an unjust denial of one's worth. Such consciousness may arise from a moment or a process of political awakening, but it may also arise from a merely reflexive act of resistance if, in performing it, one becomes sensible of one's powers and, through them, of one's dignity. This was one of the insights gained through his "slave experience" that Douglass labored hardest to impart to his readers.[57]

CHAPTER SEVEN

"Nothing Less Than a Radical Revolution"

Douglass's Struggle for a Democracy without Race

Throughout the post–Civil War decades, Douglass continued to deploy the political philosophy we have seen him putting to work as an activist from the late 1840s through the 1850s. Although he elaborated that philosophy because he believed that the United States and the Black community within it needed a more effective basis on which to meet and repudiate racism, in the postwar years he put it to other purposes also, most notably in his arguments on behalf of women's rights and free and open immigration. Indeed, as we have already seen, it was through his crafting of arguments for women's rights that he may have discovered the gender bias inherent in the term "manhood," and perhaps for that reason turned increasingly to "natural dignity" as his term for a human worth that deserves political rights. In any case, he now used "dignity" as the word that allowed him to speak of the rights of both genders, as when he observed in an 1868 speech: "I know of no argument that can be adduced in favor of the right of man to suffrage which is not equally forcible, and equally applicable to woman. If it be essential to the dignity of man; if it be necessary to protect the rights of man, it must be equally essential and necessary to protect the rights of woman."[1]

Douglass also engaged in national debates over immigration after the Civil War. Here, too, his philosophy shaped his positions. His belief in the interconnectedness of all members of the human species logically suggested a transnational conception of national democratic citizenship. The very purpose of democracy, as Douglass understood it, was to support the fullest possible expression of humanity; it made perfect sense, then, to welcome all humanity to the nation's democratic polity. In December 1869, he made these points explicit in his speech, "Our Composite Nationality." He began with a philosophical defense of the nation-state that was based on his belief that humans can form large political communities in which citizens agree to govern themselves only by submitting to the self-restraining influence of their innate moral powers. "The simple organization of a people into a National body, composite or otherwise, is of itself an impressive fact," he declared. "As an original proceeding it marks the departure of a people, from the darkness and chaos of unbridled barbarism, to the wholesome restraints of public law and society. It implies a willing surrender and subjection of individual aims and ends, often narrow and selfish, to the broader and better ones that arise out of society as a whole."[2] He had made the same point about the dependence of freedom on restraint in *My Bondage and My Freedom*, when he observed that his first master, Captain Anthony, "had he been brought up in a free society, surrounded by the just restraints of a free society . . . [he] might have been a humane man" (171).

From this view of the origins of a democratic political order, it was but a small step to his position that democracy implies unrestricted immigration. Addressing the question of Chinese immigration specifically, he took an unequivocal position: "Do you ask if I would favor such immigration? I answer, I *would*. . . . Would you have them naturalized? And have them invested with all the rights of American citizenship? I *would*" (251; emphasis added). He also asserted, with abundant optimism, that unrestricted immigration would inevitably become the policy of the United States. Naturally seeking the benefits of democratic life because these allow individuals to unfold their human nature, many persons would "want to come to us." By the same logic, as Americans saw ever more clearly that their democracy was the political expression of a deep commitment to humanity and the human species, they would become more welcoming: "As we become more liberal, we shall want them to come, and what we want done will naturally be done" (249). No coercion or sacrifice would be necessary, according to Douglass, since open immigration policy is what Americans would "want" to have. "Man is man the world over," Douglass declared. "This fact is affirmed and admitted in any effort to deny it. . . . A smile or a tear has no nationality. Joy and sorrow speak alike in all nations, and they above all the confusion of tongues proclaim the brotherhood of man."[3] This statement expresses essentially the same position as his 1855 claim that "the slave is bound to mankind, by the powerful and inextricable net-work of human brotherhood."

At the same time, however, Douglass also recognized that valuable human *differences* exist; they arise, inevitably, from the fact that "the point from which a thing is viewed is of some importance." Different persons occupy different standpoints and see the world differently. Now, he argued that these differences were actually beneficial to democratic national unity, not a threat. This is because "all great qualities are never found in any one man or in any one race. The whole of humanity, like the whole of everything else, is ever greater than a part. Men only know themselves by knowing others, and contact is essential to this knowledge."[4] But if "contact is essential," then disagreement is unavoidable. In order to sustain a polity that allows for such disagreement, therefore, democratic citizens must cultivate a disposition that is prepared to acknowledge its own limitations and to give others a careful, open-minded hearing.

Still, despite his deep interest in women's rights and open immigration, whites' anti-Black racism remained Douglass's primary concern after the war. "The work before us is nothing less than a radical revolution in all the modes of thought which have flourished under the blighting slave system," he declared in 1862.[5] He believed that only by fundamentally altering their conceptions, habits, and dispositions of citizenship, especially their notions of race and humanity, could Americans become a genuinely multiracial democracy in which all women and men enjoyed equal rights. "It seems to me," he observed, "that the relationship subsisting between the white and colored people of this country is, of all other questions, the great, paramount, imperative and all commanding question for this age and nation to solve."[6] In 1866, he described the Civil War as "at once the signal and the necessity for a new order of social and political relations among the whole people."[7]

As his words "relationship" and "relation" suggest, *relationality* was both the means and the objective of Douglass's radical revolution. This was partly because, ever since his childhood, he had been strongly attuned to relationality: it was thanks to his grandmother and mother, after all, that he understood that he was "*somebody's* child," and therefore had worth in the eyes of others. His attunement to relationality was strongly reinforced later when he observed the ways the slavery system worked through, and depended on, its flesh-and-blood human agents who disavowed their own relations with the enslaved and strove to destroy relations among them. Finally, when he arrived in the North, he saw with increasing clarity that anti-Black racism circulated through social attitudes, not just political institutions. Indeed, when he spoke of "social and political relations," he was not distinguishing between the social and the political, but conjoining them. Because he believed that dignity is the "foundation" of human rights and that dignity is both inherent within us and collaboratively produced and affirmed though our relations with others, at least since the late 1840s he had understood that "interrelation" was "the social ontology of politics" (to use political theorist Emily Beausoleil's apt phrase).[8] When he wrote that "men only know themselves by knowing others," he succinctly identified the source, or wellspring, of this ontology: to know oneself as a self, he believed, was to know oneself as a human self. And to know the *worth* or dignity of that human self, one had to engage in dignity-displaying and dignity-affirming relations with others. Democratic politics arose from the need to affirm the importance and protect the possibility of those relations over and against those—such as slaveholders and racists—who would repress or disavow them.

As we track Douglass's effort to undo "all the modes of thought that have flourished under the blighting slave system," we will look first at the speeches and writings he directed to his Black audiences, urging them to more consciously exercise their powers—including their combined political power—in order to assert their dignity and win their rights. Next we will turn to Douglass's message to white audiences, to whom he insisted that anti-Black racism was fundamentally a white problem that only whites themselves could solve. Douglass seems to have believed further that whites could be induced to jettison their racist attitudes if they were spurred to do so not by pity or by guilt, but by a desire to emulate admirable models of antiracist white comportment. In his third autobiography, *Life and Times of Frederick Douglass*, he crafted three stories that present such models. Like his entire approach to the "radical revolution" he called for, these stories risk giving undue emphasis to individual behavior while downplaying the deeper structural and systemic aspects of anti-Black racism. Yet, they also remind us—as many Black writers since then have—that racism works in significant measure through attitudes and dispositions that must be acknowledged and transformed.

"To Organize and Combine to Defend Themselves from Outrage"

With the postwar demise of the abolitionist movement, which had provided some opportunities for Black and white citizens to convene publicly together, Douglass found himself facing segregated audiences more often than previously. Consequently, the bivocal nature of his addresses and lectures intensified: he had one thing to say to Black audiences, and something different to say to white audiences. As he admitted in 1885: "To colored people and white people I present two views and both are just."[9] That two such different views could *both* be just was, for him, no problem; for, as we have seen, throughout most of his career as an orator and activist, he had employed a single "method" that, like the songs sung by the enslaved on the Lloyd plantation, aimed to express different or even "opposite" things.

Before the Civil War, Douglass had labored to persuade his Black audiences that the world could not respect them unless they manifested their dignity by exercising their powers. In 1847, for example, he had said: "The colored people . . . must maintain self-respect, if they would be respected; they must demand their own rights, if they would obtain them."[10] Eleven years later, likewise, he had observed: "This impression is, that we ourselves are unconcerned and even contented with our condition; that we, both slave and free, are unwilling to struggle and make sacrifices for our rights. I hold that next to the dignity of being a freeman, is the dignity of striving to be free."[11] After the war, he continued to pound home this message—one that holds in tension two seemingly opposite recommendations. On the one hand, he urged Blacks to build Black organizations; these would nurture Black self-respect, promote Blacks' self-consciousness of their powers, and position Blacks to demand respect from whites. On the other, because of what he took to be the relational ontology of democratic politics, he warned his Black audiences not to form separate communities, but instead to seek to become "incorporated" into the American body politic. "Our salvation," he declared at the final meeting of the American Anti-Slavery Society, "is in becoming an integral part of the American government, becoming incorporated into the American body politic, incorporated into society, having *common aims, common objects,* and *common instrumentalities* with which to work with [whites], side by side" (emphasis added).[12]

We will misconstrue this recommendation, however, if we do not fully appreciate that the "work" Douglass proposed Black and white Americans perform "side by side" was that of transforming the U.S. polity by re-establishing it on the basis of a new understanding of citizenship. He believed, as Robert Gooding-Williams argues, that "the reconstruction of the nation required the reconstitution of the opinion, ideals, and practices constituting and intrinsic to the identity of the nation."[13] Such reconstitution would require Black Americans *not* to assimilate to existing norms but rather "to organize and combine" in order to change them:

> If the six millions of colored people of this country, armed with the Constitution of the United States, with a million votes of their own to lean upon, and millions of white men at their back whose hearts are responsive to the claims of humanity, have not sufficient spirit and wisdom to organize and combine to defend themselves from outrage, discrimination and oppression, it will be idle for them to expect that the Republican party or any other political party will organize and combine for them or care what becomes of them.[14]

Such incorporation, for Douglass, did not imply mere acquiescence, or surrender. Quite the contrary, it required that one become conscious of one's powers, assert them, and thereby claim one's dignity and one's rights. This is why, in 1883, he urged African Americans to meet in separate conventions and form separate organizations to combat white racism. The purpose of these organizations would be to change the nature of Blacks' relation to whites:

> I once flattered myself that the day had happily gone by when it could be necessary for colored people to combine and act together as a separate class, and in any representative character whatever. . . . [But] the latent contempt and prejudice towards our race, which recent political doctrines with reference to our future in this country have developed, the persistent determination of the present executive of the nation, and also the apparent determination of a portion of the

people to hold and treat us in a degraded relation, not only justify the present such associate effort on our part, but make it eminently necessary.[15]

In a similar vein, Douglass was so conscious that "slavery has left its poison behind it, both in the veins of the slave and in those of the enslaver," that he could also call for preferential treatment for Black Americans in light of their "250 years of bondage" in this country: "Whenever the black man and the white man, equally eligible, equally available, equally qualified for an office, should present themselves for that office, the black man, at this juncture of our affairs, should be preferred. That is my conviction."[16]

Yet even as Douglass recommended Black solidarity and acknowledged a distinctive Black identity shaped by long experience of white oppression, he warned against "race pride."[17] We can understand why if we bear in mind his long-standing commitment to the notion of a universal humanity with a species identity that compels species loyalty. The very idea of race would split the rock of human brotherhood, or species unity, on which the entirety of his political thought arose. Only race distinction untainted by race pride could support the cultivation of Black dignity without giving ontological status to race itself. As he declared in an 1889 speech, just six years before his death: "I see no benefit to be derived from this everlasting exhortation by speakers and writers among us to the cultivation of race pride. On the contrary, I see in it a positive evil. It is building on a false foundation. Besides, what is the thing we are fighting against, and what are we fighting for in this country? What is it, but American race pride: an assumption of superiority upon the ground of race and color?"[18]

Douglass's approach to Black strategy was shaped in multiple ways by his standpoint epistemology. As political theorist Jack Turner has argued in a perceptive analysis of Douglass's post-Reconstruction political thought, Douglass was deeply attuned to "asymmetries of power" and "skeptical of legal formalism that obscured those asymmetries."[19] This is why he had no qualms about advocating for Black organizations and Black solidarity even as he warned his Black audiences not to cultivate separatist forms of Black racial pride. For Douglass, Turner argues, "moral equality between black and white Americans does not imply equality of political and economic power. The racial nature of African

Americans' subordination requires them to cultivate forms of political consciousness and methods of political action that take that racial nature into account" (211). Turner argues further that, for Douglass, "good political judgment privileges neither legal status nor formal contractual parity in power assessments; rather, it attends to the social and material prerequisites of free and effective action" (218). This is absolutely right. And it prompts us to ask: What exactly is it about racial subordination that distinguishes it from other forms of oppression? What, for Douglass, were the "prerequisites of free and effective action"? The answer, I would suggest, is that he took anti-Black racism to differ from other forms of oppression insofar as it deliberately attacks the humanity, or human dignity, of persons of African descent. This was also David Walker's and Maria Stewart's view before Douglass, and Charles Mills's after him. Consequently, what Turner calls the "social and material prerequisites of free and effective action" must include above all whites' acknowledgment of Black dignity, not just their concession that Blacks formally possess the same rights as whites.[20]

Douglass's political philosophy informed his approaches to a "radical revolution" in the nation's "modes of thought" in another important way: he repeatedly emphasized that the exercise of freedom must be accompanied by, and indeed felt to be, the fulfillment of an obligation. In his mind, when freedom was rightly understood, freedom and duty were conceptually fused. By contrast, freedom understood as something standing apart from moral responsibility was a continuing expression of the public philosophy that had tolerated, and perhaps underwritten, "the blighting slave system." Therefore, not just "spirit and wisdom" but duty called Black Americans to organize and exercise their power. He wrote in an 1870 editorial that, having at last won their freedom, "the time has now come for the colored men of the country to assume the duties and responsibilities of their own existence. Our friends can do much for us—have done much for us—but there are some things which colored men can and must do for themselves."[21] This smooth transition from duties to doing appeared frequently in his postwar speeches. In 1873, for example, he observed: "They [whites] are ahead of us. What is our duty in view of this fact? It is to build up, is it not? It is to use the opportunities that we have for the improvement of our condition, for improving our intellect, for improving our manners, improving our order, improving our punctuality, and improving our integrity."[22]

There were times, it must be said, when Douglass blamed Black Americans themselves for the treatment they received from whites. In an 1870 speech, he complained: "The truth with us as a class is, that while we work hard and make small wages, we spend what we make too hastily and freely and lay up but little for a rainy day. . . . This is all wrong, and till we reform in this respect we shall be a despised and degraded people."[23] In an 1870 speech he asked: "What does this Fifteenth Amendment mean to us? I will tell you. It means that the colored people are now and will be held to be, by the whole nation, responsible for their own existence and their well or ill being. It means that we are placed upon an equal footing with all other men, and that the glory or shame of our future is to be wholly our own."[24] As Saidiya Hartman has argued, such talk of Black responsibility risked playing into the hands of those who claimed that the freed men were not yet fit for citizenship and suffrage because they had not yet demonstrated that they could be responsible citizens. Responsibility was one of the weights that constituted what she calls the freedmen's "burdened individuality" and the "double bind of emancipation—the onerous responsibilities of freedom with the enjoyment of few of its entitlements."[25] Yet Douglass's criticisms of his Black audiences must be read with an eye to two contexts. First, his words were not intended for whites' ears; he never criticized Black Americans when he was speaking to white, or primarily white, audiences. Second, he never took "respectability" and "responsibility" to be means of winning the *approval* of others, as if that were an end in itself. He recommended them because he believed that the key to political empowerment was consciousness of and respect for one's own innate human powers. And because of the relational nature of any individual's sense of dignity, it had to command and receive the *respect* of others in order to sustain itself.

"The Real Problem Lies in the Other Direction"

While Douglass strove to persuade his Black audiences to exercise and become conscious of their powers, and to engage collaboratively in the production of their dignity, he also insisted that "the real problem lies in the other direction": by far the greater burden of responsibility for the affirmation of Blacks' dignity lay upon the shoulders of whites, both because they had more power and because anti-Black racism was their creation. Douglass underscored this point by repeatedly denying that there was any such thing as a "negro problem":

> I deny and utterly scout the idea that there is now, properly speaking, any such thing as a negro problem now before the American people. It is not the negro, educated or illiterate, intelligent or ignorant, who is on trial or whose qualities are giving trouble to the nation. The real problem lies in the other direction. It is not so much what the negro is, what he has been, or what he may be that constitutes the problem. . . . The real question . . . is whether American justice, American liberty, American civilization, American law, and American Christianity can be made to include and protect alike and forever all American citizens in the rights which, in a generous moment in the nation's life, have been guaranteed to them by the organic and fundamental law of the land.[26]

Just as he had before the war, Douglass continued to argue that the "malignant spirit" of white racism aimed not merely to dominate Black Americans but to humiliate them, not just to curtail their freedom but to convince them that they were unworthy of freedom. As he declared in an August 3, 1869 speech: "In the unwillingness to allow the negro to own land, in the determination to exclude him from all profitable trades and callings, there is clearly seen the purpose to crush our spirits, to cripple our enterprise and doom us to destitution and degradation below all other people in America."[27] Again and again, he urged white audiences to understand that they had a moral obligation and a civic duty to fight racism and offer support to their Black fellow citizens. "Every thoughtful man," he declared in 1872, "is bound by his love of country to do what he can to help solve that problem," by which he meant improving "the relations existing between the white and black people of this country."[28] But such improvement would require whites to undergo a revolution in their attitudes, habits, and practices of citizenship. Could he move them to it? And if so, how?

One method he used was to stress the transformative effect of action itself. An action, however small, was a visible expression of disposition and intent, one that could establish or change a "relation" between two persons. In his view, as we have seen, race prejudice was at bottom a culturally acquired, not a natural, disposition. A good deed somehow had the power to neutralize malignant cultural training and permit the more natural feelings of goodwill to surge to the surface of one's being. "I know there is prejudice here," he told a white audience in 1869. "There has always been prejudice. The only way to get rid of your prejudice is to begin to treat the negro as though you had no prejudice, and very soon you will find that you have got none." He then proceeded to tell a story. While traveling as an abolitionist, he had found himself one day in a hostile town, with no place to eat and no place to stay. Eventually he passed a white man who, even though he abhorred abolitionism, took pity on him. He led Douglass to his own home, where his wife was visibly displeased to have to receive him, flinching when he asked for a glass of water and sugar to ease his sore throat. "But," Douglass recalled, "the moment she brought the water and the sugar, and set them down before me, and said 'Help yourself,' and I thanked her, there was *a relation established between us*; there was a human heart answering to another human heart. The very moment she performed this deed for a suffering fellow creature, that very moment she felt her prejudice removed."[29] This power of face-to-face human relations to reestablish human solidarity was, Douglass believed, the core reason why racists sought to segregate Blacks from whites: to prevent them from coming face-to-face and thereby forming such relations. It made sense, therefore, to combat racism by using the platform of his fame to disseminate examples of Black and white individuals breaking through the iron veil of racism and forming relationships with one another.

As Russ Castronovo and Dana D. Nelson have argued, Douglass often sought "to supplement scenes of political demonology with models of civil dialogue and public rationality."[30] He provided such models primarily through storytelling, especially of stories that dramatized the kind of transformation he hoped whites would undergo. In his third and final autobiography, *Life and Times of Frederick Douglass*, he narrates a series of such stories that invite being read less as autobiography than as parables of a more relational understanding of white democratic citizenship committed to antiracist activism. As Robert Levine suggests, we should read these scenes not simply as records of his life but as scenes in a carefully wrought drama that has a "performative (or staged) dimension."[31]

Today, however, we are well aware that such an anti-racist strategy has grave risks. It can deflect attention away from the deep history, the material motives, and the structural underpinnings of racism. It can also absolve from responsibility whites who believe that they cannot be racists or benefit from racism simply because they harbor no ill will toward Blacks. As historian and critic John Ernest has observed: "What is white about white people . . . is not the color of their skin (which is not, after all, white) but rather the historical situation that has made 'white' bodies such able predictors of experience, understanding, and access to privilege and cultural authority—a whiteness, in other words, that cannot be transcended merely by good intentions or by the reach of an individual's consciousness."[32] Thus, the dangers inherent in Douglass's individual gestures of white antiracist comportment are two-fold: they might suggest that whiteness can "be transcended merely by good intentions or by the reach of an individual's consciousness," and they might underestimate the degree to which racism works through structures and institutions that are far less visible to whites than, say, a snarling police dog at the end of a short leash. Viewed from our historical standpoint today, these risks are major shortcomings of Douglass's parables.[33]

Yet, while the structural nature of racism must always be borne in mind, so too should the fact that it engages the lived world through the dynamics of attitudes and entitlements that most whites benefit from, yet remain conveniently unconscious of. They are happy to go on living as "tacitly positioned . . . white persons, culturally and cognitively European, racially privileged members of the West" while simultaneously disavowing that privilege.[34] That privileged positioning produces countless acts of what we now call "microaggression," both deliberate and inadvertent. It also produces an innocent complacency toward matters of race that allows widespread white disavowal of racism alongside white indifference to the ways racist aggression works at a structural level through law enforcement, the judicial system, housing policies, and so on. It was and still is crucial, therefore, to transform these white habits of citizenship that permit structural racism to continue flourishing. What Iris M. Young argued about poverty is true as well of race: "A thorough account of [its] sources and causes . . . must appeal to structures. However, such an account is compatible with, indeed requires, a notion of individual agency and responsibility."[35]

One obvious way to produce such transformation is to make visible to whites the many ways that their racist entitlements and attitudes injure Black Americans and other persons of color. But Douglass was always sensitive to the unintended consequences of such critical exposure: it could be read as an appeal for pity, not a demand for respect; it could lodge the problem in the suffering mind and body of the victim, not in the psyche of the perpetrator. Consequently, in *Life and Times* he adopted an unusual strategy that we might call "white uplift," one that sought to transform whites' habits of citizenship not by painting vivid scenes of Black suffering but by presenting whites with compelling and attractive models of white antiracist comportment.[36] He appears to have decided that admiration would be a more effective motivator than guilt. He had observed, after all, that Mrs. Hugh Auld's guilt only exacerbated her cruelty, and he had reasonably concluded that "men are apt to hate most those whom they have most injured." Perhaps the attractive force of admiration would work better, especially since he believed that "the deepest wish of a true man's heart is that good may be augmented and evil, moral and physical, be diminished."[37]

"Neither Afraid nor Ashamed to Own Me as a Brother"

In 1866, Douglass was elected by the city of Rochester to represent it in Philadelphia at the Southern Loyalists Convention, a national gathering of mainly Republican political figures from around the country. Douglass was the only non-white in attendance. The convention was designed as a counter-demonstration to a meeting of the National Union Convention that same day, at which Democrats hoped to muster support for the already embattled administration of President Andrew Johnson. However, when organizers of the Southern Loyalists Convention learned that Douglass would be attending, they worried that his presence would spark white racist outcry, and they asked him not to join them. Douglass, characteristically, insisted on doing so. They responded by ostracizing him ruthlessly, and on the morning of the convention's grand parade, he faced acute embarrassment:

> The members of the convention were to walk two abreast, and as I was the only colored member of the convention, the question was, as to who of my brother members would consent to walk with me? The answer was not long in coming. There was one man present who

was *broad* enough to take in the whole situation, and brave enough to meet the duty of the hour; one who was neither afraid nor ashamed to own me as a man and a brother; one man of the purest Caucasian type . . . and that man was Mr. Theodore Tilton. He came to me in my isolation, seized me by the hand in a most brotherly way, and proposed to walk with me in the procession. (828; emphasis added)

In this story, significantly, he does *not* represent Tilton as acting on principle—on a firm conviction in the equality of all men, for example. Nor does he suggest that Tilton's act was reasoned or rational; indeed, it flew in the face of public opinion and set aside self-interest. Rather, Douglass emphasizes that Tilton's gesture was spontaneous and instinctive. It was an expression of *character*, of Tilton's "broad" and "generous" disposition: "I think I never appreciated an act of courage and generous sentiment more highly than I did of this brave young man when we marched through the streets of Philadelphia on this memorable day" (828). In short, Tilton was one of the "millions of white men . . . whose hearts"—Douglass averred—"are responsive to the claims of humanity."

"Broad" and "generous" were key terms in Douglass's lexicon of democratic citizenship. Across a wide range of circumstances and topics, he used them to describe a disposition characterized by flexibility, open-mindedness, compassion, and worldliness. Speaking at a celebration of West Indian Emancipation in 1857, he had said, "We celebrate this day on the *broad* platform of Philanthropy—whose country is the world, and whose countrymen are all mankind."[38] In a critique of the postwar Democratic Party, he had written: "The party can only thrive where pride of race and *narrow* selfishness would appropriate to a class the right which belong to the whole human family."[39] Advocating unrestricted immigration to the United States, as we have seen, he had argued that "the simple organization of a people into a National body . . . implies a willing surrender and subjection of individual aims and ends, often *narrow* and *selfish*, to the *broader* and better ones that arise out of society as a whole."[40] And in his impassioned response to the Supreme Court's 1883 decision to overturn the Civil Rights Act of 1875, he had denounced the Court for having "seen fit in this case affecting a weak and much persecuted people, to be guided by the *narrowest* and most *restricted* rules of legal interpretation. It has viewed both the Constitution and the law with a strict regard to their letter, but without any *generous* recognition and application of their *broad* and *liberal* spirit."[41]

These disposition-naming words figure importantly in a second parable of democratic citizenship Douglass crafted in *Life and Times*—his account of his 1881 return to the Great House Farm. This vast estate of Colonel Edward Lloyd was once, as he had written in *My Bondage and My Freedom*, a "dark domain . . . stamped with its own peculiar iron-like individuality," where "crimes, high-handed and atrocious, could be committed with strange and shocking impunity!" (160). Now, Douglass planned to return there, still calling it "home." He had been told by friends that the current Colonel Lloyd was "a liberal-minded gentleman" who "would take a visit" from Douglass "very kindly" (879), but he remained uneasy: Would Lloyd really be willing to greet a "runaway slave," and one who had unsparingly criticized his father?

When the steamship pulled up at the Lloyds' jetty, Douglass learned that Colonel Lloyd himself had been called away, but that his son was there to greet him. This young man escorted Douglass around the estate where, as Douglass later recollected, "I found the buildings, which gave it the appearance of a village, nearly all standing, and I was astonished to find that I had carried their appearance so accurately in my mind for so many years" (881). He noticed that "the little closet in which I slept in a bag . . . had been taken into the room," and "the dirt floor, too, had disappeared under a plank" (881). He surely knew that these words would call to many of his readers' minds the most famous scene in all three versions of his autobiography—the one in which he peeps out of this closet and sees his own Aunt Hester being whipped. As he had written in the 1845 *Narrative*, "I shall never forget it whilst I remember anything. It was the blood-stained gate, the entrance to the hell of slavery through which I was about to pass" (18). When Douglass says that he remembered the details of the physical landscape of his enslavement with astonishing fidelity, he is implicitly telling his readers that although he was disposed to forgive descendants of Colonel Lloyd, he could never forget what the Lloyd family had done to him and thousands of other enslaved Blacks.

Lloyd and Douglass then toured the Lloyds' family cemetery, and while Douglass walked among the headstones, Lloyd gathered "a bouquet of flowers and evergreens" (882) and presented it to him. Douglass later wrote that he was so moved by this gesture that he took the bouquet back to his new home in the Washington suburb of Uniontown and kept it in memory of the visit. Finally, Lloyd invited Douglass into the Lloyd mansion itself and onto "its stately old verandah, where we could have a full view of its garden, with its broad walks, hedged with box and adorned with fruit trees and flowers of almost every variety. A more tranquil and tranquilizing scene I have seldom met in this or any other country" (883).

Two dramas intersect in this story, and both portray what two individuals—one white, one Black—might be and do together in order to defeat the racist legacy of slavery. In one, the grandson of an imperious former slaveholder shows a former slave around the estate. He has been instructed by his father, or perhaps merely by his upbringing, to show perfect courtesy to this guest despite his having been a slave, despite his having "run off," and despite his long and public animosity toward his grandfather. In so doing, young Lloyd refuses to identify citizenship and status with whiteness, while also showing enormous tact and skill in negotiating this difficult intersubjective encounter. As Lloyd accompanies Douglass, his silence signals his intuitive understanding that he and Douglass are walking on the same ground but occupying two radically different ontologies; he understands that he cannot possibly know what Douglass is experiencing, so that even a word of sympathy would likely be misplaced. Yet, he does find a way to make a telling gesture, which is to gather a bouquet of flowers and present it to his guest.

In the other drama, a Black man returns to the site of his enslavement and finds it much as he had left it many years before. He speaks hardly a word about his feelings, so his readers (and his host) are left to surmise how turbulent and conflicted they must be. But he shows no anger or hatred, and he does not visit the sins of the grandfather on the father and grandson. Quite the contrary: he extends to young Lloyd a silent acceptance. Or, perhaps, with a tact that surpasses even Lloyd's, he merely allows his silence to speak volumes that his young host might spend a lifetime trying to understand. We do not know. But what we may fairly surmise is that when Douglass crafted these dramas he was deliberately providing his readers with a double portrait of how "liberal-minded" persons—one white, one Black—might act against racism in and through their conduct toward each other.[42]

Douglass's dramas of intersubjective democratic citizenship might strike some of his readers today as mawkish and sentimental, too quick to forgive oppressors and too ready to forget the past. But if we place them in the context of Douglass's other writings and speeches of this period, such criticism might come less readily. Historian David Blight has shown that Douglass was a staunch and outspoken critic of any rapid reconciliation between the North and the South.[43] Far from being ready to forget the crimes committed by the slavery system, he bitterly opposed the nation's rush to leave the past behind and hasten toward reunion with the rebels. "The South has a past not to be contemplated with pleasure, but with a shudder," Douglass wrote in 1870, when the nation was already beginning to succumb to nostalgia for Dixie and its plantation life. "She has been selling agony, trading in blood and in the souls of men. If her past has any lesson, it is one of repentance and thorough reformation."[44] A year later, in 1871, he told an audience, "I am no minister of malice . . . but . . . may my tongue cleave to the roof of my mouth if I forget the difference between the parties to that . . . bloody conflict. . . . I may say if this war is to be forgotten, I ask in the name of all things sacred what shall men remember?"[45] Not surprisingly, then, Douglass was infuriated by the nation's adulation of Robert E. Lee and its rush to pardon other leaders of the rebellion. "Fellow citizens," he declared in a speech in 1882, "I am not indifferent to the claims of a generous forgetfulness, but whatever else I may forget, I shall never forget the difference between those who fought for liberty and those who fought for slavery, between those who fought to save the republic and those who fought to destroy it."[46]

In short, Douglass can hardly be construed as an advocate of swift reconciliation based on forgetfulness. But he did see that repentance and reformation were precisely the qualities most leading citizens of the South *refused* to demonstrate as they fought hard instead to recover their power and reestablish their regime of white supremacy. In his portrayal of young Lloyd, then, he would have shown his white readers— especially his white Southern readers—the example of a son who spurns his grandfather's Old South legacy and embraces a radically different style of new Southern leadership. With his courtesy, silence, and flowers, Lloyd acknowledges the evils of slavery and implicitly seeks Douglass's forgiveness. Most crucially, he can acknowledge Douglass's dignity without fearing that, in doing so, he will compromise his own. Doubtless, Douglass would have been pleased if Lloyd had given more explicit signs of reformation and repentance. Still, he was willing to meet Lloyd halfway because, by his own account, he too had a generous and "liberal-minded" disposition.

Douglass's advocacy of a sense of citizenship infused with friendship and trust strikingly resembles ideas advanced more recently by political theorist Danielle S. Allen. Taking note of the nation's continuing failure to actualize even the formal mandates of the 1954 *Brown v. Board of Education* decision, she suggests that it points to an even deeper failure to construct an understanding and practice of citizenship that militates against the formation of racist dispositions. Observing that the citizenship instruction most commonly given to citizens is "don't talk with strangers," she argues on behalf of "a new mode of citizenship in friendship understood not as an emotion but a practice": "Political friendship consists finally of trying to be like friends. Its payoff is rarely intimate, or genuine friendship, but it is often trustworthiness and, issuing from that, political trust. Its art, trust production, has long gone by the abused name of rhetoric. Properly understood, rhetoric is not a list of stylistic rules but an outline of the radical commitment to other citizens that is needed for a just democratic politics."[47]

Like Allen, Douglass does not suggest that he and young Lloyd became lifelong friends and intimates. Rather, he precisely choreographs an exchange of simultaneous and reciprocal gestures that build trust across immeasurably deep chasms of different experience and outlook. Like Allen, therefore, he is interested in a "rhetoric" of citizenship, one in which citizens communicate with one another through styles of deportment and shared commitments to a particular disposition. And, like Allen, he tries to dramatize and model a conception of citizenship as what she calls "trust production." "Mankind are not held together by lies," he once declared. "Trust is the foundation of society. Where there is no truth, there can be no trust, and where there is no trust, there can be no society. Where there is society, there is trust, and where there is trust, there is something upon which it is supported."[48]

The last of Douglass's three parables is the most dramatically compelling; it also was, and is, the most controversial because it involves Douglass's relationship with his former master, Thomas Auld.[49] When in 1881 Auld heard that Douglass was in the area of Saint Michaels, Maryland, he sent word inviting him to come see him. Douglass claimed he was shocked. "To me, Captain Auld had sustained the relation of master— a relation which I held in extremest abhorrence. . . . He had struck down my personality, had subjected me to his will, had made property of my body and soul. . . . I, on my part, had traveled through the length and breadth of this country and of England, holding up this conduct of his . . . to the reprobation of all men who would hear my words" (875).[50]

Nonetheless, Douglass agreed to see Auld, and he relates that when the two men met, they "addressed each other simultaneously, he calling me 'Marshal Douglass' and I, as I had always called him, 'Captain Auld.'" Douglass was deeply moved by Auld's gesture of calling him "Marshal" (Douglass at this time held the position of marshal of the District of Columbia), and he demonstrated a reciprocal generosity. "Hearing myself called by him 'Marshal Douglass,' I instantly broke up the formal nature of the meeting by saying, 'not Marshal, but Frederick to you as formerly'. . . . We shook hands cordially," Douglass recalled, "and he, having been long stricken with palsy, shed tears as men thus deeply afflicted will do when excited by any deep emotion. The sight of him . . . his tremulous hands constantly in motion, and all the circumstances of his condition affected me deeply, and for a time choked my voice and made me speechless" (786–87).[51]

Douglass was afterward strongly criticized by some Black leaders for having paid this visit, but in *Life and Times* he remained unapologetic: "Now that slavery was destroyed, and the slave and master stood upon equal ground, I was not only willing to meet him, but very glad to do so. . . . He was to me no longer a slaveholder either in fact or in spirit, and I regarded him as I did myself, a victim of the circumstances of birth, education, law, and custom" (875). At the same time, however, it is important to hear the note of restraint in Douglass's account—as in the sentences just quoted, for example—and not to read more sentimentality into it than it actually has. One of Douglass's biographers has claimed that "love" is at work in Douglass's meeting with Auld. But actually *respect* is the operative affect here.[52]

Douglass's stories of his reunions with former masters at least partially model, I would argue, what Alexander Hirsch has called "fugitive reconciliation." Taking issue with the liberal model of reconciliation that, in its wish to avoid conflict and achieve consensus, buries past crimes under a blanket of forgetting, Hirsch proposes a more "agonistic" model inflected by Sheldon Wolin's notion of "fugitive democracy." It would preserve rather than deny the lingering anger experienced by victims of crimes, and it would stage moments of reconciliation rather than institutionalizing them: "Reconciliation, an experimental temporal struggle, would ebb and flow. . . . Rather than something that is about to come, reconciliation would be conceived as something *which actually takes place*, albeit fleetingly, bursting onto the scene only to vanish at the moment it is sublimated into an institutionalized form."[53] By presenting his examples of reconciliation as stories of "something which actually takes place," and by narrating them *as* stories, that is, as moments in his life, Douglass did lend them these qualities of "fugitive" reconciliation. He also took some pains to ensure that he was not misunderstood as simply forgetting the past and its crimes. Before introducing the scene of his reconciliation with Thomas Auld, he reminds his readers of Auld's crimes:

> He had struck down my personality, had subjected me to his will, made property of my body and soul, reduced me to chattel, hired me out to a noted slave breaker to be worked like a beast and flogged into submission, taken my hard earnings, sent me to prison, offered me for sale, broken up my Sunday school, forbidden me to teach my fellow-slaves to read on pain of nine and thirty lashes on my bare back, and had, without any apparent disturbance of his conscience, sold my body to his brother Hugh and pocketed the price of my flesh and blood. (875)

Taken together, then, with their strengths and their flaws, these three parables offered Douglass's readers a richly textured account of the disposition he thought the times demanded, one he described as "generous," "broad," and "liberal-minded." This disposition exhibits a radical openness to others, to change, and to the unfamiliar. It opposes closure. It mocks meanness. It acknowledges our common mortality, and it subordinates resentment to compassion. But it does so in a manner that is also restrained and modest, aware of its limitations, and mindful of what it does not know and cannot know. It is skeptical of all rigidities, and it is angered by selfishness, egotism, and arrogance. Perhaps most notably, it acts promptly—and, if need be, courageously—to affirm what it sees as the basic truth of human solidarity.

These qualities are required, Douglass suggests, in order to rise to a fundamental challenge embedded in his political philosophy of dignity: How do we as citizens redress injuries to others' dignity without thereby inflicting further injury? The mere glance that conveys the knowledge that a person is hurt can inadvertently send a message of pity and condescension. One way to forestall that further wounding, Douglass indicates, is to convey that the message has been motivated not by pity but by duty—a sense of duty that has no element of self-sacrifice but instead spontaneously achieves self-actualization through acts of solidarity. The glance must convey the recognition of "I *see* you" along with the admission that "I cannot *completely* know you" and the acknowledgment that "we have no choice but to be in this *together*." Indispensable to such a glance, thought Douglass, is a prior relinquishment of individual sovereignty and an embrace instead of human brotherhood, one that is both driven and necessitated by a consciousness of shared human powers and shared human precarity.

With such exceptional attunement to relationality, Douglass's political thought resonates strongly with some contemporary feminist political theory. I have already discussed Douglass's attention to the political work performed by practices of love and caring, especially as these nurture an early sense of individual dignity that in turn makes possible perceptions of injustice and spurs claims to rights. We have seen, too, how deeply Douglass ascribed to standpoint theory, which was developed formally by Black feminists in the 1970s and 1980s. Now I want to underscore his thought's affinity with feminist political theory concerned with citizenship as a practice, taking the work of Susan Bickford as a representative example. Like Douglass, Bickford emphasizes the degree to which democracy creates ineluctable challenges for citizens rather than somehow automatically solving all their problems. Consequently, citizens must develop and sustain a disposition that enables them to grapple with these challenges, perhaps endlessly. In her account of the political disposition she recommends, which she calls "political listening," she writes that "it requires an attitude somewhere between sheer defiance and sheer docility, one that allows us neither to ignore others nor to privilege them." Like Douglass, she believes that listening to other citizens whose views may be significantly different from our own requires a radical openness to their perspective, a brave willingness to acknowledge one's own inevitable fallibility, and, at the same time, an equally courageous resolve to act in the moment guided by one's beliefs as they appear at that moment. For this reason, she writes: "The conception of citizenship that I have developed here is characterized by tension between openness and commitment, a tension that is never finally or fully resolved. Such resolution would in fact mean the end of citizenship, for citizenship is the practice of living with that tension."[54] That phrase—*tension between openness and commitment*—perfectly describes the disposition Douglass called a "method" that could express and hold opposites. He used this method himself, and he believed all citizens would have to do so in order to practice democracy effectively.

Such a commitment to tension, or rather to a disposition that can sustain tension, has been a long-standing characteristic of a good deal of African American political thought. "I am not afraid of the word tension," Martin Luther King Jr. declared, and he named one tension that he recommended with the phrase "militantly nonviolent."[55] Militant and nonviolent are usually seen as opposite and even incommensurable dispositions; King proposed that we yoke them. Likewise, Malcolm X urged his Black audiences to carry themselves in a way that signaled that they were prepared to use violence to defend themselves: "I don't mean go out and get violent, but at the same time you should never be nonviolent unless you run into some nonviolence. I'm nonviolent with those who are nonviolent with me. But when you drop that violence on me, then you've made me go insane, and I'm not responsible for what I do. And that's the way every Negro should get."[56] This was precisely the disposition Douglass adopted, and the attitude he projected, when he refused to obey Jim Crow laws, when he fought back against antiabolitionist mobs, and when he coolly faced down Captain Isaiah Rynders with the warning: "I throw out this remark in order that you may know in what light I should regard the man who would offer me an insult. The fact is, I, who have endured the whip of the slaveholder, who bear the marks of the lash upon my back, who have been driven to the slave market in the town of Easton, Talbot County, Maryland, and exposed for sale, like a brute beast, to the highest bidder—I cannot well appreciate an insult. Therefore, let no man hope to succeed in insulting me."[57]

As I transcribe these words today, John Lewis's valedictory words to the American people have appeared in the *New York Times*. Expressing his belief that "millions of people [can be] motivated simply by compassion" while also emphasizing the importance of "power," of *demanding* "respect for human dignity," and of the duty to "act" against injustice, Lewis's words also strike the balance sought by Douglass, King, and Malcolm X:

While my time here has now come to an end, I want you to know that in the last days and hours of my life you inspired me. You filled me with hope about the next chapter of the great American story when you used your power to make a difference in our society. Millions of people motivated simply by human compassion laid down the burdens of division. Around the country and the world you set aside race, class, age, language and nationality to demand respect for human dignity. . . . When you see something that is not right, you must say something. You must do something. Democracy is not a state. It is an act.[58]

Lewis, King, Malcolm, and Douglass all understood democratic politics as the practice of living with and working through the tension expressed by the phrase "militant nonviolence" (or, in Douglass's and Malcolm's case, by defensive violence). Although similar to theirs, Bickford's practice of living with the tension between openness and commitment is by no means identical. Bickford's practice certainly is a challenging one. But, as Malcolm's word "insane" hints, and as a number of Black artists, writers, and sociologists have made clear, the challenge for Black Americans of maintaining a balanced disposition in the face of anti-Black racism has always been psychologically and physically punishing. For this reason, among others, the standpoints of white Americans and other Americans of color are not equivalent or reversible; they cannot be translated into one another. To say that all citizens must build trust or be open to difference is wise, but only when we acknowledge how different are the meanings of these very words—"trust," "open," and "difference"—to white citizens and to citizens of color.

Given this difference, perhaps opacity, indirection, hints, and metaphors that acknowledge the limits to what can be thought, felt, and shared are more appropriate than bald statements. This appears to be poet Claudia Rankine's assumption in *Citizen: An American Lyric*, where she reveals that, as a woman who has learned "to hear the meaning behind words," she may not be inclined to suppose that she can put all her meaning into them. Likewise, if one "suffers from the condition of being addressable," then one might refrain from direct address herself.[59] Forthright and explicit as he usually was, Douglass also wove a thread of the ineffable and unspeakable throughout his work, from his reference in an 1850 speech to "the mysterious powers by which man soars above the things of time and sense" (420–21) to his remark in *Life and Times* that the music of the red-winged blackbirds "awakened in my young heart sensations and aspirations deep and undefinable" (882). Perhaps Emily Beausoleil's recommendation of a "dispositional ethics" that acknowledges what is "beyond one's grasp" can help us understand Douglass's own: such a disposition "is a means to prepare oneself for what is currently beyond one's grasp; to negotiate the ever-shifting balance between reliance on established terms with which to make sense of and evaluate the world, and the need to call these frames into question to truly encounter what is 'other'; to perceive and respond with care within even the most difficult moments of encounter that result too often in disavowal, defensiveness, and revenge."[60]

"I Cannot Shut My Eyes to the Ugly Facts before Me"

In 1892, the year he published his revised and expanded version of *Life and Times* (from which I have drawn the stories just narrated), Douglass met and became friends with Ida B. Wells. Wells was a young Black activist intellectual who had launched, almost singlehandedly, a campaign to expose and denounce the mass murder of Blacks by white lynch mobs—mainly in the South, but increasingly in other parts of the nation. Perhaps because Wells managed to persuade him, Douglass now turned his full attention to this crisis. In July of that year, he published "Lynch Law in the South" in the *North American Review*, and a year later he composed and began to deliver his great speech, "Why Is the Negro Lynched?" (published in 1894 as a pamphlet titled *Lessons of the Hour*).[61]

This speech is remarkable for many reasons, but here I will focus on just two: it draws heavily upon the political philosophy we have been tracing throughout this book, yet it also seems to acknowledge the futility—even the wrongheadedness—of that philosophy in the face of white racism's escalating war on Black life and dignity. This is not to suggest that Douglass ever assumed that America's racism would disappear with the defeat of the slavery system. In a speech delivered in Boston in December 1862, he predicted: "Law and the sword can and will in the end abolish slavery. But law and the sword cannot abolish the malignant slaveholding sentiment which has kept the slave system alive in this country during two centuries. Pride of race, prejudice against color, will raise their hateful clamor for oppression of the Negro as heretofore. The slave having ceased to be the abject slave of a single master, his enemies will endeavor to make him the slave of society at large."[62] Eight years later, he again predicted what we now refer to as "the afterlife" of slavery: "No two races of men sustaining the relation to each other that the white and colored people have sustained could have those relations instantly changed by any change in the laws however stringently worded or faithfully enforced. Slavery has left its poison behind it, both in the veins of the slave and in those of the enslaver."[63] Nonetheless, prepared though he was for a long struggle against "republican Negro hate," the anti-Black fury of the lynching mobs surprised and depressed him. Along with the fact that in 1892 the Democratic Party—which he always called "the party of slavery"—had won the presidency and both houses of Congress, the nation's "epidemic" of lynching indicated that the poison in the American body politic was more virulent than ever.

Characteristically, Douglass begins this speech with an announcement of his own standpoint and an implicit suggestion that standpoint is always limited, yet enabled, by one's "environment": "I propose to give you a colored man's view of the so-called 'Negro Problem.' We have had the Southern white man's view of this subject . . . colored by his peculiar environment. . . . We have also had the Northern white man's view of the subject, tempered by his distance from the scene" (491). He then delivers a scathing denunciation of white mobs "gratifying their brutal instincts." There is a "perfect epidemic of mob law and persecution now prevailing at the South," he declares. "Great and terrible as have been its ravages in the past, it now seems to be increasing, not only in the number of its victims, but in its frantic rage and savage extravagance." Douglass repeatedly underscores the excess and the perverse eroticism of anti-Black violence: "In its thirst for blood and its rage for vengeance, the mob has blindly, boldly, and defiantly supplanted sheriffs, constables, and police. . . . There is nothing in the history of savages to surpass the blood-chilling horrors and fiendish excesses perpetrated against the coloured people of this country. . . . the Southern mob, in its rage, feeds its vengeance by shooting, stabbing, and burning its victims, when they are dead" (492–93). Unsparingly, he details how the accused victim "is tortured. Till by pain or promises, he is made to think he can possibly gain time or save his life by confession—confesses—and then, whether guilty or innocent, he is shot, hanged, stabbed or burned to death amid the wild shouts of the mob" (493).

Having aroused his audience's indignant horror, Douglass proceeds to systematically rebut the widely believed claim that lynch law is a justifiable white response to Black violence. The myth of Black men sexually violating white women is "intended to blast and ruin the Negro's character as a man and a citizen," both to alienate him from whites and to make him suffer the despondence that saps political will itself (503). Drawing on his theory of the intersubjective, relational dynamic of citizenship and dignity, he continues: "I need not tell you how thoroughly it has already done its work. The Negro may and does feel its malign influence in the very air he breathes. He may read it in the faces of the men among whom he moves. . . . Its perpetual reiteration in our newspapers and magazines has led men and women to regard him with averted eyes, dark suspicion and increasing hate" (503). The real purpose of lynching, then, is political: to disenfranchise Blacks by destroying their dignity in the eyes of whites: "To degrade the Negro by judicial decisions, by legislative enactments, by repealing all laws for protection of the ballot, by drawing the color line in all railroad cars and stations and in all other public places in the South, thus to pave the way to a final consummation which is nothing less than the Negro's entire disenfranchisement as an American citizen" (503).

The language and the argument here are familiar, echoing many of Douglass's speeches going all the way back to 1848. But he strikes a solemn note now that, while not exactly new, has graver implications for his own philosophy than he had ever before countenanced. We hear it first when he addresses white Northerners who are skeptical of his reading of anti-Black mob violence, and who believe that white Southerners must have some good reason for their outrageous behavior. White Northerners, he retorts, are so "humane themselves" that they "are slow to believe that mobocrats are less humane" (505). And how much "less humane" did Douglass think they were?

> The point I make, then, is this. That I am not, in this case, dealing with men in their natural condition. I am dealing with men brought up in the exercise of irresponsible power. I am dealing with men whose ideas, habits, and customs are entirely different from those

of ordinary men. It is, therefore, quite gratuitous to assume that the principles that apply to other men, apply to the lynchers and murderers of the Negro. The rules resting upon the justice and benevolence of human nature do not apply to mobocrats, or to those who were educated in the habits and customs of the slave-holding communities. . . . We must remember that these people have not now and have never had such respect for human life as is common to other men. They have had among them for centuries a peculiar institution, and that peculiar institution has stamped them as a peculiar people. They were not before the war, they were not during the war, and they have not been since the war, in their spirit or in their civilization, a people in common with the people of the North, or the civilized world. (505)

These words come very close to repudiating the belief on which all of Douglass's political thought rests—namely, a conviction that all humans share a common human nature with a moral power that inclines most of them to do more good than evil. Douglass had always believed that culture and custom can pervert what men are "in their natural condition." In *My Bondage and My Freedom*, he had quietly noted that "a man's character greatly takes its hue and shape from the form and color of things about him" (171). Douglass had argued many times that continued use of "irresponsible power" triggers a vicious circle in which, goaded by guilt and self-recrimination, men are driven to ever more ghastly excesses. But now he goes further. Now he seems doubtful that the mob that lynches a Black man may still accurately be called a group of "men": "It is commonly thought that only the lowest and most disgusting birds and beasts, such as buzzards, vultures and hyenas, will gloat over and prey upon dead bodies; but the Southern mob, in its rage, feeds its vengeance by shooting, stabbing, and burning their victims when they are dead" (493). These creatures, whatever they are, seemed no longer to possess the faculties and powers that constitute humanness itself: "a vulgar, popular prejudice which we all know strikes men with moral blindness" has made them "incapable of seeing any distinction between right and wrong where coloured people are concerned" (498). Lacking such a capacity, incapable of obeying "the laws of their own being," they seemed to have degraded themselves beneath the level of a common humanity. And would they ever change by returning to their "natural condition"? Douglass does not think so:

Chief Justice Taney told the exact truth about these people when he said: "They did not consider that the black man had any rights which white men were bound to respect." No man of the South ever called in question that statement, and no man *ever will*. Any Southern man, who is honest and frank enough to talk on the subject, will tell you that he has no such idea as we have of the sacredness of human rights, and especially, as I have said, of the life of the Negro. Hence it is absurd to meet my arguments with the facts predicated of our common human nature. (506; emphasis added)

Douglass had spent much of his life meeting racist arguments "with the facts predicated of our common human nature." Now, reversing perspectives, he dismisses those who would downplay or even deny the evil of lynchers by asserting that our common human nature is not capable of it. Now he thinks that the human nature of the people of the South has been so twisted by their culture that they never will share Northerners' belief in "the sacredness of human rights." Recall that in his condemnations of the Southern slavery system, he had managed to preserve his belief in (or notion) of a unified humanity by emphasizing that many slaveholders were themselves "victims" of that system. They had been born and raised and educated within it, and they had been corrupted to such a degree that their very humanity was in jeopardy. Knowing this at a subconscious level, they were "at war" with themselves. Now, however, Douglass perceives no signs of such a war, neither within each individual who joined a mob nor among "the upper classes of the South" who "seem to be in full sympathy with the mob and its deeds" (494). Even though he had been cruelly mistreated by Captain Anthony, Mrs. Hugh Auld, and Thomas Auld, Douglass felt some "compassion" for them because he saw, or thought he saw, evidence that they were struggling against (though being defeated by) their culture's command that they violate their conscience and disobey the laws of their being. Now, seeing no such signs of remorse or conflict within the millions of whites who composed or supported these lynch mobs, he feels nothing for them but anger and disgust. These men and women have permanently removed themselves from the network of human brotherhood. They have placed themselves "outside of the government, outside of the law, outside of society" (492). It is not merely that they refuse to "hear the cry of a man in distress," but that they *delight* in hearing such a cry precisely because they *know* their victim to be a man.

The "humanity" that presented itself to Douglass in 1893, then, appeared to be riven in two, with millions of self-degraded white subhumans composing a bloodthirsty mob on one side of the rift, and actual, full humans on the other. And because the entire edifice of his political philosophy rested atop the predicate of a single humanity whose members feel themselves to be bound together by species loyalty, the lynch mob dismantled it as ruthlessly as it attacked Black life itself. As a consequence, Douglass seems to succumb to the despondency he had spent a lifetime urging his Black audiences to resist:

> Do not ask me what will be the final result of the so-called Negro problem. I cannot tell you. I have sometimes thought that the American people are too great to be small, too just and magnanimous to oppress the weak, too brave to yield up the right to the strong, and too grateful for public services ever to forget them or reward them. . . . But events have made me doubtful. . . . I hope and trust that all will come out right in the end, but the immediate future looks dark and troubled. I cannot shut my eyes to the ugly facts before me. (511)

Poignantly, the seventy-six-year-old Douglass tries to shake free of this despairing mood, but his recuperative effort is feeble compared with the energy of his denunciation and the pathos of his discouragement. For the thousandth time in his long career, he slips his word "humanity" into the traditional lexicon of American public philosophy: "Let the American people cultivate kindness and humanity," he advises (520). For the thousandth time, he reminds white Americans that the Declaration of Independence "announced the advent of a nation based on human brotherhood and the self-evident truths of liberty and equality" (523). And for the thousandth time, he affirms that Americans' only hope is to recognize that their nation and their democracy are "based upon the eternal principles of truth, justice, and humanity" (523).

But were the Black men and women in his audiences convinced that such arguments would work? Was *he?*

CHAPTER EIGHT

"That Strange, Mysterious, and Indescribable"

The Fugitive Legacy of Douglass's Political Thought

As I have underscored many times throughout this book, Douglass's thought remains elusive today because the philosophical lexicon at his disposal to articulate it was inadequate to the task. But there also is a second, related reason. Douglass was not a unitary thinker. The split in his being was not just the hyphenated African-American identity that Du Bois called "double consciousness"; it was also the split indicated, yet also masked, by the conjunction "and" in his autobiography *My Bondage and My Freedom*. His bondage and his freedom were two very different states, and as a consequence, he could never be entirely at one with himself. In his speech titled "The Nature of Slavery," which he included as an appendix to *My Bondage and My Freedom*, he declared: "But ask the slave what is his condition—what his state of mind—what he thinks of enslavement? and you had as well address your inquiries to the silent dead. There comes no voice from the enslaved" (423). Then and now, a reader's first response to these words would be to object that surely Douglass himself was such a voice, speaking from within the memory of enslavement if not from within the condition itself. But I would suggest instead that Douglass was making an admission here: that in stepping from bondage into freedom, he had profoundly and irrevocably changed. He was no longer the man he once had been, and never could be again. Aspects of his past, and of the being of millions of his brethren in bondage, were now unknown to him. Consequently, all his statements to the contrary notwithstanding, he could not truly "stand here identified with the American slave, and . . . see this day as he does"; such identification had become a trope, it was no longer a fact. And from his oscillation back and forth between these conditions came forth a fugitive philosophy with a profound attunement to the unknown and the unknowable within himself and others. I want to close this book with his cautionary words ringing in my ears, heeding his challenges to our conventions, and listening into the unknown that is Frederick Douglass, not just to the words we believe we can hear and understand.[1]

"Here, on a Bare Theory"

In 1855, well after Douglass had begun to think of himself as something of a political philosopher, he delivered a speech that called the very enterprise of political philosophy into question. Titled "The Anti-Slavery Movement," the speech offered both a historical overview of abolitionism and an implicit, philosophical justification for his break with Garrison and the American Anti-Slavery Society. The quarrel between them, as we have seen, had as much to do with their different ways of thinking as with their different positions. In this speech, Douglass gives his own account of those differences.

He begins by asking several large questions about abolitionism: "What is this mighty force? What is its history? And what is its destiny?" Yet he also acknowledges that to pose such questions is to risk indulging in idle "speculation":

> Excellent chances are here for speculation; and some of them are quite profound. We might, for instance, proceed to enquire not only into the philosophy of the Anti-Slavery movement, but into the philosophy of the law, in obedience to which, that movement started into existence. We might demand to know what is that law or power which, at different times, disposes the minds of men to this or that particular object—now for peace, and now for war—now for Freedom, and now for Slavery; but this profound question I leave to the Abolitionists of the superior class to answer. The speculations which must precede such an answer would afford, perhaps, about the same satisfaction, as the learned theories which have rained down upon the world, from time to time, as to the origin of evil. I shall, there-

fore, avoid water in which I cannot swim, and deal with Anti-Slavery as a fact, like any other fact in the history of mankind, capable of being described and understood, both as to its internal forces, and its external phases and relations.[2]

Multiple streams of irony permeate these remarks. Douglass's words at first seem to enforce a pejorative distinction between "philosophy" or "speculation," on the one hand, and "fact" and "history," on the other. Feigning to believe that the philosophical questions are "profound," Douglass goes on to mock them, indeed to mock profundity itself, and philosophy and theory along with it. Although these afford some "satisfaction," he acknowledges sarcastically, they resemble the innumerable "theories" about "the origin of evil" that tell us nothing new and get us nowhere. Ironically pretending to honor such theorizing as the work of "abolitionists of the superior class," he leaves no doubt in the minds of his audience about where he stands himself: he believes that his own humble recital of facts is more valuable than philosophical speculation.

This disparagement of theorizing gradually emerges as a theme in this speech; yet, when we have read or heard the speech in its entirety, we realize that Douglass has actually taken up and answered the very questions he mocked at the outset: "What is this mighty force? What is its history? And what is its destiny?" Not only that, but as I hope my account of his political thought has shown, Douglass himself was deeply concerned "to know what is that law or power which, at different times, disposes the minds of men to this or that particular object—now for peace, and now for war—now for Freedom, and now for Slavery." Far from leaving "this profound question . . . to the Abolitionists of the superior class," he made it the engine that drove his own philosophical speculations. We can only conclude, then, that in Douglass's mind, the questions themselves were not faulty. What was mistaken was a particular way of approaching or handling them. Douglass uses irony to criticize one mode of speculation, thereby implicitly opening up space for his own rather different kind.

After these opening feints, he proceeds to deliver a direct rebuttal of Garrison's argument that slavery's abolition could only be achieved by individual states seceding from the Union and then forming a new nation with a purified Constitution. "I dissent entirely from this reasoning," Douglass declares. "It assumes to be true what is plainly absurd, and that is, that a population of slaves, without arms, without means of concert, and without leisure, is more than a match for double its number, educated, accustomed to rule, and in every way prepared for warfare, offensive or defensive" (42). Not content with exposing the absurdity of Garrison's position, Douglass goes on to ridicule the *way* of thinking that had produced it. And here is where he implicitly identifies his own, quite different way of thinking: "As a mere expression of abhorrence of Slavery, the sentiment [no union with slaveholders] is a good one; but it expresses no intelligible principle of action, and throws no new light upon the pathway of duty. . . . Here, on a bare theory, and for a theory which, if consistently adhered to, would drive a man out of the world—a theory which can never be made intelligible to common sense—the freedom of the whole slave population would be sacrificed" (42). The precise object of Douglass's ironic critique, then, is not speculation or theory per se, but what he calls "*bare* theory." What characterizes *bare* theory is that it contains "no intelligible principle of action," "throws no new light upon the pathway of duty," and "can never be made intelligible to common sense."[3] Conversely, he implies, a more robust and legitimate way of theorizing would be one without such flaws. It would have value only if, after speculating about a topic (the origin of evil, the nature of civil government), it produced a "principle" that could guide our actions, point out to us the path of action we are duty-bound to take, and did both these things in a manner "intelligible to common sense." Theorizing that is more than *bare* theory does not rest content with a speculative account of the way things *are*; it also explains what this account requires us to *do*. Douglass believed that good theorizing should be both analytical and prescriptive. It should not split thought from action but instead take these to be a unitary whole.

This is why a number of his readers have called him a protopragmatist, arguing that his unitary conception of thought and action strikingly anticipates the thinking of William James and John Dewey. But are we hearing a "pragmatist" when Douglass explains in this speech why the abolitionist movement, with all its setbacks and reversals, will "go on"? It will persist, he claims, because "the moral life of human society . . . cannot die, while conscience, honor, and humanity remain" (45). Moral life, being intrinsic to the powers that constitute humanity itself, cannot die unless humanity itself perishes. If even a single person remains to sustain it, Douglass asserts, "the [abolitionist] cause lives" because "its incarnation in any one individual man leaves the whole world a priesthood—occupying the highest moral eminence—even that of disinterested benevolence. Whoso has ascended this height, and has the grace to stand there, has the world at his feet, and is the world's teacher, as of divine right" (45).

As David Blight and political theorist George Shulman have shown, Douglass often spoke in this *prophetic* mode, one in which he called an errant people to cease sinning and to honor their founding covenant with their Creator.[4] Strongly influenced by his religious education under the tutelage of "Uncle" Lawson and by decades of reading the Bible, and doubtless shrewdly cognizant of the cultural power of the Puritan tradition of the jeremiad sermon, Douglass often figured himself as a prophet come to warn his people of their certain doom unless they found their way—with his help—back to the path of righteousness. Such a prophet, he continues, in what is probably a self-description too, "may sit in judgment upon the civilization of the age, and upon the religion of the age" because, knowing the truth of the higher law, "he has a test, a sure and certain test, by which to try all institutions" (45).

At just this point, however, Douglass reverses course and shifts from this prophetic mode back to the mode of "pragmatism."[5] Such rendering of judgment, he asserts, "is *not* the chief business for which he is qualified":

> The man who has thoroughly embraced the principles of Justice, Love, and Liberty, like the true preacher of Christianity is less anxious to reproach the world for its sins than to win its repentance. The great work to which he is called is *not* that of judgment. . . . His great work on earth is to exemplify, and to *illustrate* and engraft those principles upon the living and practical understandings of all men within the reach of his influence. . . . It is to snatch from the bosom of nature the latent facts of each man's individual experience, and with steady hand to hold them up fresh and glowing, enforcing, with all his power, their acknowledgment and *practical adoption*. (45–46, emphasis added)

Emersonian notes are unmistakable here, as are the tones and the posture of the Old Testament prophets, but Douglass gives these the coloring of his distinctive intellectual method by underscoring the *unity* of word and deed, of thought and action, of reproach and repentance. The Mosaic figure of the man who has ascended this "height" of vision is also the more down-to-earth and intelligible thinker who addresses "the living and practical understandings of all men" and seeks their "practical adoption" of his message.

A theory that is "living and practical" was thus, for Douglass, the preferred alternative to one that was "bare" and speculative. In his view, the "truth" of such theory coordinates simultaneously with its fidelity to higher law, its ironic acknowledgment of the limits of its own perspective, and its commitment to practical application. In yet another of his stunning reversals, Douglass makes this point vividly: even the "slaveholder himself," he argues, has assented to the principles of higher law and agreed with the antislavery man's appeals to justice, liberty, and humanity—but only with reference to himself. "You have only to keep out of sight your manner of applying your principles, to get them endorsed every time. Contemplating himself, he sees truth with absolute clearness and distinctness. He only blunders when asked to lose sight of himself. In his own cause he can beat a Boston lawyer, but he is dumb when asked to plead the cause of others" (46–47). In other words, the slaveholder, too, has only a "bare theory." It is *bare* because it is indifferent to the *manner of applying* its principles.[6]

Perhaps it was to warn readers against approaching Douglass as though he were a more conventional thinker that James McCune Smith, in his introduction to *My Bondage and My Freedom*, offered such a rich analysis of Douglass's "plantation education" (126), repeatedly emphasizing that it had given Douglass a manner or method of thinking that was significantly different from that of most of his presumed readers. After listing what he took to be Douglass's most striking qualities of character, Smith contrasts the "formulas of deductive logic" typically learned in "the schools" with the method of "induction" Douglass learned from "nature and circumstances." Referring specifically to "the first ninety pages" of *My Bondage and My Freedom*, Smith suggests that they "afford specimens of observing, comparing, and careful classifying . . . that [make it] difficult to believe them the results of a child's thinking." He then went on to claim, "To such a mind, the ordinary processes of logical deduction are like proving that two and two make four. Mastering the intermediate steps by an intuitive glance . . . it goes down to the deeper relation of things, and brings out what may seem, to some, mere statements, but which are new and brilliant generalizations, each resting on a broad and stable basis" (122–34).

In these sentences, Smith alerts readers that they will not find formulaic and "ordinary" reasoning but rather "induction" in Douglass's writings; he also teases out the implications of inductive logic itself. (Inductive reasoning starts from observations about the world and then moves to laws and generalizations about it. Deductive reasoning, by contrast, begins with a theory or hypothesis and then seeks to test it, or prove it, through a close examination of evidence.) Inductive reasoning, Smith suggests, is quicker than deductive to perceive and explain "the deeper relation of things," probably because it starts at the bottom and thinks upward. (Inductive reasoning is sometimes described as "bottom-up" reasoning.) Consequently, as we might infer, inductive reasoning also has the potential to evade, challenge, and reform the assumptions and concepts ("formulas of deductive logic") that have already been put in place to explain the world. It goes "deeper" because it is trying to *find* the meaning of phenomena rather than trying to test or prove a meaning that has already been hypothesized or claimed. Inductive reasoning is often accused (rightly) of drawing overly broad conclusions based on too little evidence, and it is to counter this charge that Smith asserts that Douglass's conclusions, though drawn from his personal experience, nonetheless rest "on a broad and stable basis" (134). Conversely, however, deductive reasoning can err by passing over phenomena it deems irrelevant, but which in truth are highly pertinent. For this reason, deductive reasoning can be more easily used to demonstrate the truth of an epistemological or political order that is already established, whereas inductive reasoning is more likely to build new conclusions that challenge those already in place. This is why inductive reasoning has been so useful to science even though, as David Hume argued, it cannot be justified in a philosophical sense without circularity. (Smith, having been trained in Edinburgh, would almost certainly have known David Hume's famous critique of induction in *An Enquiry Concerning Human Understanding*.)[7]

Smith also remarks on the *political* efficacy of inductive reasoning when he declares that wherever Douglass traveled, "the people" would "earnestly say, '*Tell me thy thought!*'"—that is, tell me how things look to you, and what I should do. "And somehow or other," Smith writes, "revolution seemed to follow in his wake" (132). Smith returns to the revolutionary potential inherent in Douglass's inductive method and standpoint epistemology when he claims that his speeches "were not the mere words of eloquence . . . that delight the ear and pass away. No! They were *work*-able, *do*-able words, that brought forth fruits in the revolution in Illinois, and in the passage of the franchise resolutions by the Assembly of New York" (132; emphasis added). Smith's account of Douglass's "work-able," "do-able" words, and of the revolutions they incited, should remind us that Douglass was always a *political* thinker not a "bare" theorist. He did not seek the truth for its own sake; he sought it because it carried him closer to justice.

All such "active thinking," as Wilson J. Moses observes, "runs into contradiction," and all "original thought is generated by the tragic and heroic struggle to reconcile conflict."[8] *Active* thinking runs into self-contradiction because it is continually adapting itself to changing circumstances; almost inevitably, some of those adaptations will conflict with earlier ones. All thought is temporal, but thinkers who situate themselves in time know what this means: one must adopt what Douglass called "a fixed principle of honesty." Therefore, Moses concludes, "It is the task of the historian to discover the processes by which thinkers seek to reconcile or, as some would say, to rationalize their own contradictions."[9] Although this is certainly the task for a historian writing a *history* of Douglass's political thinking, it does not quite describe the task of either a political theorist or a literary critic who studies Douglass. In both a theoretical and literary inquiry, the work also requires delving into these "contradictions," listening to them and learning from them what is self-limiting about one's own thinking and one's language. It requires softening one's tacit belief in the comparative truth of one's perspective—the assumption that one can perceive the truth of the past more readily than the past itself could—and instead to be open to the unknowable that lies in the space between now and then, between speech and silence, between what is "full of meaning" and what is "unmeaning jargon." One name for that unknowable is "gap." Another is "aporia." Yet another is "fugitivity."

Was Douglass a Black Nationalist?

As I have aimed to show from the start of this book, Douglass's political thought emerged from his experience of raced enslavement and took form as he brought what he had learned from that experience not just to abolitionism but to a wider set of issues of concern to the Black community and the U.S. polity. Chief among these was race or, more precisely, white racism. For these reasons, Douglass was first and foremost a Black political philosopher. But this is not to imply that he is a representative Black theorist, or that he initiates or stands in a particular tradition of Black theory. Here, too, we encounter Douglass's fugitivity as he (like many other Black thinkers, activists, and artists) evades the categories and taxonomies—assimilationism, Black nationalism, Black egalitarian liberalism, the Black radical tradition—that continue to play such an important part in the academic study of Black American cultural production.

If we ask, for example, *Does Douglass stand in the Black radical tradition?* or *Was Douglass a Black nationalist?*, the answers depend entirely on what we mean by these terms. If they entail commitments to a Black racial identity or to an independent Black community and culture living within the territorial United States, then I would argue that the answer to both of them is *no*. If these terms indicate a commitment to the enduring value—for Black and white Americans—of modes of thought and expression that have arisen within "the muck and more" of distinctively Black historical experience, then the answer is *yes*. Likewise, if these terms connote a willingness to use violence in self-defense, in defense of one's community, and in defense of human dignity and rights everywhere, then again the answer is *yes*. If the terms express a belief in the value of racial *pride*, the answer is no. But if they express a belief in the importance of Black *dignity*, then the answer is *yes*. If they mean a commitment to revolution, then again everything depends on what one means by that term. Douglass was skeptical if not hostile to the notion that significant historical change can be accomplished overnight and cemented in place afterward. He admired the 1848 revolutions in Europe, and he urged his Black readers to draw inspiration from them, but he did not think that any revolution could usher in a new era overnight. Rightly understood, revolution meant endless struggle.

Was Douglass a humanist? Yes, but in a particular sense of that word.

As we have seen, in order to address the problem of whites' anti-Black racism, he developed a more substantive theory of the human than could be found in U.S. public philosophy, based as it was so largely upon natural rights liberalism. He argued that our human rights are not just "endowed" such that we "possess" them, and he urged instead that we understand our rights as deriving from the powers that constitute us as humans. He warned that unless we have an opportunity to exercise those powers freely, we will not become conscious of them, and of the dignity and the rights that they confer. Nor will others. This far more relational and action-oriented understanding of rights and citizenship provided Douglass with a far better explanation of the dynamics of racial oppression—and how to combat them—than did Locke's natural rights philosophy.

Was Douglass an assimilationist? On the one hand, in an obvious way, the answer is *yes*: Douglass urged Black Americans' "incorporation" into the United States. On the other hand, the answer is *no*, since the nation he envisioned would have to be "composite," not white. Douglass's antiracist strategy therefore amounts to far more than just "assimilation" or "integration." It also calls for whites to purge themselves of racism and to redescribe the citizen and the human as an assemblage of powers, not as a mere blank abstraction bearing human rights. At the same time, it calls on Black Americans to do more than appeal to whites for recognition of Blacks' rights by invoking the morality they share with them; they must also struggle to empower themselves through the exercise of their distinctive human powers and thereby to command the respect of whites. In short, if "assimilationist" signifies conformity to established white norms, then Douglass was no assimilationist, since he clearly wished to transform those norms. Why would he have aimed "to instruct the highly educated [white] people" of the United States "in the principles of liberty, justice, and humanity" if he had wished merely to assimilate with them? Why would he have elaborated a political philosophy applicable to them if he believed that appeals to the public philosophy they already had would suffice? But if "assimilationist" means a total commitment to a universal human community, then the answer is *yes*. And not just Blacks, but also whites and all other races, would have to assimilate to it.

Michael Dawson has posited that a signature trait of Black nationalism is that it takes "race as *the* fundamental analytical category of concern to African Americans."[10] By this measure, Douglass definitely qualifies as a Black nationalist, since throughout his long career he took white racism to be the most urgent problem facing both the Black community and U.S. democracy. Recall his words: "The relationship subsisting between the white and colored people of this country is, of all other questions, the great, paramount, imperative and all commanding question for this age and nation to solve."[11] More important, his most distinctive contribution to democratic political thought—his theory that human powers and dignity are core values of democracy—arose in the first place from his analysis of what white racism is and seeks to do. As well, we must bear in mind that Douglass often advocated for all-Black political organizations, and at times for all-Black schools.[12] But if Douglass was a Black nationalist, he was also in an important sense a Black liberal insofar as he was fully committed to an abstract universality of citizenship. However, if, as Dawson writes, "black nationalism . . . cannot be made to march under the liberal banner," then Douglass could not have been a Black nationalist.[13] How can we resolve this paradox? One way, I suggest, is to acknowledge that Douglass espoused an unfamiliar but deeply radical conception of Black nationalism: one that is not *separatist*, but instead places the perspective of Black Americans at the *center* of the nation, as a generating force of its understanding of democracy. To put this formulation in its most provocative form: Black nationalism, for Douglass, would have meant striving to turn a white democracy Black.

"To Get at the Soul of Things"

Despite the effort of some thinkers to rehabilitate the term "humanism"—including, notably, Frantz Fanon and Sylvia Wynter—within the academy today it still lingers under a cloud of suspicion, and for good reason: its long-standing and often covert usefulness to Eurocentrism, colonialism, and the subtle enforcing of the racial contract. Douglass's political thought, however, asks us to rethink and reconsider whether *all* forms of humanism deserve this judgment, and it does so first and foremost by redefining the site at which political theorizing comes into being as a site of endless struggle. Douglass believed that all citizens, indeed all humans, must commit themselves to such struggle, and that once they do, they will have to look around for the resources they need in order to sustain their efforts *forever*. Even after a revolution, no reign of democratic flourishing ever will set in and last indefinitely. Endless struggle is the democratic condition. Or, as John Lewis so pointedly puts it, "Democracy is not a state. It is an act, and each generation must do its part to help build what we called the Beloved Community, a nation and world society at peace with itself."[14]

What would Americans—Black and white—need in order to sustain such a struggle? Along with transformed conceptions of the freedom and dignity of all persons, thought Douglass, they would need transformed conceptions of time, progress, the universal, and the human. Time, in most of Douglass's writings and speeches, is not simply a temporal *dimension* of existence—as in the familiar notion of time as the "fourth dimension." Time, for Douglass, is the temporal movement of action. He urges us to think less of actions as occurring in moments of time, and more of time as coming into being only as the occasion or expression of an action. We can grasp this difficult thought if we hold in our minds simultaneously both senses of the word "occasion": as a noun, it means "opportunity, or grounds for action," and as a verb, it means "to bring about." This way of thinking about time was an extension of Douglass's tendency to distrust the category of existence, or being, in human affairs, and to replace it with action or acting. His view resembles somewhat John Dewey's admonition that human experience is in truth an "undergoing": in every moment of life, we are not just being, but doing *and* being done to. But, as I have noted earlier, where pragmatists tend to think of undergoing as experimentation, Douglass gave it a more urgent cast: it is struggle.

Here I want to borrow an insight and a word from literary historian Jeffrey Insko, who has written the most searching and profound account of Douglass's temporality, which he characterizes as "anticipation." Insko writes: "An affective rather than an analytical mode, anticipation suggests a complex of feelings, experiences, or even bodily sensations one can have toward and of the future."[15] This way of thinking about time strongly disposed Douglass to prioritize the present, pay tribute to the future (since action in the present aims to bring it into being), and downgrade but not dismiss the value of the past. Recall that in his March 1849 editorial titled "The Constitution and Slavery," he had crystallized his understanding of the relation between time and human knowing in his phrase "the ever-present now": "True stability consists not in being of the same opinion now as formerly, but in a fixed principle of honesty, even urging us to the adoption or rejection of that which may seem to us true or false at the ever-present now."[16] Douglass's emphasis on the present appears most famously in his July Fourth speech, where he called it "the ever-living now" and emphasized that "now is the time, the important time": "My business, if I have any here to-day, is with the present. The accepted time with God and his cause is the ever-living now. . . . We have to do with the past only as we can make it useful to the present and to the future. To all inspiring motives, to noble deeds which can be gained from the past, we are welcome. But now is the time, the important time. . . . You live and must die, and you must do your work."[17]

As Insko argues, however, Douglass's "present" was "ever-present" because it was a present of anticipation, a *future-oriented* present. About five years after his July Fourth Address, Douglass's distinctive democratic temporality informed his May 1857 response to the Supreme Court's recent *Dred Scott* decision. This moment was almost certainly one of the gloomiest of his life. The culmination of a series of setbacks that had begun in 1850 with the passage of the Fugitive Slave Act, the decision dealt a devastating blow both to abolitionism's hopes and to the prospects of free Blacks living anywhere in the United States. While the 1850 act had extended slavery by permitting slaveholders to override the local laws of the free, northern states, the 1857 decision extended slavery even further by implicitly denying the very possibility of citizenship to all Black Americans, including those who were already nominally free. Yet this was not how Douglass chose to interpret the decision's impact. Instead, he argued that by making the injustice of slavery more "open" and "glaring," it marked an inevitable stage in a long struggle whose steady intensification augured the certain defeat of the slavery system.

Douglass's retrieval of hope from the "lengthening shadows" of despair was far from optimistic about the future, however; rather, it seemed to deny the usefulness of the temporal category we call the "future." He begins his speech with a subtle but effective framing that emphasizes his temporal location in a present of great urgency. His key rhetorical device here is anaphora: "*While* four millions of our fellow countrymen are in chains—*while* men, women, and children are bought and sold on the auction-block with horses, sheep, and swine—*while* the remorseless slave-whip draws the warm blood of our common humanity—it is meet that we assemble as we have done to-day."[18] These repetitions of "while" underscore that the "to-day" of that meeting is located firmly within a cotemporal, circumscribing present of slavery's continuing existence. In the next paragraph, Douglass strengthens this frame through an insistent repetition of the phrase "than now": the enemies of abolition claim that "the price of human flesh has never been higher *than now*"; that the people of the South have never been more attached to slavery "*than now*"; that "slavery has never reposed on a firmer basis *than now*" (407; emphasis added).

Having thus firmly placed his audience in this discouraging *now*, Douglass goes on to confess his own inclination to look to the future for respite or deliverance. He begins in an unabashedly affective register: "With an earnest, aching heart I have long looked for the realization of the hope of my people" (408). He then describes this stance of looking forward using shockingly material metaphors intended to convey that, in the "present" from which he looks forward, he is still an embodied, "barefoot" consciousness: "Standing, as it were, barefoot, and treading on the sharp and flinty rocks of the present, and looking out upon the boundless sea of the future, I have sought, in my humble way, to penetrate the intervening mists and clouds, and, perchance, to descry, in the dim and shadowy distance, the white flag of freedom, the precise speck of time at which the cruel bondage of my people should end" (408). Abruptly, however, Douglass closes down this futural prospect: "But of that time I can know nothing, and you can know nothing. All is uncertain at that point" (408). By thus eschewing the consolations of futural thinking, Douglass places his audience, too, on the "sharp and flinty rocks of the present," where one thing only is "certain": "slaveholders are in earnest and mean to cling to their slaves as long as they can, and to the bitter end" (408).

For Douglass, then, political time is hammered out by exigency and exists only as the site of struggle. From the past, we take only what we need for that struggle. Of the future, we can know nothing. And although the present may feel like sharp and flinty rocks beneath our feet, it can also be experienced as an "ever-present now," an "ever-living now," a forward-looking now. Pessimism and optimism, the grip of the past and the possibilities of the future, converge in this existential commitment to struggle. It is a struggle without end because it is a struggle against power that "concedes nothing without a demand, and . . . never will." "Parties, like men, must act in the living present or fail. It is not what they have done or left undone that turns the scale, but what they are doing, and what they mean to do now."[19] There, in that phrase "mean to do now," we catch the blending of present and future that Insko calls "anticipation."

To be sustained, thought Douglass, such struggle must be fueled by a firm belief in progress (or by a resolute *anticipation* of progress). At times, he expressed this belief as if it were something he had to will, or even to pretend, in order to sustain the struggle. As he put it in his lecture "Pictures and Progress," "He who despairs of progress despises the hope of the world—and shuts himself out from the chief significance of his existence—and is dead while he lives."[20] But more often he stated his anticipation of progress as a logical induction from facts he had observed. In his response to Lincoln's Emancipation Proclamation, he avowed: "I believe in the millennium—the final perfection of the race, and hail this Proclamation, though wrung under the goading lash of a stern military necessity, as one reason of the hope that is in me." And so he was critical of pessimism: "I have somewhere seen a doubt expressed that there is any such thing as human progress. Some go so far as to say that this world is growing worse. To this view—this disheartening view, I may say—there is no more impressive contradiction than in the history of the anti-slavery cause."[21] One might say, then, that Douglass holds in tension present-day theories that either emphasize the ongoingness of the past of slavery or underscore the need to aspire and work toward alternative futures. He moves back and forth in the interval between "the not yet" and the "no longer," refusing to be defined by either of them.[22]

Yet Douglass would also go beyond such practical and historical arguments for progress to assert a metaphysical claim: that progress is the expression of the immutable laws of the universe: "the world, like the fish preached to in the stream, moves on in obedience to the laws of its being, bearing away all excrescences and imperfections in its progress."[23] As he grew older, he rested his understanding of progress increasingly on his particular conception of the human: it posits that the source of all "higher" law is *not* the will of a divine being but human nature itself, with all its distinctive powers. As he affirmed in 1863: "But little hope would there be for this world covered with error as with a cloud of thick darkness . . . if there were not in man, deep down, and it may be very deep down, in his soul or in the truth itself, an elective power, or an attractive force, call it by what name you will, which makes truth in all her simple beauty and excellence, ever preferred to the grim and ghastly powers of error."[24] This "elective power" is an aspect of our "moral power," which may be why he shifts from the adjective "elective" to "attractive": we do not *elect* to exercise this power so much as we find ourselves *obeying* its commands, which are as irresistible as gravity. In an 1865 speech, he associates this inward moral force with another "element of progress" that lies within our very nature: "Man is distinguished from all other animals, but in nothing is he distinguished more than in this, namely, resistance, active and constant resistance, to the forces of physical nature. . . . To lack this element of progress is to resemble the lower animals, and to possess it is to be men."[25]

Douglass's faith in a human nature whose powers work unceasingly for progress was also the foundation of his belief in the viability of democracy as a form of human governance:

If I believed in the doctrine that human nature is totally depraved, that it is an evil nature unmixed with good, I should hold with Carlyle that it is better to restrict the right of suffrage among the masses of the people. If I believed that there was a prevailing disposition to evil and a preponderance of evil over good in human nature, I should say that the less the masses have to do with governing the better, for the less of humanity there was in it, the more of divinity there would be. But I believe that men are rather more disposed to truth, to goodness and to excellence, than to vice and wickedness, and for that reason I wish to see the elements of humanity infused throughout all human government.[26]

Somehow, then, Douglass was able to hold fast to two seemingly opposite views of time. One was an extreme form of presentism in which the "ever-present now" absorbs both past and future and constitutes the only meaningful temporality of human life. The other was a strong anticipation of progress, which does imply a futurity of some kind, but one understood as endless struggle undertaken where all action occurs: in the present. He neither reconciled these two conceptions of time nor subsumed one within the other. He accepted the tension between them just as he accepted that progress is both an inevitable expression of human nature *and* an accomplishment won by countless actions performed by persons living in their moment of "the ever-present now." A belief in the inevitability of progress, for Douglass, was not an encouragement to complacence or even hope, but a recognition of the human capacity for endless struggle and sacrifice to bring about a better world: "The world has made some progress since then: it is making progress all the time, but it so happens that every step in the world's progress costs terribly; every inch of man's disputed way upwards is bought at the cost of agony and often of blood."[27]

As I have noted earlier, Douglass gradually moved from a Christianity-based philosophy to a more human-centered one. We may also describe this movement as his heading steadily toward a mystery he called soul. In 1855, he had defined humanity as being "endowed with those mysterious powers by which man soars above the things of time and sense, and grasps with undying tenacity, the elevating and sublimely glorious idea of God."[28] In 1863, as we have just seen, he had declared that there is "in man, deep down, and it may be very deep down, in his soul or in the truth itself, an elective power, or an attractive force, call it by what name you will, which makes truth in all her simple beauty and excellence, ever preferred to the grim and ghastly powers of error."[29] In his remarks in 1870 at the final meeting of the American Anti-Slavery Society, he had said: "I want to express my love to God and gratitude to God, by thanking those faithful men and women, who have devoted the great energies of their souls to the welfare of mankind. It is only through such men and women that I can get any glimpse of God anywhere."[30] In 1883, he had affirmed: "What is true of external nature is also true of that strange, mysterious, and indescribable, which earnestly endeavors in some degree to measure and grasp the deepest thought and to get at the soul of things; to make our subjective consciousness, objective, in thought, form and speech." And in an April 1885 speech, he called the struggle against racism a struggle for "the soul of the nation"; then, as if to acknowledge that by using the word "soul" he was asking his audience to risk uncharted depths with him, he came back to it again: "Let me say one word more of the soul of the nation and of the importance of keeping it sensitive and responsive to the claims of truth, justice, liberty, and progress. In speaking of the soul of the nation I deal in no cant phraseology. I speak of that mysterious, invisible, impalpable something which underlies the life alike of individuals and of nations, and determines their character and destiny."[31]

When Douglass says that we may call soul "by what name you will," he is frankly admitting that the deepest source of his anticipation of progress and belief in humanity is so mysterious as to be beyond the reach of language. It is fugitive. Or, as political theorist Melvin Rogers might say, it "runs ahead of the evidence."[32] We may call it by whatever name we like, he suggests, because all names for our reasons for faith are inadequate. As he puts the matter in his lecture "It Moves": "Contemplated as a whole, it [truth] is too great for human conception or expression, whether in books or creeds. It is the illimitable thought of the universe, upholding all things, governing all things, superior to all things. Reigning in eternity, it is sublimely patient with our slow approximations to it, and our imperfect understanding of it, even where its lessons are clearly taught and easily understood."[33]

Like Douglass's belief in human brotherhood, like his eternal now that has no patience with either pessimism or optimism, like his melding of the certainty of progress in the future with the necessity of endless struggle in the present, Douglass's soul language admonishes us to name our deepest value commitments even when we know that our words will fail us. These commitments come to rest, like it or not, on our suppositions about human nature. Do we believe, then, with Douglass, "that men are rather more disposed to truth, to goodness and to excellence, than to vice and wickedness"? If so, what gives us reason to think so? If not, on the basis of what alternative view of human nature may we remain committed to democracy? Having seen the worst that human beings can be, and the worst that they can do to one another, Douglass felt that the obligation to ask these questions was foundational to political philosophy and political struggle. Yet he also acknowledged that the answers to them would vary, and that no answer could offer more than a glimmering—and fugitive—vision of "that mysterious, invisible, impalpable something which underlies the life alike of individuals and of nations."

NOTES

Abbreviations and Citations to the Autobiographies

FDP *The Frederick Douglass Papers, Series One: Speeches, Debates, and Interviews*, ed. John W. Blassingame et al., 5 vols. (New Haven, CT: Yale University Press, 1979–92)

LW *The Life and Writings of Frederick Douglass*, ed. Philip S. Foner, 5 vols. (New York: International Publishers, 1950–75)

All three of Douglass's autobiographies—*Narrative of the Life of an American Slave, My Bondage and My Freedom*, and *Life and Times of Frederick Douglass*—are included in *Frederick Douglass: Autobiographies*, edited by Henry Louis Gates Jr. (New York: Library of America, 1994). With few exceptions, which are clearly indicated in the text, citations to the autobiographies, indicated by page numbers in parentheses, refer to this volume. For clarity, I also indicate in the text which of Douglass's three autobiographies I am discussing at that point.

Notes to Introduction

1. Douglass, *My Bondage and My Freedom*, 387 (emphasis added). All further page references will appear in the text.

2. Mills, *Blackness Visible*, xv.

3. FDP 4:160. Douglass's political philosophy is the subject of two excellent book-length studies, both of which argue that it is a form of natural rights liberalism. I have learned a great deal from both works, even while disagreeing with their theses. See Myers, *Frederick Douglass*, and Buccola, *Political Thought of Frederick Douglass*. I am also indebted to two superb intellectual histories of Douglass: Martin, *Mind of Frederick Douglass*, and Blight, *Frederick Douglass' Civil War*.

4. Quoted in Dawson, *Black Visions*, 29.

5. Gooding-Williams, *In the Shadow of Du Bois*; Myers, *Frederick Douglass*; Buccola, *Political Thought of Frederick Douglass*; Lee, *Slavery, Philosophy, and American Literature*;

Jones, "Douglass' Impersonal," 1–35. Jack Turner, too, has made a powerful case for an Emersonian Douglass in *Awakening to Race*.

6. My approach to Douglass thus joins the work of other scholars who, in a fairly recent critical and historical turn, urge that "our own approaches be shaped by the theories and practices developed by the black men and women who lived with the print we study." Fagan, *Black Newspaper and the Chosen Nation*, 10.

7. Davis, "Lectures on Liberation."

8. Yancy, *Black Bodies, White Gazes*, 157.

9. FDP 3:204.

10. FDP 2:9.

11. FDP 2:327.

12. FDP 2:261.

13. Davis, "Lectures on Liberation," 114.

14. Roberts, *Freedom as Marronage*, 53–88.

15. Spires, *Practice of Citizenship*, 3.

16. FDP 3:209.

17. Hooker, "'Black Sister to Massachusetts,'" 692.

18. Nick Buccola, too, argues that Douglass intended to renovate the nation's public philosophy: his aim "was to persuade the American people to accept a new liberal creed that would replace narrowness with egalitarianism and selfishness with humanitarianism." This, as I hope to show, is a partially true but too limited account of Douglass's aspiration and achievement, which cannot accurately be described as a "new liberal creed." Buccola, *Political Thought of Frederick Douglass*, 1.

19. Douglass repeatedly affirmed and famously described the Declaration as the "ringbolt to the nation's destiny." Nonetheless, he would not have elaborated his own chapter of political philosophy if he had thought that the Declaration's principles, as understood by his contemporaries, would suffice to defeat anti-Black racism. FDP 2:363.

20. By the early 1850s, as historian John Stauffer has shown, Douglass had affiliated himself with a band of radical abolitionists who belonged to both the moral suasion and political wings of the movement. They were prepared to work politically to end slavery, and they did not shrink from the use of violence if necessary. However, the most revolutionary aspect of their enterprise, Stauffer suggests, was an "ethic" that sought "to dismantle the various cultural dichotomies that posed obstacles to the new age"—"those of black and white, body and soul, sacred and profane, ideal and real, civilization and savagery, and masculine and feminine." Stauffer, *Black Hearts of Men*, 19, 7.

21. As we shall see, Douglass also deployed his political philosophy to counter the exclusion of women and immigrants from the U.S. polity. Unfortunately, he failed to take such strong positions in favor of Native Americans, whom he believed to be so different as to be incommensurable with it.

22. Robin Kelley's account of the differences between Paul Gilroy's and Cedric Robinson's "agendas" is instructive in this respect: "Gilroy's point, and one of his most important critical interventions, is . . . that Black people are products of the modern world, with a unique historical legacy rooted in slavery; Blacks are hybrid people with as much claim to the Western heritage as their former slave masters. Robinson, on the other hand, takes the same existential condition but comes to different conclusions: slavery did not define the Black condition because we were Africans first, with worldviews and philosophical notions about life, death, possession, community, and so forth that are rooted in that African heritage." Framed by this distinction, Douglass lends himself more to Gilroy's agenda than Robinson's, though with two caveats. First, Douglass was less interested in Blacks' "claim" to Western heritage than in a Black transformation of it. Second, as we shall see, Douglass offers a tantalizing hint that the ultimate source of his attunement to the values of self-respect, respect, and dignity was a quality of African culture kept alive within the slave community. Robin Kelley, foreword to Robinson, *Black Marxism*, xix.

23. LW 4:351.

24. As another example of what I've been describing as an entwining of the familiar and the unfamiliar in Douglass's thought as I describe it in this book, consider this statement by one of the guiding lights of my own work, Angela Y. Davis: "Let's attempt to arrive at a philosophical definition of the slave," she writes. "We have already stated the essence: he is a human being who, by some reason or another, is denied freedom. But is not the essence of the human being his freedom?" She states this definition of the slave a second time: "the very existence of the slave is a contradiction: he is a man who is not a man—that is, a man who does not possess the essential attribute of humanity, freedom." While there can be no doubt that freedom looms large in Douglass's political thought, and that he believed the enslaved knew something about it that free persons do not, a closer reading of it raises a searching question about Davis's assertions. Is freedom the "essential attribute of humanity"? If it is, then a man wholly deprived of freedom would *not* be a "contradiction": he would simply have become a being who is *no longer* a man. But, as Davis herself seems to believe, and as Douglass repeatedly affirmed, the slavery system never could succeed in utterly crushing the "spirit," "manhood," "soul," or "dignity" of the enslaved. In his mind, it followed therefore that the essential attribute of humanity must consist not just of freedom, but as well of human dignity. This insight, born of his "experience of slavery," is what Douglass brought to his reformulation of America's public philosophy. Davis, "Lectures on Liberation," 113, 122.

25. The terms "fugitivity" and "Black fugitivity" have been used in various ways by a number of scholars. For a helpfully succinct account of Black fugitivity, see Hooker, "'Black Sister to Massachusetts,'" 691–92. The fugitivity of Douglass's thought that I have been trying to describe in this book is perhaps best seen as, in Hooker's words, "embracing the intellectual orientations arising from fugitivity . . . and imagining alternate racial orders, futures, and forms of subjectivity" (691). However, I am not sure that Douglass himself saw his intellectual orientation as arising from his fugitivity—a state of perpetual flight and marginality he was eager to leave behind. Rather, as I have been trying to show, he traced it to his "slave experience" and refined it in his work as a comparatively free Black activist intellectual. See also Best and Hartman, "Fugitive Justice"; Hesse, "Escaping Liberty," 288–313.

26. Blight, *Frederick Douglass' Civil War*, 1.

27. Dawson, *Black Visions*, 254.

28. Patterson, *Slavery and Social Death*, 100. Orlando Patterson frequently uses "dignity" and "self-respect" as if they were synonymous and interchangeable, but as we shall see, Douglass (like some philosophers today) sharply distinguishes between these.

29. Martin, *Mind of Frederick Douglass*, 92, 93.

30. Jones, "Douglass' Impersonal," 27.

31. FDP 3:210; FDP 4:253.

32. Notable exceptions, as we shall see, include Bernard R. Boxill, Frank Kirkland, and Robert Gooding-Williams. However, while they carefully investigate what "dignity" might have meant to Douglass, they do not appreciate its value as one of the key terms in his philosophical lexicon.

33. Gooding-Williams, *In the Shadow of Du Bois*, 17.

34. Jacques Rancière defines politics as "an extremely determined activity antagonistic to . . . the tangible configuration whereby parties and parts or lack of them are defined by a presupposition that, by definition, has no place in that configuration—that of the part of those who have no part. . . . Political activity is whatever shifts a body from the place assigned to it or changes a place's destination. It makes visible what had no business being seen, and makes heard a discourse where once there was only place for noise." Political subjectification, for him, is that moment of "shift" in which a "body" (he prefers not to say "person") insists on a "place in that configuration." Rancière, *Dis-agreement*, 30–31. For an account of the ways Rancière's political thought does not quite account for Black American political struggle and reflection, see Bromell, "'That Third and Darker Thought,'" 261–88.

35. FDP 5:291.

36. FDP 4:173.

37. LW 2:188.

38. LW 2:185.

Notes to Chapter One

1. Blight, *Frederick Douglass*, 216.

2. Levine, *Martin Delany, Frederick Douglass*, 5. See also Peterson, *Doers of the Word*; Vogel, *Black Press*; Fanuzzi, *Abolition's Public Sphere*; J. Brooks, "Early American Public Sphere," 67–92; Foster, "Narrative of the Interesting Origins," 714–40; Fagan, *Black Newspaper*; Spires, *Practice of Citizenship*.

3. Peterson, *Doers of the Word*, 11.

4. As Derrick Spires points out, "We have yet to describe the degree to which black writers themselves conceptualized and transformed the meaning of citizenship in the early Republic." Spires, *Practice of Citizenship*, 2.

5. LW 1:94. McCune Smith goes on to sketch the pre-history of Douglass's involvement in the Black public sphere when he writes: "The Church question, the school question, separate institutions, are questions he enters upon and argues about as our weary but active young men thought about and argued about years ago, when we had Literary societies"(94). These words remind us that the Black public sphere Douglass entered full-time, so to speak, in 1848, had a history dating back to the eighteenth century if not earlier. As Joanna Brooks has argued: "The birth of black institutions and black print production in the 1780s and 1790s constitutes a crucial moment in the history of black thought about the public sphere, when black people articulate in practice and enact for the first time in print key principles of black counterpublicity: collective incorporation, conscious differentiation, and criticism of dominant political and economic interests." J. Brooks, "Early American Public Sphere," 75.

6. Martin, *Mind of Frederick Douglass*, esp. 55–106.

7. As Jeannine DeLombard has shown, Douglass's shift from a nearly exclusive focus on abolitionism to the broader arena of the antebellum Black public sphere can also be understood in terms of his wish to *advocate* through legal argumentation, not just to bear witness: "Douglass's own reassessment of his role in the antislavery movement . . . should prompt a corresponding reevaluation of the ongoing critical emphasis in African American studies and in the legal academy on black testimony's purportedly liberating quality." Douglass believed that "African American civic participation required a black advocacy that foregrounded forensic argumentation even as it retained the personal narrative of racial oppression." DeLombard, *Slavery on Trial*, 126.

8. As we shall see, Douglass did not use the word "dignity" exclusively or consistently, relying often on cognate terms like "manhood," "respect," and "self-respect"; however, as we shall also see, an analysis of what those words meant to him suggests that "dignity" is what he was driving at, and he uses that word increasingly from the early 1850s until the end of his life.

9. Martin, *Mind of Frederick Douglass*, 119.

10. FDP 2:59.

11. LW 1:128–29.

12. FDP 2:3.

13. Roediger, *Wages of Whiteness*, 49.

14. Quoted in Spires, *Practice of Citizenship*, 126.

15. Spires, *Practice of Citizenship*, 126–27.

16. Spires, *Practice of Citizenship*, 127.

17. Quoted in Spires, *Practice of Citizenship*, 127.

18. Douglass never defined explicitly what he meant by "dignity." We have to infer that meaning from his many uses of the word and its cognates ("manhood," "self-respect," "soul") over many years. These uses make plain where he stood on two issues that concern philosophers who ponder the nature of human dignity. First, he was comfortable thinking of dignity as being both inherent in human nature and contingent on recognition from others. Second, he never mistook it for "honor," which is a different quality. As Meir Dan-Cohen succinctly puts it in his introduction to Jeremy Waldron's *Dignity, Rank, and Rights*: "Honor is of social origin: it derives from and reflects one's social position and the norms and attitudes that define it. . . . Consequently, honor is in principle limited in scope, capable of privileging only those who occupy certain positions while excluding others who occupy different ones." By contrast, worth (Kant's word for dignity) "is evenly distributed over humanity as a whole" and "is categorical, attaching to all its possessors by virtue of their being human, no matter what." However, Douglass's understanding of dignity is not identical with Kant's, for Douglass is among those philosophers who argue that dignity straddles the line that separates the natural from the social, the eternal from the contingent. He understood dignity as being *both* inherent in all human beings *and* dependent to some degree on its affirmation by others. Waldron, *Dignity, Rank, and Rights*, 4.

19. FDP 3:212.

20. Arendt, *Origins of Totalitarianism*, 296.

21. FDP 2:109.

22. Myers, *Frederick Douglass*, 62. Myers was the first scholar to note the importance of "faculties and powers" in Douglass's political thought. As will become clear,

however, our understandings of what he meant by these terms differ. Myers's full discussion of them can be found in pp. 54–57.

23. LW 1:410.

24. FDP 2:111.

25. In his definitive history of postbellum Black American uplift ideology, Kevin K. Gaines shows how often it was structured by—and accepted—class stratification as a permanent fixture of American society. Black elites believed that Black progress in the United States could be measured and effected by their own upward class mobility. Douglass, too, believed that Black elites had to perform a leadership role in demonstrating self-respect and demanding respect from whites. However, Douglass's uplift exhortations, especially before the Civil War, are comparatively uninterested in class-based markers of progress. As we shall see, his consistent emphasis is on Black *self-empowerment*, not merely Black upward mobility through emulation of white bourgeois norms. Gaines, *Uplifting the Race*.

26. LW 1:282–83.

27. LW 1:314.

28. Marrs, "Frederick Douglass in 1848," 447–48. Marrs's focus in this essay is on Douglass's temporality and its implications for transnationalism. For a more comprehensive account of Douglass's engagement with the events of 1848, see Fagan, "North Star," 51–67. For a broader view of U.S. literary culture and 1848, see Reynolds, *European Revolutions*.

29. LW 1:322.

30. LW 1:325 (emphasis added).

31. Quoted in Fagan, "North Star," 58.

32. Foner and Walker, *Proceedings of the Black State Conventions*, 190. All further page references will appear in the text.

33. This was true of virtually all the colored conventions. However different their policy recommendations and rhetorical strategies were, their most vital work was to assert a Black presence in a polity that wished for it to disappear.

34. The other authors were J. M. Whitfield, H. O. Wagoner, Rev. A. N. Freeman, and George B. Vashon.

35. LW 2:254. All further page references will be made in the text.

36. Hence the appeal of the idea of Black emigration. But as Juliet Hooker shows, Douglass's occasional and at times only implicit interest in Black emigration (that is, when he was not dead-set against it) was frequently infused by his search for "models" of Black activism and self-government that could inspire his Black readers. This interest began early: "In 1852," Hooker writes, "*Frederick Douglass' Paper* was the discursive site of African-American reflections about Central America that

directly contested U.S. racism in light of political models of multiracial democracy drawn from Nicaragua and the Mosquito Kingdom." Hooker, "'Black Sister to Massachusetts'," 692.

37. FDP 2:428.

38. FDP 3:209, 211, 212.

39. Melish, *Disowning Slavery*, 88.

40. The antebellum history of what political theorists call "public philosophy"—the public understanding of democracy's nature and principles—has not been sufficiently studied, perhaps because it has been regarded by as "ideology" and thus by definition a form of mystification that produces false consciousness. The brief account I offer here draws mainly on the following scholars and studies: Nelson, *National Manhood*; Sandel, *Democracy's Discontent*; K. Smith, *Dominion of Voice*; Roediger, *Wages of Whiteness*; Schudson, *Good Citizen*; R. Smith, *Civic Ideals*; Wilentz, *Rise of American Democracy*.

41. K. Smith, *Dominion of Voice*, vii.

42. FDP 2:363.

43. Arendt's proposal of a "right to have rights" is no solution, since it simply begs the question of what gives us the right to have rights. Arendt, *Origins of Totalitarianism*.

44. Nelson, *National Manhood*, 34, 37. Nelson's and Roediger's accounts of the emergence of anti-Black racism stress class dynamic and competition. See also Reginald Horseman's attention to the role played by Anglo-Saxonism as a racial idea and by American claims of manifest destiny. Horseman, *Race and Manifest Destiny*. On Douglass and Anglo-Saxonism specifically, see Hanlon, *America's England*, 41–44.

45. Tocqueville, *Democracy in America*, 482.

46. Whitman, *Democratic Vistas*, 15.

47. Wilentz, *Rise of American Democracy*, 485.

48. Roediger, *Wages of Whiteness*, 57.

49. R. Smith, *Civic Ideals*, 470.

50. Goodell, *Views of American Constitutional Law*, 149. Goodell argues that "common law" provides this foundation, but then specifies that it "speaks . . . in the name of universal, essential, uncreated, unalterable law, or in other words, in the name of the most high and eternally supreme God" (151). As we shall see, Douglass's conception of such law was usually more humanistic than this and, by the end of his life, emphatically so.

Notes to Chapter Two

1. LW 5:79.

2. Ellis, *Antebellum Posthuman*, 25. Cristin Ellis argues further that Douglass develops an argument that "brackets the question of Black humanity and embraces the materiality and animality of the human. . . . Douglass invokes a rhetoric of assertive Black 'manhood' that is paradoxically animalistic" (27). In my view, as will become clear, this intriguing argument goes too far.

3. To a considerable degree, Douglass's conviction that his times required a more adequate idea of the human anticipates Sylvia Wynter's belief that "the struggle of our new millennium will be one between the ongoing imperative of securing the well-being of our present ethnoclass (i.e., Western bourgeois) conception of the human, Man, which overrepresents itself as if it were the human itself, and that of securing the well-being, and therefore the full cognitive and behavioral autonomy of the human species itself/ourselves." However, in my reading of Douglass's work, he is more concerned with the dignity and interdependence of the human species than with its "cognitive and behavioral autonomy." Wynter, "Unsettling the Coloniality of Being," 260.

4. As Britt Rusert has observed, Douglass's interest in the category of the human was shared, and would have been supported, by many other Black intellectuals of the time, including his close friend and mentor, James McCune Smith. As Rusert writes, "More than simply establishing the fact of Black humanity, African Americans used natural science to profoundly meditate on the category of the human itself—on its possibilities, limits, and its complex relationship to blackness, a concept that exceeds simply biological or even transparently empirical relationship to race." Rusert, *Fugitive Science*, 6.

5. As I have noted earlier, however, because Douglass never gave such elaboration the form of a full-blown treatise, we must piece it together from many fragments. The two most important of these are an 1866 editorial he penned on women's suffrage and an 1883 lecture discussing what he called "the philosophy of reform." In this chapter, I will be using these later works to unpack some of what is only implicit in earlier ones. In doing so, I am not suggesting that his thought developed teleologically toward these end points of greater self-consciousness, nor am I claiming that his political philosophy never changed. Rather, I am taking account of the fact that as an activist thinker, he seldom had time to set forth in explicit form the fundamental philosophical principles, or commitments, that underlie his political actions and positions. The political philosophy he elaborated from his experience of enslavement is far more often the animating spirit of his work than its explicit subject. If we wish to reconstruct and understand it, we have no choice but to examine a range of his work across time.

6. Combe, *Constitution of Man*, 164. Combe's understanding of "man," and of man's "faculties and powers," was by no means unique. To a considerable degree such thinking was part of a broader tendency, which we associate with Romanticism, to shift creative and agentic powers from the realm of the divine and supernatural to that of the human and the natural. Nonetheless, the affinities between Combe's language and Douglass's are noteworthy.

7. Combe, *Constitution of Man*, 8, 10.

8. As Douglas Jones has compellingly argued, another important influence on Douglass came from Emerson and the "transcendental logic of essential and immutable human sameness"—"a theory that demands we recognize how the impersonal that produces the infinitude of the world works through all persons without bias and produces the very same dignity and infinitude in every person" (Jones, "Douglass' Impersonal," 4, 3). What Jones misses, however, is the degree to which Douglass's experience of enslavement shaped the way he received and modified this logic—in particular, the way that experience led Douglass to emphasize the vulnerability and importance of human dignity and to work out a theory of what, exactly, composes human dignity.

9. As we shall see later, after 1859 Douglass also drew upon the language he found in Ludwig Feuerbach's *The Essence of Christianity* to give a fuller account of Combe's act of recognition of one's self as an "intelligent and accountable subject."

10. FDP 2:454.

11. Stepto, "Storytelling in Afro-American Fiction," 109; Krause, "Frederick Douglass," 1.

12. FDP 2:261 (emphasis added). Myers was the first to notice Douglass's use of this phrase, but he does not allow it to trouble his argument that Douglass was fundamentally a natural rights liberal whose major political value was freedom. In his analysis of the phrase, he argues that the two words ("powers" and "faculties") mean significantly different things to Douglass (Myers, *Frederick Douglass*, 53–57). In any case, "powers" was the word Douglass used most often, and it accords better with his tendency to regard thought and action, doer and deed, as a comprehensive whole rather than as fundamentally distinct from each other.

13. FDP 2:454–55.

14. FDP 2:501, 502. See Myers's excellent discussion of the logic at work in this speech, in *Frederick Douglass*, 51–54. Myers concludes that in arguing for the slaves' natural possession of moral and intellectual powers, Douglass was "presenting a core Lockean argument . . . that the right of self-ownership depends on the capacity for self-ownership" (54–55). As I hope will become clear, I believe that because Douglass's conception of these matters arose from his reflections on his enslavement, not from his reading of Locke, his political and moral theories are

also marked by profound differences from Locke's, differences we overlook if we affiliate him too closely with Lockean theory.

15. LW 4:232–33.

16. LW 4:237.

17. As we shall see, a deep interest in power and human powers animates all three of Douglass's autobiographies and appears in many of his speeches and editorials. If we turn, for example, to what is perhaps the most famous passage in all of Douglass's writings, in which he described his physical resistance to the "slave-breaker" Edward Covey, we find that here, too, his more easily recognized celebration of freedom is accompanied by a less noticed interest in power. Christa Acampora, one of the very few scholars to have noted Douglass's interest in power, notes that this physical struggle seems to have produced within him "the felt quality or aisthesis of freedom"; this feeling in turn opened up an "imaginary domain" in which he experienced freedom as the power to be the "author" and "sources" of his own life. In her view, then, Douglass believed that the exercise of power is the means by which we secure our felt sense of having freedom. To this I would add that, at bottom for Douglass, the feeling of having freedom is itself the feeling of having powers, of being a power on earth (Acampora, "Unlikely Illuminations," 176, 180). Acampora derives the term "imaginary domain" from Cornell, At the Heart of Freedom, x.

18. LW 4:236, 237.

19. FDP 4:273.

20. Philosophers who believe that we must choose between these two ways of thinking about dignity include, recently, Michael Rosen and Jeremy Waldron. Both argue (though in different ways) for a cultural rather than natural derivation of human dignity. Rosen, Dignity; Waldron, Dignity, Rank, and Rights.

21. FDP 2:327.

22. FDP 2:9.

23. FDP 3:212.

24. Boxill, "Douglass against the Emigrationists," 36. All further page references will be made in the text.

25. Frank M. Kirkland argues (correctly, in my view) that "it is the sense of being vulnerable to moral injury, not the fear of mortality, that provokes Douglass's resistance and gives resistance or struggle for recognition its moral force." Kirkland, "Enslavement, Moral Suasion, and Struggles," 287.

26. FDP 5:135.

27. Bernard Boxill and Frank Kirkland have led the way in arguing that Douglass's political philosophy was rooted in a moral philosophy. Peter C. Myers, in his de-

tailed account of Douglass's moral theory, analyzes many of the features I discuss in this chapter, including its fusion of human powers with the laws of the universe, and its emphasis on human responsibility as both a perquisite and a right of democratic citizenship. I am enormously indebted to his account. However, Myers and I differ insofar as he sources Douglass's moral philosophy in his affiliation with Locke's (and some of the founders') natural rights liberalism, whereas I source it in Douglass's suspicion that the liberal tradition of political thought—at least as it was understood in the United States—provided an insufficient basis on which to combat anti-Black racism. See especially Myers, *Frederick Douglass*, 47–82.

28. It seems likely that Douglass acquired at least some of his high regard for moral power and individual duty from William Lloyd Garrison. See McDaniels, *Problem of Democracy*.

29. As we shall see in more detail in chapter 6, Douglass's account of his childhood in *My Bondage and My Freedom* describes the process through which he became conscious of his intellectual, moral, and what I will be calling aesthetic powers. He relates there that, as he became increasingly conscious of these, he became determined to claim and exercise them, to assert and create his own dignity, and to resist the powers that sought to prevent him from doing so.

30. After the Civil War, Douglass would apply the same psychological analysis to anti-Black racism, observing that "we may easily forgive those who injure us, but it is hard to forgive those whom we injure" (LW 4:347). Waldo Martin does not state this self-punishing psychological dynamic as I have, but I believe he is making nearly this point when he writes that in Douglass's view "the moral dilemma of the oppressor is . . . to cease oppression, to love the formerly oppressed, and to rise above the will to dominate others while also rising above guilt and self doubt" (Martin, *Mind of Frederick Douglass*, 113). What I would add here is that, for Douglass, the slaveholders' "guilt and self-doubt" actually drove, or even constituted, their "will to dominate others."

31. FDP 3:173.

32. FDP 5:137, 129. Compare with George Eliot's translation of Feuerbach, which Douglass almost certainly read, perhaps in the summer of 1860: "But what is this essential difference between man and the brute? The most simple, general, and also the most popular answer to this question is—consciousness. . . . Consciousness in the strictest sense is present only in a being to whom his species, his essential nature, is an object of thought. . . . But only a being to whom his own species, his own nature, is an object of thought, can make the essential nature of things or beings an object of thought." Feuerbach, *Essence of Christianity*, 1–2.

33. Feuerbach, *Essence of Christianity*, 1–2.

34. FDP 5:135, 138, 139. What is this law? Through most of his life Douglass called it "natural law." Here, not helpfully perhaps, he calls it "Truth." His account of it makes room for pluralism and for differing interpretations, but only by retreating into the ineffable: "Contemplated as a whole, it is too great for human conception of expression, whether in books or creeds. It is the illimitable thought of the universe, upholding all things, governing all things, superior to all things. Reigning in eternity. It is sublimely patient with our slow approximation to it, and our imperfect understanding of it, even where its lessons are clearly taught and understood" (FDP 5:141).

35. Wynter, "Unsettling the Coloniality of Being," 329 (emphasis added). And with his deep attunement to standpoint epistemology, and his awareness of human fallibility, Douglass might also have shared her willingness to think in terms of "genres" of the human rather than a single form of the human species. But perhaps not, since he believed with equal firmness that the idea of a single human community composed of all human beings was an indispensable foundation for politics that honored dignity and strove for justice.

36. But is such submission to, and exercise of, one's moral powers in actuality just an internalization of social discipline—as Nietzsche, Foucault, and others have suggested? Perhaps. But Douglass testifies that, to radically unfree persons who are enslaved, the governing of oneself through obedience to the moral law feels to be the exercise of a power that constitutes one's human being and human worth. From their standpoint and perspective, the idea that one's moral power is an introjection of social power could only be advanced by someone who, not having experienced conditions of extreme oppression, can take his or her human status for granted. The same could be said about broader skepticism of the very idea of the human: it can flourish best among those who feel relatively secure that they have a human worth of some kind. And although they may disavow having such a feeling, that disavowal too is shaped by their standpoint, for not having experienced what it is like to have their worth denied, they cannot know the comparative security they feel about their own.

37. Although a re-description of the human lies at the heart of Douglass's political thought, I think it can be misleading to call him a "humanist" and link his thought to "humanism" unless we define precisely what those terms mean. While it is true that Douglass drew upon a tradition of philosophy and a cultural orientation that can be broadly described as "humanist," his reason for investigating the very idea of "the human" was triggered by this tradition's inclination—intensifying in his time—to exclude persons of African descent from it. Another problem with these terms is that they encourage us to think of Douglass's interest in "the human" as a settled question—"He was a humanist"—rather than looking into the specific historical reasons why he became so interested in it. One of these, as I have tried to show, was his belief that the nation's public philosophy, and in particular its

natural rights elements, offered an insufficiently robust conception of the human to effectively combat racism—perhaps because its earliest spokesmen had been able to take their own status as humans for granted.

Notes to Chapter Three

1. As Lloyd Pratt has shown, Douglass self-consciously figured himself as just such a stranger. Pratt also demonstrates that "the stranger persona" in Douglass's writings plays "a key role . . . in his projected vision of political community. [It] posits credible experiences of strangerhood as pathways to a democratic community of the human emerging not from identification, but rather from open-ended scenes of encounter. If Douglass figures strangerhood as an escape route from the dubious terrain of sympathetic identification and as a condition available to all comers, he is also careful to specify the rules of the game called strangerhood." Pratt, *Strangers Book*.

2. Wilshire, *William James*, 55.

3. The body of scholarship on Douglass's rhetoric and performance is small but growing. See, especially, Dorsey, "Becoming the Other," 435–50, and Ganter, "'He Made Us Laugh Some,'" 535–52. Of particular interest also are the earliest books on Douglass, written when he was admired more for his oratory than for his writing. For this, see Brown, *Black Man*, 180–87; Gregory, *Frederick Douglass the Orator*; Holland, *Frederick Douglass*.

4. Collins, "Learning from the Outsider Within," s16.

5. FDP 2:368.

6. FDP 4:152.

7. FDP 5:576.

8. Gates, *Figures in Black*, 80–97; Gikandi, *Slavery and the Culture of Taste*, 236.

9. This puzzle only intensifies when he goes on to say, "To those songs I trace my first glimmering conception of the dehumanizing character of slavery" (24). Did those glimmerings occur when he stood within the circle or when he stood without it? Did not the whippings of Aunt Hester provoke such a glimmering conception? And what, for that matter, is a *glimmering* conception?

10. As I note also in chapter 6, I think literary scholars have tended to read Douglass's autobiographies (after the *Narrative*) too exclusively as efforts at self-representation. They were also efforts at self-discovery and self-understanding, and Douglass was not always as much in control of them as many critics have suggested.

11. See P. Sterling Stuckey's brilliant account of the implications of Douglass's fusion of opposites for our understanding of Black American music: Stuckey, "Afterword," 451–58.

12. Gates, *Figures in Black*, 93.

13. Roberts, *Freedom as Marronage*, 71–80.

14. On Baldwin's caustic analysis of whites' "innocence," see Balfour, *Evidence of Things Not Said*, 87–112.

15. Young, "Asymmetrical Reciprocity," 342, 351. Iris M. Young is taking issue here with Seyla Benhabib's Kantian universalism; by contrast, Young joins other feminist theorists in combining standpoint theory and Derridean appreciation of difference to critique universalism of this kind. As we shall see, however, Douglass's position is slightly but crucially different from Young's. He believed that the oppressed require a universalism of some kind, for without it, they and their oppressors have no shared moral framework within which they can demand justice.

16. LW 4:351.

17. *Douglass Monthly*, October 1860, quoted in Martin, *Mind of Frederick Douglass*, 122.

18. Pratt, *Strangers Book*, 44.

19. Gates, *Figures in Black*, 93.

20. Gorodeisky, "19th Century Romantic Aesthetics."

21. LW 1:361 (emphasis added).

22. FDP 2:261.

23. In other words, we should not overlook the distinctiveness of Douglass's subject position and mistake his fugitivity for mere "inconsistency." Martin Jay made the same point differently when he argued in a 1990 essay that we should not judge Douglass's frequent appeals to Christian dogma simply "as a maneuver that allows just a bit of rebellion" while ceding too much ground to the era's dominant discourse. "The practice of that discourse, historically, by Douglass, reinscribes a difference that white hegemony cannot efface. As a speaking subject Douglass constantly trades on the shock value of his eloquent literacy, on the irony of his appearance and speech. Dialectically, one cannot understand Douglass without recognizing his humanity, and to recognize his humanity is to transform the history and category of the 'human' as his era conceives it." Jay, "The Example of Frederick Douglass," 241.

24. Bromell, "Democratic Indignation," 287. For a complementary reading of Douglass that argues that anger more generally can be a productive democratic emotion, see Sokoloff, "Frederick Douglass," 330–45.

25. Walker, *David Walker's Appeal*; Stewart, *Maria Stewart*.

26. Stewart, *Maria Stewart*.

27. FDP 2:168.

28. FDP 2:427. Further page references will appear in the text.

29. FDP 2:492.

30. Thus, while it is true that, as Waldo Martin has argued, "Douglass perceived an inherent conflict between race consciousness and humanism," at moments Douglass actually drew upon his humanism to assert and defend his race consciousness. The point where these two dispositions joined without conflict was in the notion of human dignity. In general, as political theorist Robert Gooding-Williams points out, Douglass did not believe "that, to be effective and legitimate, black politics must avow and embody a racially specific and collectively shared spiritual or cultural orientation that antecedently unites all black Americans." On this occasion, however, he broke from that position and implicitly advocated solidarity based on the spiritual and cultural orientation that arose in response to white racism. But this may be explained by the fact that many whites were in his audience that day. As we shall see when we turn to Douglass's thinking about Black emigration schemes, he was sometimes comfortable couching as a veiled threat to whites the very policies he rejected when he discussed them with Blacks. Martin, *Mind of Frederick Douglass*, 106; Gooding-Williams, *In the Shadow of Du Bois*, 188.

31. Levine, *Martin Delany, Frederick Douglass*, 23.

32. Ture and Hamilton, *Black Power*, 165.

33. LW 1:314.

34. LW 1:291.

35. Bromell, "Democratic Indignation," 292.

36. FDP 2:129.

37. FDP 2:130.

38. FDP 2:238. Douglass's words mirror these by Ture and Hamilton: "Nothing more quickly repels someone bent on destroying you than the unequivocal message: 'O.K., fool, make your move and run the same risk I do—of dying.'" Ture and Hamilton, *Black Power*, 52.

39. FDP 2:29.

Notes to Chapter Four

1. Turner, *Awakening to Race*, 27.

2. Bernard Boxill also emphasizes this point: "Douglass believed that emigration... encouraged the false belief that black and white people could not live peacefully together in the same society." But whereas Boxill goes on to argue that "the crux

of Douglass's case against emigrationism" was that "it would perpetuate the sense of alienation and homelessness that he thought already devastated the black population," I suggest that the crux was that it would reinforce Blacks' despondence and thus further discourage Black political mobilization. Boxill, "Douglass against the Emigrationists," 29, 30.

3. Levine, *Martin Delany: A Documentary Reader*, 190, 191.

4. Levine, *Martin Delany: A Documentary Reader*, 212, 213, 219–20.

5. Levine, *Martin Delany: A Documentary Reader*, 247, 248–49.

6. Delany also claims that "the English, French, Irish, German, Italian, Turk, Persian, Greek, Jew and all other races, have their native or inherent peculiarities, and why not our race?" What Delany overlooks here, however, is that all these other "races" have seen fit to become "white" for political and social purposes in the United States. He elides this fact precisely because he does not wish people of African descent to do likewise. Levine, *Martin Delany: A Documentary Reader*, 252.

7. Levine, *Martin Delany: A Documentary Reader*, 252.

8. LW 2:129.

9. Hooker, "'Black Sister to Massachusetts,'" 690–702.

10. LW 2:252.

11. Douglass's position on violence has been discussed by many scholars. On the broader topic of violence and Black self-representation, see Takaki, *Violence in the Black Imagination*. On violence and the antislavery movement, see McKivigan and Harrold, *Antislavery Violence*. One of the earliest and still most helpful treatments of Douglass and violence is Leslie F. Goldstein's "Violence as an Instrument for Social Change."

12. FDP 2:484.

13. "I am a peace man. I am opposed to the shedding of blood in all cases where it can be avoided. But this Convention ought to say to Slaveholders that they are in danger of bodily harm if they come here, and attempt to carry men off to bondage" (FDP 2:275).

14. FDP 2:390.

15. FDP 2:281.

16. Robert Levine reads the restraint Douglass claims to have exercised as a strategic appropriation of the values and language of the antebellum temperance movement. See Levine, *Martin Delany, Frederick Douglass*, 126–32.

17. Lawson and Kirkland, *Frederick Douglass*, 287.

18. However, neither scholar explains what Douglass understood self-respect, or dignity, to be. While Margaret Kohn does see that this fight is a "struggle for rec-

ognition," she is more interested in a particular Hegelian reading of this passage, one in which Douglass achieves a form of pure self-consciousness made possible by a negativity that detaches him from "mortal life" and "sensuous pleasures." "In that experience," according to Hegel, the slave "has been quite unmanned, has trembled in every fiber of its being, and everything solid and stable has been shaken to its foundations. But this pure universal movement, the absolute melting-away of everything stable is the simple, essential nature of self-consciousness, absolute negativity, pure being for itself." Consequently, Kohn argues, "understanding of the universal emerges out of 'negativity,' . . . which severs the connection to the world of appearances. Through negativity, the slave acquires the idea of freedom. Possessing the idea of freedom and not being free, the slave is led to transform the conditions of his existence, thereby realizing historical progress." Kohn, "Frederick Douglass's Master-Slave Dialectic," 91, 101.

19. As Robert Levine has pointed out, whereas Douglass had portrayed himself as acting alone in *Narrative*, "in *Bondage and Freedom*, he presents himself on his own terms, and one of the selves he chooses to present is that of a Black freedom fighter who has joined hands with his Black compatriots" (Levine, *Lives of Frederick Douglass*, 163). To this view that focuses on Douglass's self-representation, I would add a complementary possibility: that his deeper interest in group solidarity, which also appears elsewhere in *My Bondage and My Freedom*, reflects Douglass's emergent self-description as a political philosopher who aims to awaken his Black readers by setting before them models of Black solidarity and political awakening. This scene of his wrestling match with Covey thus dramatizes his belief that individual dignity, while emanating from the exercise of an individual's powers, also requires recognition and support from others.

20. FDP 3:210.

21. As Robert Gooding-Williams concisely points out, "Where Emerson explains that self-reliance is aversion to conformity . . . Douglass depicts it as aversion to domination." What that domination sought first and foremost was to crush Black dignity by reducing the enslaved to the level of the "brutes." Gooding-Williams, *In the Shadow of Du Bois*, 163, 177.

22. LW 2:437.

23. Cognizant of arguments by Glen Coulthard (among others) that the politics of recognition may simply reproduce a fundamentally "colonial" relation despite "a seemingly more conciliatory set of discourses and institutional practices," I want to emphasize that Douglass's version of a politics of recognition is profoundly different from that exercised by a state (e.g., Canada) in relation to its colonized subjects. The recognition Douglass called for was not a relation between the state and a group of its subjects, nor between a dominant and an oppressed group in a society or polity. Rather, Douglass's interest was in intersubjective recognition, which he believed occurred spontaneously and naturally among all humans by virtue of

their shared possession of certain powers that defined their humanity. He was well aware, of course, that many persons disavow such recognition of others in order to establish social hierarchies. Coulthard, *Red Skin, White Masks*, 6.

24. See, for example, the introduction by editors Levine, Stauffer, and McKivigan in Douglass, *The Heroic Slave*, xi–xxxvi.

25. Douglass, *The Heroic Slave*, 42. All further page references will appear in the text.

26. Douglass, *The Heroic Slave*, 6.

27. Fanon, *Wretched of the Earth*, 51. And even Frantz Fanon himself would seem to agree when he writes that violence "restores" the "self-respect" of the colonized individual.

28. As several critics have pointed out, Douglass here (and elsewhere, in his speeches) was laying claim to the white revolutionary tradition of the founders to justify Black revolutionary violence against the slavery system. We should notice also, however, this distinction: while the leaders of the rebelling colonies justified their action by invoking the "self-evident" truths of natural law, which included certain "inalienable rights," Douglass's understanding of those rights was that they arose from the natural powers of every human being.

29. Of course, as to the facts of the matter and how Douglass actually did fight, we cannot be certain. On the one hand, he writes that "the fighting madness had come upon me" and describes the action of combat as though his will had played little or no part in it: "I found my strong fingers firmly attached to the throat of my cowardly tormentor" (282). On the other hand, he unequivocally states, "Every blow of his was parried, though I dealt no blows in turn. I was strictly on the *defensive*, preventing him from injuring me, rather than trying to injure him" (283; emphasis in original). All we may conclude with certainty is that in his representation of this struggle, Douglass took pains to offset "fighting madness" with cool resolve and self-restraint.

30. Goldstein, "Violence as an Instrument," 69, 70.

31. Goldstein, "Violence as an Instrument," 71.

32. Goldstein, "Violence as an Instrument," 68.

33. LW 4:278.

34. LW 3:84.

Notes to Chapter Five

1. LW 2:53–54.

2. "Throughout the 1850s," Waldo Martin observes, "Douglass followed a pattern in which at first he would align himself primarily with the Liberty Party and Radical Abolitionists in principle. Come election time, however, he would opt for expediency." David Blight calls Douglass's inconsistency a struggle between "pragmatism," on the one hand, and "moral principle," on the other, with pragmatism winning the day. Wilson Moses is even more critical: "Douglass' ideology was thoroughly inconsistent, usually opportunistic, and always self-serving." Martin, *Mind of Frederick Douglass*, 33; Blight, *Frederick Douglass's Civil War*, 50; Moses, *Creative Conflict*, 48.

3. LW 2:480.

4. LW 2:63.

5. Garrison, "Dissolution of the Union," 42–44.

6. Garrison, "Dissolution of the Union," 43 (emphasis added).

7. LW 2:115.

8. LW 1:361. Further page references will appear in the text.

9. I borrow my language here from Sharon Krause in *Civil Passions: Moral Sentiment and Democratic Deliberation*. See also Jacques Rancière's discussion of logos and pathos in *The Aesthetic Unconscious*. Rancière suggests that the writer, or artist, is at once an archaeologist who finds the logos within pathos, and a doctor who gets to the pathos within logos. We might say, similarly, that Douglass identifies the logos (or "system") within the pathos (or lawless suffering) of slavery, but also finds the pathos within the logos, as when he sees slaveholders as victims of their own claim to mastery, or logos.

10. LW 1:370.

11. LW 1:379.

12. LW 2:155–56.

13. LW 1:377.

14. LW 2:150 (emphasis added).

15. LW 2:157.

16. FDP 1:253. Nick Buccola offers a nuanced account of what he calls Douglass's "malleability–free will duality" in his essay "'The Human Heart,'" 269–74. Buccola argues persuasively, "On the one hand, we find Douglass saying that human nature can be 'corrupted and perverted by long abuse of irresponsible power.' . . .

On the other hand, we find Douglass defending a strong theory of moral agency" (273).

17. LW 1:356.

18. LW 2:141.

19. LW 1:379. There were two other reasons, as well. As we shall see later, Douglass believed that when enslaved persons made appeals to slaveholders, they reached out to, or called to, the slaveholders' natural moral faculty, that is, to their sense of personal responsibility for their immoral actions. The enslaved could neither have outwardly appealed to their masters nor inwardly condemned them if they had not believed that the slaveholders *intended* their wicked actions. Finally, while evil and destructive in itself, the slaveholders' negation of standpoint and intentionality also short-circuited the hermeneutic that in Douglass's view came closest to finding the truth of any matter: movement back and forth among differing standpoints, even those regarded as opposites, such as "without" and "within" the circle of slavery.

20. LW 1:361.

21. LW 2:155–56.

22. Quoted in Spires, *Practice of Citizenship*, 126.

23. FDP 5:139.

24. LW 2:479.

25. LW1:109 (emphasis added).

26. LW 1:323 (emphasis added).

27. Literary scholar Kelvin Black has arrived at a similar understanding of Douglass's constitutional thought by way of Jacques Derrida's theoretical account of the Declaration of Independence. According to Black, Derrida argues that "there is always a pragmatic gap between the speech act of declarations of freedom and their actual performance" (145). That gap is the space where politics can happen; for democratic politics is in essence an ongoing, endless effort to close that gap by making good on the promises made by the Declaration. Black suggests that Douglass came to believe there was such a gap between the Preamble to the Constitution and the articles that, as Wendell Phillips and others had argued, were intended to protect the institution of slavery. Douglass eventually concluded also that all subsequent interpretations of the Constitution were justified in stepping into and attempting to close that gap. Both Black's argument and my own trouble, and perhaps even efface, the distinction that is regularly drawn between Douglass's principles and his pragmatism, such that his principles align with his Garrisonian position and his pragmatism with his embrace of political abolitionism. Black, "Frederick Douglass' Differing Opinions," 145–69.

28. Sullivan, *Political Class Book*, first page of introduction (unpaginated). Further page references will appear in the text.

29. Story, *Constitutional Class Book*, 142.

30. Hooker, "'Black Sister to Massachusetts,'" 692. Juliet Hooker persuasively shows that Douglass's political thought can be understood as a complex—and tension-filled—combination of Sheldon Wolin's notion of "democratic fugitivity" and the "tradition of black fugitivity."

31. Wolin, "Fugitive Democracy," 43.

32. Barber, "Foundationalism and Democracy," 353.

33. This is the title Douglass gave to the speech when he included a portion of it in *My Bondage and My Freedom*. However, Eric Foner refers to it as "The Meaning of July Fourth for the Negro."

34. FDP 2:368. All further page references will appear in the text.

35. Jason Frank makes precisely this point in somewhat different terms, arguing that Douglass's July Fourth speech is an example of a "constituent moment" in which the very meaning of "the people" is transfigured by one who has been excluded from it. Likewise, in his autobiographies, "Douglass aspires not to bring African American life into conformity with the constitutive norms of the polity but to radically reimagine those norms." Frank, *Constituent Moments*, 227.

36. Hooker, "'Black Sister to Massachusetts,'" 691.

37. Barber, "Foundationalism and Democracy," 351.

38. Douglass's post-1851 attitude to the Constitution partially resembles what Jack Balkin has called the "faith" or "fidelity" that constitutionalism requires of all citizens. Balkin argues that because no constitution can be just all of the time, citizens must sometimes have faith that in the long run its principles will produce justice more often than not—that over time, the constitution redeems itself. Balkin calls such commitment "fidelity" (and takes Douglass to be a prime exemplar of it). Balkin's *fidelity*—"a discipline of self"—is his way of describing what Douglass called a "fixed principle of honesty." This discipline, which Balkin calls an "attitude" and "orientation," subtends conscious thought and rational reflection and is not a *solution* to a dilemma intrinsic to constitutional, democratic governance and citizenship, but rather the *fortitude* needed in order to meet these dilemmas responsibly. Yet there is also a significant difference between their views, one that rests in their differing understandings of democratic temporality. Balkin's faith looks to the future, seeing U.S. democracy as a "transgenerational project; it is *in the future* that today's apparent constitutional injustices will be redeemed by the greater justice the Constitution affords over the long run" (emphasis added). Douglass, as we have seen, shifted the location of faith to the "ever-present now." Just as we have no right to dismiss the past unless we accept our responsibilities

to the present and future, so only if we work now do we have a right to look to the future with any hope for progress. Balkin, *Constitutional Redemption*, 127, 16.

39. FDP 5:261 (emphasis added).

Notes to Chapter Six

1. Andrews, *My Bondage and My Freedom*, 134. William L. Andrews thus sees Douglass as expressing his determination "to reidentify himself as a leader and spokesman of a nationwide Afro-American community" while also writing self-consciously in a "distinctly Emersonian" mode with the intention of placing himself among his "Romantic literary contemporaries" and indeed within the mainstream (white) "literary climate of the 1850s" (143, 134, 145, 134).

In a second major study published six years later, literary historian Eric Sundquist similarly read *My Bondage and My Freedom* in terms of Douglass's dual commitments to "self-definition as an *American* who happened to have been a slave of African descent" and to self-assertion as a Black man engaged in a "further rebellion against the new bondage imposed on him by white antislavery liberalism," i.e., William Lloyd Garrison and his colleagues in the American Anti-Slavery Society. Whereas Douglass had written the *Narrative* in a way that conformed closely to the "script" Garrison and his colleagues in the AAS had encouraged him to follow, Sundquist argued, in *My Bondage and My Freedom* he shaped the story of his life according to his own aims and principles. Sundquist, *To Wake the Nations*, 85, 87.

Invoking Douglass's "creation of a persona" and his "power as a narrator," Sundquist gave even more emphasis than Andrews to the self-fashioning involved in self-representation, and thus to the constructed nature of the text. The thrust of Sundquist's interpretation of the book is that it accomplishes a "blending of a campaign for black freedom and black rights with a telling of his own representative story" by affiliating both with the Black revolutionary tradition embodied in "Toussaint L'Ouverture, Gabriel Prosser, Denmark Vesey, Nat Turner, and Madison Washington, among others" *and* with the founding fathers and "America's revolutionary tradition of liberal individualism and . . . the principles of autonomy, property, and equal rights" (86, 87, 87, 85, 90).

More recently, in *Martin Delany, Frederick Douglass, and the Politics of Representative Identity* and *The Lives of Frederick Douglass*, Robert Levine has carried forward this tradition of reading *My Bondage and My Freedom* as a discursive cultural intervention by a Black man negotiating his place in a white-dominated nation. In the first book, Levine shows the many ways in which Douglass deliberately synthesized two antebellum discourses—that of the temperance movement and that of abolitionism—both to give the latter more cultural traction and to enhance the self-image he wished to promote. In the second study, Levine skillfully uncovers the many resemblances between *My Bondage and My Freedom* and Douglass's novella, *The Heroic Slave*, published just two years earlier, arguing that in both works Douglass "links himself with the cause of black freedom fighters" and represents himself as a "prideful black leader" while also "making clear that he has been developing new interracial friendships." Levine, *Lives of Frederick Douglass*, 159, 173, 172.

2. However, I am inclined to read *My Bondage and My Freedom* not just as Douglass's fashioning of a self-representation for readers white and Black but also as a record of his process of self-discovery. In other words, I believe that the book was the outcome of a dialectical process, one in which the particular representation of himself that he wished to project was continuously modified by the discoveries about himself that he made as he wrote. We must also take into account the challenges he faced as he tried to articulate his discoveries about his experience of enslavement within the generic and discursive frameworks at his disposal.

3. Beginning with Caroline Levander's pathbreaking 2005 essay, many scholars have understood these added chapters as expressing not so much Douglass's deepened interest in his childhood per se as his concern to manipulate "the figure of the child" in the field of cultural representations. "Douglass includes an account of himself as a child subject," argues Levander, "as part of his project of reconfiguring the ground rules of U.S. national belonging." Levander, "Witness and Participate," 183–92.

Yet, as Marissa Carrere warns, we should not forget that the children we see in *My Bondage and My Freedom*—not just Douglass but the other children of whom he writes—are both figural and actual. "Douglass's child . . . calls us to a more complex recognition of the enslaved child as a human subject, and then further to the challenges of representing humanity within slavery without reducing subjects to rhetorical objects that might best serve political narratives." Carrere, "'As Child in Time,'" 141.

4. See, for example, Mandoki, *Everyday Aesthetics*; Leddy, *Extraordinary in the Ordinary*.

5. As Bernard Boxill points out, Douglass's strong feelings for the home and its values informed his dispute with Martin Delany over the wisdom of Black emigration. Douglass believed that "insofar as the emigrationists' plan accepted the [white] majority's claim that blacks were strangers in the land they identified with and called home, it would perpetuate the sense of alienation and homelessness that he thought already devastated the black population." Boxill, "Douglass against the Emigrationists," 30–31.

6. Likewise emphasizing how "Douglass presents himself" in *My Bondage and My Freedom*, Robert Levine has shown that Douglass's portrait of his grandmother promotes "the values of free labor" and underscores his "difference (and distance) from the slave community." Levine, *Martin Delany, Frederick Douglass*, 119.

7. Quoted in Boxill, "Douglass against the Emigrationists," 31.

8. Stuckey, "'Ironic Tenacity,'" 25. Douglass's account of his grandmother and mother thus lends support to Gerald Mullin's claim that "whatever the precise meaning of procurement for the African as a person, his fellowship of affectivity, a core area of human behavior, remained intact as a slave." Mullin, quoted in Robinson, *Black Marxism*, 169.

9. Stephanie A. Smith was one of the first critics to perceive that in *My Bondage and My Freedom* Douglass is concerned with personal identity, Black agency, and the well-being of national polity. She argues in a 1992 essay on Douglass's "strategic" use of sentimentality that his representation of his years with his grandmother "offers . . . a blueprint for imagining an autonomy that both is and is not autonomous." S. Smith, "Heart Attacks," 208.

10. Bromell, "Democratic Indignation," 285–311.

11. Yancy, *Black Bodies, White Gazes*, 163.

12. See, for example, Leverenz, "Frederick Douglass's Self-Fashioning," 108–34; Zafar, "Franklinian Douglass," 199–217; Drake, "Rewriting the American Self," 91–108; Willett, *Soul of Justice*, 189–202; Moses, *Creative Conflict*, 46–48.

13. Although she emphasized the masculine, individualistic Douglass, Kimberly Drake was one of the few feminist critics of Douglass in the 1980s and 1990s to note that in his later autobiographies "he takes steps to restore, however minimally, his reliance on community." Drake, "Rewriting the American Self," 102.

14. McDowell, "In the First Place," 172–83; Franchot, "Punishment of Esther," 141–65. In the *Narrative* Douglass refers to his aunt as Aunt Hester, in *My Bondage and My Freedom* as Aunt Esther.

15. It is a testament to the enduring power of the *Narrative* to shape our understanding of Douglass that both Saidiya Hartman and Fred Moten focus on the *Narrative's* version of the whipping of Aunt Hester as the "primal scene" in Douglass's autobiographies. If his revisions in *My Bondage and My Freedom* are considered, the scenes of his discovery of standpoint and of his mother defending his dignity are arguably more primal. Hartman, *Scenes of Subjection*, 4; Moten, *In the Break*, 1–5.

16. Alfaro, "Black Masculinity," 236, 238.

17. Patterson, *Slavery and Social Death*, 97.

18. Patterson, *Slavery and Social Death*, 7; Hahn, *Nation under Our Feet*, 16–17. See also Blassingame, *Slave Community*; Gooding-Williams, *In the Shadow of Du Bois*, 172–76.

19. Many slave narratives, not just Douglass's, celebrated relationships for this reason. In doing so, many also deploy the terms and tropes of the antebellum culture of sentiment in which their authors found themselves in the North. Scholars today whose conception of power and the political is either Foucauldian or Arendtian tend to regard this representational strategy with suspicion, failing to

perceive that the enslaved undertook a political act whenever they tried to create for themselves a private space where their relationships with one another could be nurtured, and where they were not always "under the eye" of the overseer. Thus, although Lauren Berlant is right to warn that sentimentality's use of "personal stories to tell us of structural effects . . . risks thwarting its very attempt to perform rhetorically a scene of pain that must be soothed politically," she slides too precipitously to the conclusion that "the political as a place of acts oriented toward publicness *becomes replaced by* a world of private thoughts, leanings, and gestures" (emphasis added). Berlant, "Poor Eliza," 297; Dawson, *Black Visions*, 11.

20. LW 5:209. All further page references will be made in the text.

21. Buccola, "'Human Heart,'" 254. Further page references will appear in the text.

22. As Maurice S. Lee has shown, Douglass read Scottish philosophy, so he was likely to have been influenced by its conception of man as born for society. However, Douglass's philosophy, being so centrally concerned with political activism, chose to emphasize human powers rather than human sentiments. Lee, *Slavery, Philosophy, and American Literature*.

23. Frederick Douglass, "Self-Made Men: An Address Delivered in Carlisle, Pennsylvania, March 1893," in McKivigan, Husband, and Kaufman, *Speeches of Frederick Douglass*, 419–20.

24. I have discussed this scene at some length already, with similar but also some different conclusions. Bromell, "'Voice from the Enslaved,'" 697–723.

25. They can also appear differently to a single person as she moves through space and time. This aspect of standpoint epistemology suggests a second reason why, along with the desire to re-fashion his self-representation, Douglass kept revising his autobiographies: he kept seeing his past differently as his standpoint relation to it changed.

26. Collins, "Learning from the Outsider Within," s16.

27. Yancy, "African-American Philosophy," 552.

28. See also Nolan Bennett's fine argument that, in Douglass's hands, "autobiography is a distinct genre of political theory, one that challenges present relations between the individual and the collective by representing not simply its author but an expanded view of 'the people.'" Bennett, "To Narrate and Denounce," 240.

29. Wagner, *Disturbing the Peace*, 1–2.

30. FDP 2:359; LW 4:491; FDP 4:149.

31. Arthur Riss has argued that Douglass came to appreciate what families are and do only *after* he had escaped to the North and acquired what Riss calls the "lexicon" of antebellum sentimental culture. He is correct to the extent that our ability to name our feelings reinforces them and makes them more real to us. But he goes

too far when he smuggles in a poststructuralist suspicion of the natural and concludes that "Douglass . . . is interested in denaturalizing the sense that the feelings one expresses are ever natural." Riss, "Sentimental Douglass," 113.

32. Jacobs, *Incidents in the Life*, 37. Harriet Jacobs's answer to her own question is, "Youth will be youth" (38). She thus conveys that, however irrational and doomed her impulsive love might have been, it was nonetheless an expression of her humanity.

33. Sundquist, *To Wake the Nations*, 88, 89.

34. Gikandi, *Slavery and the Culture of Taste*, 238. However, for reasons that will become evident as this chapter unfolds, I believe that Simon Gikandi sees only one aspect of Douglass's view of aesthetics when he claims that he "detested any suggestion that the experience of slavery would generate any kind of pleasure for the enslaved" and argues that Douglass implicitly questioned "the notion that sensuousness itself could have value outside the domain of rationality" (197–99). To be sure, Douglass exposes the slaveholders' manipulation of the pleasures of the enslaved, and he criticizes the enslaved for acquiescing in that manipulation. But, as we shall see, Douglass also suggests that some forms of "sensuousness" could actually catalyze political awakening and resistance.

35. A number of critics have discussed Douglass's deepened interest in nature in *My Bondage and My Freedom*. See Buell, *Environmental Imagination*; Finseth, *Shades of Green*; Ellis, "Amoral Abolitionism," 275–303.

36. I am grateful to John Stauffer's essay "Frederick Douglass and the Aesthetics of Freedom," which prompted me to begin thinking about Douglass's thoughts on aesthetics and on the relationship of aesthetics to politics. Stauffer, "Frederick Douglass and the Aesthetics," 114–36.

37. FDP 3:460.

38. FDP 5:143.

39. Stephanie Camp borrows the phrase from Edward Said. Her book is a noteworthy addition to recent historical studies that expand and enrich our understanding of the multiple forms of resistance by the enslaved. Camp, *Closer to Freedom*, 7.

40. Finseth, *Shades of Green*, 277.

41. Quashie, *Sovereignty of Quiet*, 6. It was Jeffrey Ferguson who first called my attention to the need for a more thoroughgoing account of the inward life of Black Americans rather than focusing so intently and exclusively on resistance. In his essay "Race and the Rhetoric of Resistance," Ferguson invites his readers to doubt whether "a theme like resistance, which focuses more on the struggle against outside forces than on inner experiences, can give the best account of how both the oppressed and oppressor exceed the frameworks that we use to explain them."

Those words were published in 2008, and since then, fortunately, both historians and literary critics have developed more subtle approaches to the dynamics of resistance, ones that do at least some justice to "inner experience." Ferguson, "Race and the Rhetoric of Resistance," 6–7.

42. In both "Pictures and Progress" and "It Moves," Douglass was almost certainly drawing on his reading not just of Combe, but also of Ludwig Feuerbach's book *The Essence of Christianity*, which he had read with the German expatriate journalist Ottilie Assing in the summer of 1860. Compare, for example, Douglass's "the process by which man is able to invert his own subjective consciousness, into the objective form, considered in all its range, is in truth the highest attribute of man[']s nature" (in "Pictures and Progress") and his "to make our subjective consciousness objective" (in "It Moves") with Feuerbach's words: "In the object which he contemplates, therefore, man becomes acquainted with himself; consciousness of the objective is the self-consciousness of man. We know the man by the object, by his conception of what is external to himself; in it his nature becomes evident; this object is his manifested nature, his true objective *ego*. And this is true not merely of spiritual, but also of sensuous objects. . . . Consciousness consists in a being becoming objective to itself; hence it is nothing apart, nothing distinct from the being which is conscious of itself" (5).

It is important to note, however, that Douglass wrote *My Bondage and My Freedom* five years *before* the summer of 1860, and that his ideas about the nature of consciousness in relation to the external world are already strongly implied in that book; thus, Feuerbach's book did not generate those ideas, but instead gave Douglass a more precise philosophical vocabulary in which to cast them.

43. Newman, "Free Soil and the Abolitionist," 134. This "radical pastoral mode" has, however, a deeper connection to English and continental romanticism than Newman acknowledges; see Neil Roberts's discussion of this topic in *Freedom as Marronage*, 63–71. On British romanticism and slave narratives in general, see Thomas, *Romanticism and Slave Narratives*. See also Kimberly Smith's illuminating and important account, "Black Agrarianism," 267–86.

44. Quoted in Levine, *Martin Delany, Frederick Douglass*, 47 (emphasis added).

45. Delany's language here is so similar to language Douglass used years later in *My Bondage and My Freedom*, and then in "Pictures and Progress," that one wonders whether Delany (not Feuerbach) was the source from which Douglass drew the language—and perhaps even the ideas that the language conveys. Notice also the resemblance between Delany's "*soar* to the extent of human susceptibility . . . my soul is *lifted up*, my bosom . . . conscious that he [God] has *endowed* me with *faculties* to comprehend them," and Douglass's language in his 1850 speech, "Slavery and the Slave Power" (discussed earlier): "*endowed* with those mysterious *powers* by which man *soars above* the things of time and sense."

46. Rogers, "David Walker," 209, 218.

47. Hartman, *Scenes of Subjection*, 88.

48. FDP 3:49. Of course, Douglass might have been wrong about this. Perhaps the appeals of the enslaved were not based on the truth of human nature but were simply a leveraging, to whatever advantage they could secure, of the slavery system's patently false ideology.

49. Douglass, "Slavery," 14.

50. Cavell, as quoted in Havercroft and Owen, "Soul Blindness, Police Orders," 749.

51. Hartman is discussing the power of seduction here, not appeal: "As a theory of power, seduction contends that there is an ostensible equality between the dominant and the dominated. The dominated acquire power based upon the identification of force and weakness" (88). In the case of appeal, according to Douglass, the power stems not from such an identification of weakness with power, but from the appellant's invocation of a shared horizon of humanness, which then forces the slave master to destroy his own humanity if he rejects the appeal.

52. A compelling theoretical elaboration of my argument that the vulnerability of the enslaved can be a source of resistance because both vulnerability and mastery are relational and socially produced can be found in Butler, Gambetti, and Sabsay, *Vulnerability in Resistance*. As Butler warns, however, when "vulnerability" is used as "the basis for group identification," this will likely strengthen "paternalistic power. Once groups are marked as 'vulnerable' within human rights discourse or legal regimes, those groups become reified as definitionally 'vulnerable,' fixed in a political position of powerlessness and lack of agency" (24–25). As we shall see in subsequent chapters, Douglass regularly fought such fixing by eschewing whites' pity and by chastising his African American audiences to overcome their "despondence."

53. Moten, *In the Break*, 1.

54. FDP 2:327.

55. Frederick Douglass, "Slavery," 7, 8. Many years later, Martin Luther King Jr. would use the same term "manhood" in essentially the same sense when he declared that "the Negro will only be free when he reaches down to the inner depths of his own being and signs with the pen and ink of his manhood his own emancipation proclamation." King, *Testament of Hope*, 246.

56. LW 1:358. I believe that Douglass always knew, though perhaps not always consciously, that what he was calling "manhood" was not restricted to the male sex. He had grown up with a grandmother who herself had such powers and faculties; he knew that his own mother was endowed with "high powers of manner as well as matter"; and he had witnessed numerous enslaved women who were conscious of and ready to assert their powers by stoutly resisting unjust punishment or by

taking the grave risk of appealing to their master for justice. Nonetheless, it was not until 1866, and while writing about women's suffrage, that he seems to have realized that the gendered word "manhood" was too restrictive for his purposes, and so he used the phrase "natural dignity" in its stead.

57. The equal weight Douglass gives to action and consciousness in his conception of dignity is one some political theorists might identify as an unsettling and unlikely yoking of Arendtian and Hegelian philosophy. But such transgression of conventional categories in political thought is typical of Douglass's method.

Notes to Chapter Seven

1. FDP 4:173.

2. FDP 4:241.

3. FDP 4:257.

4. FDP 4:255.

5. LW 3:292.

6. FDP 3:570.

7. FDP 4:131.

8. Beausoleil, "Responsibility as Responsiveness," 295.

9. FDP 5:208.

10. FDP 2:91.

11. FDP 3:210.

12. FDP 4:206. Gooding-Williams argues that Douglass was not "an assimilationist (in Du Bois's sense) for unlike Du Bois and Myrdal he does not propose to bring [Black] group practices into conformity with norms of behavior or development corresponding to prevailing [white] group ideals." Gooding-Williams, *In the Shadow of Du Bois*, 195–96.

13. Gooding-Williams, *In the Shadow of Du Bois*, 197.

14. FDP 5:95.

15. FDP 4:90–91.

16. FDP 4:284.

17. As Gooding-Williams has put it, "the Douglass of *Bondage* had no truck with [Black] political expressivism" and "lets us see that African American politics need not be the expression of antecedently given, kinship and descent-based identity that the participants have in common." The rising power of white racism after the war

made Douglass even more hostile to racial thinking, white or Black, than when he had written *My Bondage and My Freedom*. Gooding-Williams, *In the Shadow of Du Bois*, 187.

18. FDP 5:411–12.

19. Turner, "Douglass and Political Judgment," 211. Further page references will be made in the text.

20. Jack Turner also argues that for Douglass (and for Supreme Court associate justice John Marshall Harlan), "in addition to a legal status, citizenship is an intersubjective condition"—or practice, rather—"of reciprocal recognition" (Turner, "Douglass and Political Judgment," 212). Again, this hits the nail on the head. But I would suggest that this formulation should also pressure us to inquire: Reciprocal recognition of *what*? Although I suspect that the words "humanity" and "dignity" will come to mind, I wonder if we political theorists today have taken the time to understand what these words mean. Too often we invoke them merely because we realize, half consciously, that words like "rights" and "freedom" will not quite suffice to make our case for democracy. The exact nature of the supplement dignity provides goes unexamined. In short, democratic theory today lacks a substantive conception of dignity, which is precisely what Douglass's understanding of dignity as composed of distinctive human powers provides.

21. LW 4:220.

22. FDP 4:372.

23. FDP 5:207.

24. FDP 4:270.

25. Hartman, *Scenes of Subjection*, 121.

26. FDP 5:409.

27. FDP 4:235–36.

28. LW 4:225; FDP 5:557; FDP 4:318.

29. FDP 4:208, 210 (emphasis added).

30. Castronovo and Nelson, "Fahrenheit 1861," 330.

31. Levine, "Frederick Douglass and Thomas Auld," 35.

32. Ernest, *Chaotic Justice*, 41.

33. As we shall see, Douglass's 1881 version of *Life and Times* does at times offer too rosy a picture of race relations in the United States, one in which racism is figured simply as an error melting in the warmth of sunbeams cast by individuals of goodwill. However, his speeches from the same period are much less sanguine, and in the final (1893) version of *Life and Times*, he seems to have added material with the specific purpose of giving a more sober account of racism's future and a more re-

alistic vision of what must be done to defeat it. These three stories should be read not in isolation but as part of that broader discursive context.

34. Mills, *Blackness Visible*, xv.

35. Young, *Responsibility for Justice*, 4.

36. William L. Andrews points out that Douglass's reunion scenes in *Life and Times* are hardly singular. A number of African American postbellum autobiographies include accounts of such reconciliation. As Andrews writes: "One may be surprised to discover how often and how easily the estrangement wrought by long-standing caste and class differences, and by time itself, is bridged in scenes in which a genuine reconciliation between black and white seems to be effected." Moreover, as Andrews shows, many such scenes depict moments in which white former masters recognize the dignity of their former slaves. But whereas Andrews reads these works as expressing "a complex of desires, some of them psychological," he also suggests that "soon after the Civil War, ex-slave autobiographers, like the majority of black activists and pundits of the Reconstruction era, decided that it was no longer in the best interests of blacks, especially black Southerners, to continue to feed the sectionalism of the past." To this astute analysis I would add that, in Douglass's case at least, such scenes also express his long-standing intention to offer instruction to white readers in "the principles of liberty, justice, and humanity"—specifically, here, in the protocols of dignity affirmation and recognition. Andrews, "Reunion in the Postbellum Slave Narrative," 6, 7, 12.

37. FDP 5:137, 129; LW 2:268.

38. FDP 2:270 (emphasis added).

39. FDP 3:200 (emphasis added).

40. LW 4:207 (emphasis added).

41. FDP 4:241 (emphasis added).

42. Because the word "liberal" is in such disrepute today, we should understand that it meant something different in Douglass's time than it has come to mean in ours. Etymologically, it derives from the Indo-European root leudh-, which in turn is closely associated with leu-, meaning "loosen" or "let go," as in the Greek λύω . Liberality is thus a quality of letting go, of being unconstrained or on the loose. In the eighteenth and early nineteenth centuries, "liberal" simply meant generous. A liberal person gave unstintingly, and his opposite was a person who was selfish, mean, or grasping. By the time Douglass wrote, "liberal" had begun to imply an open stance toward life and a broad-minded attitude toward other people's ideas and values. "Meanness," by contrast, came to connote a strict, close-minded disposition that could become prejudiced, unkind, or even cruel. He never used the word "liberal" in the sense we now give it, which derives from nineteenth-century British advocates of free trade known as the Manchester school liberals.

43. Blight, *Frederick Douglass's Civil War*, 213.

44. LW 4:257.

45. FDP 4:290.

46. FDP 5:47.

47. Allen, *Talking to Strangers*, 156, 157.

48. FDP 4:257.

49. For an illuminating account of this controversy, see Laski, *Untimely Democracy*, 66–71.

50. Douglass wrote in an 1865 letter to Lydia M. Child: "The story of an interview between us [Douglass and Auld] is a newspaper story for which I am in no way responsible. Any such meeting could not fail to be awkward. . . . Still I should be glad to see him especially if I could do so simply by meeting him halfway. I do not fancy making a journey to see a man who gave me so many reasons for wishing the greatest distance between us. . . . I learn from my sister who still lives near Master Thomas, that he would be glad to see me. He has but to say so to me by letter—and considering his age, and forgetting his past, I will make him a visit." LW 4:170.

51. Douglass's own self-conscious performance here calls to mind political theorist William Connolly's *A World of Becoming*, in which he urges his readers to recognize that their subjectivity consists of the multiple "roles" they play and to exploit this performativity by redefining and recombining them: "The accumulation of rapid shifts in role performance might introduce new pressures into the world. . . . The point of individual and group experimentation with role assignments is simultaneously to make a direct difference through our conduct, to open us to new experiences that might alter our relational sensibilities even further, to unscramble role assumptions assumed by others, to form operational connections with others from which larger political movements might be generated, and to make connections with noble role warriors in other regions and walks of life to enlarge the space and visibility of positive action." Douglass portrayed himself, Tilton, Lloyd, and even Auld as such "noble warriors," suggesting that the "operational connections" among such persons were an effective way to build "larger political movements." Connolly, *A World of Becoming*, 144–45.

52. Robert S. Levine also stresses this point in "Frederick Douglass and Thomas Auld," 34–45.

53. Hirsch, "Fugitive Reconciliation," 181; emphasis added.

54. Bickford, *Dissonance of Democracy*, 168, 186. See also Noble, "Sympathetic Listening."

55. King, *Testament of Hope*, 291, 348.

56. Malcolm X, "The Ballot or the Bullet," in *Malcolm X Speaks*, 9.

57. FDP 2:238–39.

58. John Lewis, "Together You Can Redeem the Soul of Our Nation." https://www
.nytimes.com/2020/07/30/opinion/john-lewis-civil-rights-america.html. July 30,
2020, 8:52 AM EST.

59. Rankine, *Citizen*, 126, 49.

60. Beausoleil, "Responsibility as Responsiveness," 298.

61. According to biographer David Blight, the speech was variously called "Lessons of the Hour," "Why the Negro Is Lynched," and "The Negro Problem" (Blight, *Frederick Douglass: Prophet of Freedom*, 740). It is doubtful that Douglass himself ever gave it this last title, but if he did, it would have been an expression of deep and bitter irony.

62. LW 3:311–12.

63. LW 4:27. The term "afterlife" is from Hartman, *Your Mother*, 6.

Notes to Chapter Eight

1. John Stauffer offers an analogous and complementary argument about the difference between Douglass's aesthetics of freedom and his aesthetics of bondage in "Frederick Douglass and the Aesthetics," 114–36.

2. FDP 3:19. Further page references will be made in the text.

3. Douglass's language here bears a strong resemblance to Lysander Spooner's. (Spooner was a principal theoretician of the political abolitionists' argument that the Constitution rightly understood was an antislavery document.) Spooner defined law as "'an intelligible principle of right, necessarily resulting from the nature of man; and not an arbitrary rule, that can be established by mere will, numbers or power.'" Spooner, quoted by Schrader, "Natural Law in the Constitutional Thought," in Lawson and Kirkland, *Frederick Douglass: A Critical Reader*, 91.

4. Blight, *Frederick Douglass: Prophet of Freedom*, 236, 445; Shulman, *American Prophecy*, 16–20, 76–80.

5. Or perhaps what Cornel West has called his "prophetic pragmatism," though he does not mention Douglass in connection with it. West, *American Evasion of Philosophy*, 234.

6. As I hope we have seen, Douglass's more integrative way of thinking expresses his commitment to relationality, connections, continuities, breadth, and generosity and his aversion to compartmentalization, separation, narrowness, and meanness. For Douglass, nothing stands alone. Everything is part of a spectrum. Ideas cannot be separated from actions. Absolute truth cannot be separated from standpoint perspective. Principles cannot be separated from the manner of applying them. Culture cannot be separated from nature, and mind is not altogether

distinct from body. Each pair should be regarded as a unitary whole that is always in tension, or in struggle, with itself.

7. Of course, as the story of the three blind men in their first encounter with an elephant conveys, the use of inductive reason is hardly foolproof. An even greater danger, in my view, is that deductive reasoning often pretends to be inductive. In his *Notes on the State of Virginia*, Thomas Jefferson gives the appearance of dispassionately observing and collecting data from which he assembles his scientific conclusions, but we have good reason to believe that about some matters—e.g., the condition of the "New World" and the nature of African persons—he arrived first at conclusions and then selected evidence that purportedly supported them.

8. Moses, *Creative Conflict*, xi–xii.

9. Moses, *Creative Conflict*, xii.

10. Dawson, *Black Visions*.

11. FDP 3:570.

12. Finally, there is at least some affinity between Delany's idea of "inherent sovereignty" and Douglass's notion that rights derive from inherent human powers that compose dignity. To put the matter bluntly: Do not both thinkers share a disposition toward what we would now call "essentialism"? In the nineteenth century, essentialism was at least as prevalent a disposition as contingency thinking. Yet the deeper reason for their affinity on this point might have been their experience as raced Black bodies living in a white racist polity. Insults to his Blackness might have triggered in Douglass, as much as in Delany, a drive to locate bedrock values in his own body. Thereafter, a fork in the road might have led him to emphasize such value in all human bodies, whereas Delany emphasized the specific value of Black human bodies. These are major differences, of course; up to that point, however, they were walking the same path, one that originated in their experience and consciousness of race.

13. Dawson, *Black Visions*, 13.

14. John Lewis, "Together You Can Redeem the Soul of Our Nation." https://www.nytimes.com/2020/07/30/opinion/john-lewis-civil-rights-america.html. July 30, 2020, 8:52 AM EST.

15. Insko, *History, Abolition*, 129. Cody Marrs offers a quite different view of Douglass's temporality: "Time, he came to believe, tends not to progress in a straight line, but to break off and return in unexpected ways." I think Marrs is correct if "in a straight line" connotes "automatically" rather than through struggle; but I would disagree with the second part of Marrs's account, which implies that, in breaking off and coming back, progress has a life of its own apart from human struggle. Marrs, "Frederick Douglass in 1848," 435.

16. FDP 1:361.

17. FDP 2:366.

18. LW 2:407 (emphasis added). Further page references will be made in the text.

19. FDP 5:178.

20. FDP 3:471.

21. FDP 3:471; FDP 3:552; FDP 4:410.

22. I am grateful to Lawrie Balfour both for pointing this out to me and helping me find the language to express it.

23. FDP 3:555.

24. FDP 3:553.

25. FDP 4:495.

26. FDP 4:173.

27. FDP 4:315.

28. FDP 2:255.

29. FDP 3:553 (emphasis added).

30. FDP 4:264 (emphasis added).

31. FDP 5:191 (emphasis added).

32. Rogers writes: "If what we are after is commending a posture toward one's ethical and political inequality, what we can say is that transformation for and by oppressed peoples, as far as I know, has never finally come about by taking the facts of the case as settled. . . . So if political struggle persists and thus the belief in transforming America into a racially just society persists, it will do so by running ahead of the evidence needed to justify or make sense of the struggle itself. This is what [Anna Julia] Cooper and [William] James meant by the term 'Faith.'" Rogers, "Running ahead of the Evidence," 2.

33. FDP 5:141.

Abrams, M. H. *Natural Supernaturalism: Tradition and Revolution in Romantic Literature*. New York: W. W. Norton, 1971.

Acampora, Christa Davis. "Introduction." In *Critical Affinities: Reflections on the Connections between Nietzsche and African-American Thought*, edited by Jacqueline Scott and A. Todd Franklin, 1–16. Albany: State University of New York Press, 2006.

Acampora, Christa Davis. "Unlikely Illuminations: Nietzsche and Frederick Douglass on Power, Struggle and the Aisthesis of Freedom." In *Critical Affinities: Reflections on the Connections between Nietzsche and African-American Thought*, edited by Jacqueline Scott and A. Todd Franklin, 175–202. Albany: State University of New York Press, 2006.

Alfaro, Ange-Marie Hancock. "Black Masculinity Achieves Nothing without Restorative Care: An Intersectional Rearticulation of Frederick Douglass." In *A Political Companion to Frederick Douglass*, edited by Neil Roberts, 236–51. Lexington: University Press of Kentucky, 2018.

Alinsky, Saul D. *Rules for Radicals: A Pragmatic Primer for Realistic Radicals*. New York: Vintage Books, 1989.

Allen, Danielle S. *Talking to Strangers: Anxieties of Citizenship since Brown v. Board of Education*. Chicago: University of Chicago Press, 2004.

Andrews, William L. "*My Bondage and My Freedom* and the American Literary Renaissance of the 1850s." In *Critical Essays on Frederick Douglass*, edited by William L. Andrews, 133–47. Boston: G. K. Hall, 1991.

Andrews, William L. "Reunion in the Postbellum Slave Narrative: Frederick Douglass and Elizabeth Keckley." *Black American Literature Forum* 23, no. 1 (Spring 1989): 5–16.

Andrews, William L. *To Tell a Free Story: The First Century of Afro-American Autobiography, 1760–1865*. Urbana: University of Illinois Press, 1986.

Archuleta, Micki. "Life, Liberty, and the Pursuit of Happiness: A Fugitive Slave on Individual Rights and Community Responsibilities." *Nineteenth Century Studies* 19 (2005): 35–45.

Arendt, Hannah. *The Origins of Totalitarianism*. New York: World Publishing, 1958.

Augst, Thomas. "Frederick Douglass, between Speech and Print." In *Professing*

Rhetoric: Selected Papers from the 2000 Rhetoric Society of America Conference, edited by Frederick Antczak, Cinda Coggins, and Geoffrey D. Klinger, 53–61. Mahwah, NJ: Erlbaum, 2002.

Baker, Houston A., Jr. Blues, Ideology, and Afro-American Literature: A Vernacular Theory. Chicago: University of Chicago Press, 1984.

Baker, Houston A., Jr. Long Black Song: Essays in Black American Literature and Culture. Charlottesville: University Press of Virginia, 1972.

Balfour, Lawrie. The Evidence of Things Not Said: James Baldwin and the Promise of American Democracy. Ithaca, NY: Cornell University Press, 2001.

Balkin, Jack. Constitutional Redemption: Political Faith in an Unjust World. Cambridge, MA: Harvard University Press, 2011.

Ball, Charles, and Thomas Fisher. Fifty Years in Chains; or, The Life of an American Slave. New York: H. Dayton, 1858.

Barber, Benjamin. "Foundationalism and Democracy." In Democracy and Difference: Contesting the Boundaries of the Political, edited by Seyla Benhabib, 348–60. Princeton, NJ: Princeton University Press, 1996.

Beausoleil, Emily. "Responsibility as Responsiveness: Enacting a Dispositional Ethics of Encounter." Political Theory 45, no. 3 (2017): 291–318.

Benhabib, Seyla. Democracy and Difference: Contesting the Boundaries of the Political. Princeton, NJ: Princeton University Press, 1996.

Bennett, Nolan. "To Narrate and Denounce: Frederick Douglass and the Politics of Personal Narrative." Political Theory 44, no. 2 (2016): 240–64.

Bentley, Nancy. "The Fourth Dimension: Kinlessness and African American Narrative." Critical Inquiry 35, no. 2 (Winter 2009): 270–92.

Berlant, Lauren. "Poor Eliza." In No More Separate Spheres: A Next Wave Reader, edited by Cathy N. Davidson and Jessamyn Hatchers, 291–323. Durham, NC: Duke University Press, 2002.

Bernier, Celeste-Marie. "From Fugitive Slave to Fugitive Abolitionist: The Oratory of Frederick Douglass and the Emerging Heroic Slave Tradition." Atlantic Studies: Literary, Cultural, and Historical Perspectives 3, no. 2 (2006): 201–24.

Best, Stephen Michael. The Fugitive's Properties: Law and the Poetics of Possession. Chicago: University of Chicago Press, 2004.

Best, Stephen, and Saidiya Hartman. "Fugitive Justice." Representations 92, no. 1 (Fall 2005): 1–15.

Bickford, Susan. The Dissonance of Democracy: Listening, Conflict, and Citizenship. Ithaca, NY: Cornell University Press, 1996.

Black, Kelvin C. "Frederick Douglass' Differing Opinions of the Pro-slavery Character of the American Union." Qui Parle 16, no. 1 (Summer 2006): 145–69.

Blassingame, John W. The Slave Community: Plantation Life in the Antebellum South. Oxford: Oxford University Press, 1972.

Blight, David W. Frederick Douglass' Civil War: Keeping Faith in Jubilee. Baton Rouge: Louisiana State University Press, 1989.

Blight, David W. *Frederick Douglass: Prophet of Freedom*. New York: Simon and Schuster, 2018.

Bogues, Anthony. "And What about the Human? Freedom, Human Emancipation, and the Radical Imagination." *boundary 2: An International Journal of Literature and Culture* 39, no. 3 (2012): 29–46.

Boxill, Bernard R. *Blacks and Social Justice*. Totowa, NJ: Rowman and Littlefield, 1984.

Boxill, Bernard R. "Douglass against the Emigrationists." In *Frederick Douglass: A Critical Reader*, edited by Bill E. Lawson and Frank M. Kirkland, 21–49. Oxford: Blackwell, 1999.

Boxill, Bernard R. "Fear and Shame as Forms of Moral Suasion in the Thought of Frederick Douglass." *Transactions of the Charles S. Peirce Society* 31, no. 4 (1995): 713–44.

Boxill, Bernard R. "Two Traditions in African-American Political Philosophy." *Philosophical Forum* 24, nos. 1–2 (1992–93): 119–35.

Broadhead, Richard H. "Sparing the Rod: Discipline and Fiction in Antebellum America." *Representations* 21 (Winter 1988): 67–96.

Bromell, Nick. "Democratic Indignation: Black American Thought and the Politics of Dignity." *Political Theory* 41, no. 2 (April 2013): 285–311.

Bromell, Nick. "'That Third and Darker Thought': African-American Challenges to the Political Theories of Axel Honneth and Jacques Rancière." *Critical Philosophy of Race* 7, no. 2 (2019): 261–88.

Bromell, Nick. *The Time Is Always Now: Black Thought and the Transformation of U.S. Democracy*. New York: Oxford University Press, 2013.

Bromell, Nick. "A 'Voice from the Enslaved': The Origins of Frederick Douglass's Political Philosophy of Democracy." *American Literary History* 23, no. 4 (2011): 697–723.

Brooks, Daphne. *Bodies in Dissent: Spectacular Performances of Race and Freedom, 1850–1910*. Durham, NC: Duke University Press, 2006.

Brooks, Joanna. "The Early American Public Sphere and the Emergence of a Black Print Counterpublic." *William and Mary Quarterly*, Third Series, vol. 62, no. 1 (January 2005): 67–92.

Brown, William Wells. *The Black Man: His Antecedents, His Genius, and His Achievements*. New York: Thomas Hamilton, 1863.

Buccola, Nick. "'The Human Heart Is a Seat of Constant War': Frederick Douglass on Human Nature." In *A Political Companion to Frederick Douglass*, edited by Neil Roberts, 252–82. Lexington: University Press of Kentucky, 2018.

Buccola, Nick. *The Political Thought of Frederick Douglass*. New York: New York University Press, 2012.

Buell, Lawrence. *The Environmental Imagination: Thoreau, Nature Writing, and the Formation of American Culture*. Cambridge, MA: Harvard University Press, 1995.

Butler, Broadus N. "Frederick Douglass: The Black Philosopher in the United States—A Commentary." In Leonard Harris, *Philosophy Born of Struggle: Anthology of Afro-American Philosophy from 1917*. Dubuque, IA: Kendall Hunt, 1983.

Butler, Judith. *The Powers of Mourning and Violence*. London: Verso, 2004.

Butler, Judith. *The Psychic Life of Power: Theories in Subjection*. Stanford, CA: Stanford University Press, 1997.

Butler, Judith, Zeyneb Gambetti, and Leticia Sabsay, eds. *Vulnerability in Resistance*. Durham, NC: Duke University Press, 2018.

Camp, Stephanie M. H. *Closer to Freedom: Enslaved Women and Everyday Resistance in the Plantation South*. Chapel Hill: University of North Carolina Press, 2004.

Carrere, Marissa. "'As Child in Time': Childhood, Temporality, and 19th Century U.S. Literary Imaginings of Democracy." PhD diss., University of Massachusetts, 2015.

Cassuto, Leonard. "Frederick Douglass and the Work of Freedom: Hegel's Master-Slave Dialectic in the Fugitive Slave Narrative." *Prospects: An Annual Journal of American Cultural Studies* 21 (1996): 229–59.

Castronovo, Russ. "'As to Nation, I Belong to None': Ambivalence, Diaspora, and Frederick Douglass." *American Transcendental Quarterly* 9, no. 3 (September 1995): 245–60.

Castronovo, Russ, and Dana D. Nelson. "Fahrenheit 1861: Cross Patriotism in Melville and Douglass." In *Frederick Douglass and Herman Melville: Essays in Relation*, edited by Robert S. Levine and Samuel Otter, 329–48. Chapel Hill: University of North Carolina Press, 2008.

Chaffin, Tom. *Giant's Causeway: Frederick Douglass's Irish Odyssey and the Making of an American Visionary*. Charlottesville: University of Virginia Press, 2014.

Chaney, Michael A. "Heartfelt Thanks to Punch for the Picture: Frederick Douglass and the Transnational Jokework of Slave Caricature." *American Literature: A Journal of Literary History, Criticism, and Bibliography* 82, no. 1 (2010): 57–90.

Christian, Barbara. "The Race for Theory." The Nature and Context of Minority Discourse, *Cultural Contexts* 6 (Spring 1987): 51–63.

Colaiaco, James. *Frederick Douglass and the Fourth of July*. New York: Palgrave Macmillan, 2006.

Coles, Romand. *Rethinking Generosity: Critical Theory and the Politics of Caritas*. Ithaca, NY: Cornell University Press, 1997.

Collins, Patricia Hill. "Learning from the Outsider Within: The Sociological Significance of Black Feminist Thought." *Social Problems* 33, no. 6 (Oct.–Dec. 1986), S14–S32.

Combe, George. *The Constitution of Man, Considered in Relation to External Objects*. New York: W. H. Colyer, 1847.

Connolly, William E. *A World of Becoming*. Durham, NC: Duke University Press, 2011.

Cornell, Drucilla. *At the Heart of Freedom: Feminism, Sex, and Equality*. Princeton, NJ: Princeton University Press, 1998.

Coulthard, Glen S. *Red Skins, White Masks: Rejecting the Colonial Politics of Recognition*. Minneapolis: University of Minnesota Press, 2014.

Crane, Gregg D. *Race, Citizenship, and Law in American Literature*. Cambridge: Cambridge University Press, 2002.

Culbertson, Graham. "Frederick Douglass's 'Our National Capital': Updating L'Enfant for an Era of Integration." *Journal of American Studies* 48, no. 4 (2014): 911–35.

Dahl, Christian. "Unfreedom and the Crises of Witnessing: A Republican Perspective on the African American Slave Narratives." In *To Be Unfree: Republicanism and Unfreedom in History, Literature, and Philosophy*, edited by Christian Dahl and Tue Anderson Nexø, 213–28. Bielefeld, Germany: Transcript, 2014.

Dan-Cohen, Meir. *Dignity, Rank, and Rights*. Oxford: Oxford University Press, 2012.

Davis, Angela Y. "Lectures on Liberation." Los Angeles: National Committee to Free Angela Davis, 1971. Reprinted in *A Political Companion to Frederick Douglass*, edited by Neil Roberts, 107–134. Lexington: University Press of Kentucky, 2016.

Dawson, Michael C. *Black Visions: The Roots of Contemporary African-American Political Ideologies*. Chicago: University of Chicago Press, 2001.

DeLombard, Jeannine. "'Eye-Witness to the Cruelty': Southern Violence and Northern Testimony in Frederick Douglass's 1845 Narrative." *American Literature: A Journal of Literary History, Criticism, and Bibliography* 73, no. 2 (2001): 245–75.

DeLombard, Jeannine. *Slavery on Trial: Law, Abolition, and Print Culture*. Chapel Hill: University of North Carolina Press, 2007.

DePietro, Thomas. "Vision and Revision in the Autobiographies of Frederick Douglass." *CLA Journal* 26, no. 4 (June 1983): 384–96.

Diedrich, Maria. *Love across the Color Line: Ottilie Assing and Frederick Douglass*. New York: Hill and Wang, 1999.

Dilbeck, D. H. "An Antislavery Constitution and a Righteous Violence." In *Frederick Douglass: America's Prophet*, edited by D. H. Dilbeck, 75–90. Chapel Hill: University of North Carolina Press, 2018.

Dillon, Robin S., ed. *Dignity, Character, and Self-Respect*. New York: Routledge, 1995.

Dorsey, Peter A. "Becoming the Other: The Mimesis of Metaphor in Douglass's *My Bondage and My Freedom*." *PMLA* 111, no. 3 (May 1996): 435–50.

Douglass, Frederick. *The Frederick Douglass Papers*. 5 vols. Edited by John Blassingame. New Haven, CT: Yale University Press, 1979–92. Cited as FDP.

Douglass, Frederick. *The Heroic Slave: A Cultural and Critical Edition*. Edited by Robert S. Levine, John Stauffer, and John R. McKivigan, New Haven, CT: Yale University Press, 2015.

Douglass, Frederick. *Life and Times of Frederick Douglass*. In *Frederick Douglass: Auto-*

biographies. Edited by Henry Louis Gates Jr., 453–1048. New York: Library of America, 1994.

Douglass, Frederick. *The Life and Writings of Frederick Douglass.* 5 vols. Edited by Philip S. Foner. New York: International Publishers, 1950–75. Cited as LW.

Douglass, Frederick. *My Bondage and My Freedom.* In *Frederick Douglass: Autobiographies.* Edited by Henry Louis Gates Jr., 103–452. New York: Library of America, 1994.

Douglass, Frederick. *Narrative of the Life of Frederick Douglass.* In *Frederick Douglass: Autobiographies.* Edited by Henry Louis Gates Jr., 1–102. New York: Library of America, 1994.

Douglass, Frederick. "Slavery." Unpublished ms. in Frederick Douglass Papers at the Library of Congress. Speech, Article, and Book File. 66 pages. http://hdl .loc.gov/loc.mss/mfd.30001.

Douglass, Frederick. *The Speeches of Frederick Douglass.* Edited by John R. McKivigan, Julie Husband, and Heather L. Kaufman. New Haven, CT: Yale University Press, 2018.

Doyle, Laura, ed. *Bodies of Resistance: New Phenomenologies of Politics, Agency, and Culture.* Evanston, IL: Northwestern University Press, 2001.

Doyle, Laura. *Freedom's Empire: Race and the Rise of the Novel in Atlantic Modernity, 1640–1940.* Durham, NC: Duke University Press, 2008.

Drake, Kimberly. "Rewriting the American Self: Race, Gender, and Identity in the Autobiographies of Frederick Douglass and Harriet Jacobs." *Melus* 22, no. 4 (1997): 91–108.

Drexler, Michael J., and Ed White, eds. *Beyond Douglass: New Perspectives on Early African-American Literature.* Lewisburg, PA: Bucknell University Press, 2008.

Duane, Anna Mae. "'Like a Motherless Child': Racial Education at the New York African Free School and in *My Bondage and My Freedom*." *American Literature* 82, no. 3 (2010): 461–88.

Egan, Hugh. "'On Freedom': Emerson, Douglass, and the Self-Reliant Slave." *ESQ: A Journal of the American Renaissance* 60, no. 2 (2014): 183–208.

Ellis, Cristin. "Amoral Abolitionism: Frederick Douglass and the Environmental Case against Slavery." *American Literature* 86, no. 2 (2014): 275–303.

Ellis, Cristin. *Antebellum Posthuman: Race and Materiality in the Mid-Nineteenth Century.* New York: Fordham University Press, 2018.

Emerson, Ralph Waldo. "Self-Reliance." In *The Collected Works of Ralph Waldo Emerson*, vol. 2. Cambridge, MA: Harvard University Press, 1979: 27–51.

Ernest, John. *Chaotic Justice: Rethinking African American Literary History.* Chapel Hill: University of North Carolina Press, 2009.

Ernest, John. "Revolutionary Fictions and Activist Labor: Looking for Douglass and Melville Together." In *Frederick Douglass and Herman Melville: Essays in Relation*, edited by Robert S. Levine and Samuel Otter, 19–38. Chapel Hill: University of North Carolina Press, 2008.

Fagan, Benjamin. *The Black Newspaper and the Chosen Nation*. Athens: University of Georgia Press, 2016.

Fagan, Benjamin. "The North Star and the Atlantic 1848." *African American Review* 47, no. 1 (Spring 2014): 51–67.

Fanon, Frantz. *The Wretched of the Earth*. Translated by Richard Philcox. New York: Grove, 2004.

Fanuzzi, Robert. *Abolition's Public Sphere*. Minneapolis: University of Minnesota Press, 2003.

Fanuzzi, Robert. "Frederick Douglass's 'Colored Newspaper': Identity Politics in Black and White." In *The Black Press: New Literary and Historical Essays*, edited by Todd Vogel, 55–70. New Brunswick, NJ: Rutgers University Press, 2001.

Fanuzzi, Robert. "The Trouble with Douglass's Body." *American Transcendental Quarterly* 13, no. 1 (1999): 27–49.

Ferguson, Jeffrey. "Race and the Rhetoric of Resistance." *Raritan* 28, no. 1 (Summer 2008): 4–32.

Feuerbach, Ludwig. *The Essence of Christianity*. Translated by George Eliot. New York: Harper and Row, 1957.

Finseth, Ian Frederick. *Shades of Green: Visions of Nature in the Literature of American Slavery, 1770–1860*. Athens: University of Georgia Press, 2009.

Foner, Philip S., ed. *Douglass on Women's Rights*. Westport, CT: Greenwood Press, 1976.

Foner, Philip S., and George E. Walker, eds. *Proceedings of the Black State Conventions 1840–1865*, vol. 1. Philadelphia: Temple University Press, 1979.

Foster, Frances Smith. "A Narrative of the Interesting Origins and (Somewhat) Surprising Developments of African American Print Culture." *American Literary History* 17, no. 4 (Winter 2005): 714–40.

Fought, Leigh. *Women in the World of Frederick Douglass*. New York: Oxford University Press, 2017.

Franchot, Jenny. "The Punishment of Esther: Frederick Douglass and the Construction of the Feminine." In *Frederick Douglass: New Literary and Historical Essays*, edited by Eric J. Sundquist, 141–65. Cambridge: Cambridge University Press, 1990.

Frank, Jason. *Constituent Moments: Enacting the People in Postrevolutionary America*. Durham, NC: Duke University Press, 2010.

Frank, Jason. "Logical Revolts: Jacques Rancière and Political Subjectivization." *Political Theory* 43, no. 2 (April 2015): 249–61.

Frey, Raymond. "Douglass, Slavery, and Original Intent." *Proteus: A Journal of Ideas* 12, no. 1 (1995): 15–17.

Fritz, Meaghan M., and Frank E. Fee. "To Give the Gift of Freedom: Gift Books and the War on Slavery." *American Periodicals: A Journal of History, Criticism, and Bibliography* 23, no. 1 (2013): 60–82.

Gaines, Kevin K. *Uplifting the Race: Black Leadership, Politics, and Culture in the Twenti-eth Century*. Chapel Hill: University of North Carolina Press, 1996.

Ganter, Granville. "'He Made Us Laugh Some': Frederick Douglass's Humor." *African American Review* 37, no. 4 (2003): 535–52.

Garrison, William Lloyd. "Dissolution of the Union Essential to the Abolition of Slavery" (September 24, 1855). In *American Datelines: Major News Stories from Colonial Times to the Present*, edited by Ed Cray, Jonathan Kotler, and Miles Beller, 41–43. New York: Facts on File, 1990.

Gates, Henry Louis, Jr. *Black Literature and Literary Theory*. New York: Methuen, 1984.

Gates, Henry Louis, Jr. *Figures in Black: Words, Signs, and the "Racial" Self*. Oxford: Oxford University Press, 1987.

Gates, Henry Louis, Jr. *"Race," Writing, and Difference*. Chicago: University of Chicago Press, 1986.

Gates, Henry Louis, Jr. *The Signifying Monkey: A Theory of Afro-American Literary Criticism*. New York: Oxford University Press, 1988.

Gavin, William J. *William James and the Reinstatement of the Vague*. Philadelphia: Temple University Press, 1992.

Gikandi, Simon. *Slavery and the Culture of Taste*. Princeton: Princeton University Press, 2011.

Giles, Paul. "Douglass's Black Atlantic: Britain, Europe, Egypt." In *The Cambridge Companion to Frederick Douglass*, edited by Maurice S. Lee, 132–45. Cambridge: Cambridge University Press, 2009.

Giles, Paul. "Narrative Reversals and Power Exchanges: Frederick Douglass and British Culture." *American Literature: A Journal of Literary History, Criticism, and Bibliography* 73, no. 4 (Dec. 2001): 779–810.

Gillman, Sandra, and Alys Eve Weinbaum, eds. *Next to the Color Line: Gender, Sexuality, and W. E. B. Du Bois*. Minneapolis: University of Minnesota Press, 2006.

Gilmore, Paul. "Aesthetic Power: Electric Words and the Example of Frederick Douglass." *American Transcendental Quarterly* 16, no. 4 (December 2002): 291–311.

Gilroy, Paul. *The Black Atlantic: Modernity and Double Consciousness*. Cambridge, MA: Harvard University Press, 1993.

Golden, Timothy J. "From Epistemology to Ethics: Theoretical and Practical Reason in Kant and Douglass." *Journal of Religious Ethics* 44, no. 4 (December 2012): 603–28.

Golden, Timothy J. "Morality, Art, and the Self: Existentialism in Frederick Douglass and Søren Kierkegaard." In *Existentialist Thought in African American Literature before 1940*, edited by Melvin G. Hill, 1–20. Lanham, MD: Lexington Books, 2016.

Goldstein, Leslie F. "Violence as an Instrument for Social Change: The Views of Frederick Douglass," *Journal of Negro History* 61, no. 1 (January 1976): 61–72.

Goodell, William. *Views of American Constitutional Law, in Its Bearing upon American Slavery*, 2nd ed. Utica, NY: Lawson and Chaplin, 1845.

Gooding-Williams, Robert. "The Du Bois–Washington Debate and the Idea of Dignity." In *To Shape a New World: Essays on the Political Philosophy of Martin Luther King, Jr.*, edited by Tommie Shelby and Brandon M. Terry, 19–34. Cambridge, MA: Harvard University Press, 2018.

Gooding-Williams, Robert. *In the Shadow of Du Bois: Afro-Modern Political Thought in America*. Cambridge, MA: Harvard University Press, 2009.

Gordon, Lewis. "Theory in Black: Teleological Suspensions in Philosophy of Culture." *Qui Parle* 18, no. 2 (2010): 193–214.

Gorodeisky, Keren. "19th Century Romantic Aesthetics." In *The Stanford Encyclopedia of Philosophy*, edited by Edward N. Zalta, last modified 2016. https://plato.stanford.edu/archives/fall2016/entries/aesthetics-19th-romantic/.

Gougeon, Len. "Militant Abolitionism: Douglass, Emerson, and the Rise of the Anti-slave." *New England Quarterly: A Historical Review of New England Life and Letters* 85, no. 4 (Dec. 2012): 622–57.

Gregory, James Monroe. *Frederick Douglass the Orator*. Chicago: Afro-Am, 1969. First published Springfield, MA: Willey, 1893.

Hahn, Steven. *A Nation under Our Feet: Black Political Struggles in the Rural South, from Slavery to the Great Migration*. Cambridge, MA: Harvard University Press, 2003.

Hamilton, Cynthia S. "Models of Agency: Frederick Douglass and 'The Heroic Slave.'" *Proceedings of the American Antiquarian Society: A Journal of American History and Culture through 1876* 114, no. 1 (Oct. 2004): 87–136.

Hanlon, Christopher. *America's England: Antebellum Literature and Atlantic Sectionalism*. New York: Oxford University Press, 2013.

Harris, Leonard. *Philosophy Born of Struggle: Anthology of Afro-American Philosophy from 1917*. Dubuque, IA: Kendall Hunt, 1983.

Hartman, Saidiya. *Scenes of Subjection: Terror, Slavery, and Self-Making in Nineteenth-Century America*. New York: Oxford University Press, 1997.

Hartman, Saidiya. *Your Mother: A Journey along the Atlantic Slave Route*. New York: Farrar, Straus and Giroux, 2007.

Havercroft, Jonathan, and David Owen. "Soul Blindness, Police Orders and Black Lives Matter: Wittgenstein, Cavell, and Rancière." *Political Theory* 44, no. 6 (July 2016): 739–63.

Hesse, Barnor. "Escaping Liberty: Western Hegemony, Black Fugitivity." *Political Theory* 42, no. 3 (June 2014): 288–313.

Hickman, Jared. "Douglass Unbound." *Nineteenth-Century Literature* 68, no. 3 (2013): 323–62.

Hirsch, Alexander. "Fugitive Reconciliation: The Agonistics of Respect, Resentment, and Responsibility in Post-conflict Society." *Contemporary Political Theory* 10, no. 2 (2011): 166–89.

Holland, Frederic May. *Frederick Douglass: The Colored Orator.* New York: Negro Universities Press, 1970. First published in New York: Funk and Wagnalls, 1895.

Honig, Bonnie. "Declarations of Independence: Arendt and Derrida on the Problem of Founding a Republic." *American Political Science Review* 85, no. 1 (March 1991): 97–113.

Honig, Bonnie. *Political Theory and the Displacement of Politics.* Ithaca, NY: Cornell University Press, 1993.

Honneth, Axel. *The Struggle for Recognition: The Moral Grammar of Social Conflicts.* Translated by Joel Anderson. Boston: MIT Press, 1996.

Hooker, Juliet. "'A Black Sister to Massachusetts': Latin America and the Fugitive Democratic Ethos of Frederick Douglass." *American Political Science Review* 109, no. 4 (2015): 690–702.

Hooker, Juliet. *Theorizing Race in the Americas: Douglass, Sarmiento, Du Bois, and Vasconcelos.* New York. Oxford University Press, 2017.

Horseman, Reginald. *Race and Manifest Destiny: The Origins of American Racial Anglo-Saxonism.* Cambridge, MA: Harvard University Press, 1981.

Hunter, William R. "To the Wilderness and Back: The Role of Nature in Frederick Douglass's Narrative of the Life." In *Literature, Writing, and the Natural World,* edited by James Guignard and T. P. Murphy, 96–107. Newcastle upon Tyne: Cambridge Scholars, 2009.

Hutchins, Zachary McLeod. "Rejecting the Root: The Liberating, Anti-Christ Theology of Douglass's Narrative." *Nineteenth-Century Literature* 68, no. 3 (2013): 292–322.

Insko, Jeffrey. *History, Abolition, and the Ever-Present Now in Antebellum American Writing.* New York: Oxford University Press, 2018.

Jacobs, Harriet. *Incidents in the Life of a Slave Girl.* New York: Signet Classics, 2010.

James, Joy, ed. *The Angela Y. Davis Reader.* Oxford: Blackwell, 1998.

James, William. *Principles of Psychology.* In *William James: The Essential Writings,* edited by Bruce Wilshire, 44–61. Albany: State University of New York Press, 1984.

Jay, Gregory S. "American Literature and the New Historicism: The Example of Frederick Douglass." *boundary 2: An International Journal of Literature and Culture* 17, no. 1 (Spring 1990): 211–42.

Jenkins, Lee. "'The Black O'Connell': Frederick Douglass and Ireland." *Nineteenth Century Studies* 13, no. 2 (Winter 1999): 22–46.

Jenkins, Melissa Shields. "'The Poets Are with Us': Frederick Douglass and John Milton." *Modern Language Studies* 38, no. 2 (2009): 12–27.

Jones, Douglas A. "Douglass' Impersonal." *ESQ: A Journal of the American Renaissance* 61, no. 1 (2015): 1–35.

Joseph, Peniel E. *Waiting 'til the Midnight Hour: A Narrative History of Black Power in America.* New York: Henry Holt, 2006.

King, Martin Luther, Jr. *A Testament of Hope: The Essential Writings and Speeches of Martin Luther King Jr.* Edited by James M. Washington. New York: Harper-Collins, 1986.

Kirkland, Frank. "Enslavement, Moral Suasion, and Struggles for Recognition: Frederick Douglass's Answer to the Question—'What Is Enlightenment?'" In *Frederick Douglass: A Critical Reader*, edited by Bill E. Lawson and Frank M. Kirkland, 243–310. Oxford: Blackwell, 1999.

Kohn, Margaret. "Frederick Douglass's Master-Slave Dialectic." In *A Political Companion to Frederick Douglass*, edited by Neil Roberts, 84–106. Lexington: University Press of Kentucky, 2018.

Krause, Sharon. *Civil Passions: Moral Sentiment and Democratic Deliberation*. Princeton, NJ: Princeton University Press, 2008.

Krause, Sharon. "Frederick Douglass: Non-sovereign Freedom and the Plurality of Political Resistance." In *African American Political Thought: A Collected History*, edited by Melvin L. Rogers and Jack Turner, 116–41. Chicago: University of Chicago Press, forthcoming.

Krause, Sharon. *Liberalism with Honor*. Cambridge, MA: Harvard University Press, 2002.

Laski, Gregory. *Untimely Democracy: The Politics of Progress after Slavery*. Oxford: Oxford University Press, 2018.

Lawson, Bill E., and Frank M. Kirkland, eds. *Frederick Douglass: A Critical Reader*. Oxford: Blackwell, 1999.

Leddy, Thomas. *The Extraordinary in the Ordinary: The Aesthetics of Everyday Life*. New York: Broadview, 2012.

Lee, Maurice S. *Slavery, Philosophy, and American Literature*. Cambridge: Cambridge University Press, 2005.

Levander, Caroline. "Witness and Participant: Frederick Douglass's Child." *Studies in American Fiction* 33, no. 2 (2005): 183–92.

Leverenz, David. *Manhood and the American Renaissance*. Ithaca, NY: Cornell University Press, 1989.

Levine, Robert S. "Frederick Douglass and Thomas Auld: Reconsidering the Reunion Narrative." *Journal of African American History* 99, nos. 1–2 (Winter–Spring 2014): 34–45.

Levine, Robert S. "Identity in the Autobiographies." In *The Cambridge Companion to Frederick Douglass*, edited by Maurice S. Lee, 31–45. Cambridge: Cambridge University Press, 2009.

Levine, Robert S. *The Lives of Frederick Douglass*. Cambridge, MA: Harvard University Press, 2016.

Levine, Robert S. *Martin Delany: A Documentary Reader*. Chapel Hill: University of North Carolina Press, 2003.

Levine, Robert S. *Martin Delany, Frederick Douglass, and the Politics of Representative Identity*. Chapel Hill: University of North Carolina Press, 1997.

Levine, Robert S., and Samuel Otter, eds. *Frederick Douglass and Herman Melville: Essays in Relation.* Chapel Hill: University of North Carolina Press, 2008.

Lloyd, Vincent. "The Affect of God's Law." In *A Political Companion to Frederick Douglass,* edited by Neil Roberts, 303–23. Lexington: University Press of Kentucky, 2018.

Locke, John. *The Works of John Locke.* Aalen, Germany: Scientia Verlag Aalen, 1963. First published in London: Printed for Thomas Tegg, 1823.

Lohman, Christoph, ed. *Radical Passion: Ottilie Assing's Reports from America and Letters to Frederick Douglass.* New York: Peter Lang, 1999.

Mailloux, Steven. "Re-marking Slave Bodies: Rhetoric as Production and Reception." *Philosophy and Rhetoric* 35, no. 2 (2002): 96–119.

Malcolm X. *Malcolm X Speaks.* Edited by George Breitman. New York: Grove, 1965.

Mandoki, Katya. *Everyday Aesthetics: Prosaics, the Play of Culture, and Social Identities.* Aldershot, UK: Ashgate, 2007.

Markell, Patchen. *Bound by Recognition.* Princeton, NJ: Princeton University Press, 2003.

Marrs, Cody. "Frederick Douglass in 1848." *American Literature* 85, no. 3 (September 2013): 447–73.

Martin, Waldo E. *The Mind of Frederick Douglass.* Chapel Hill: University of North Carolina Press, 1984.

Massumi, Brian, and Joel McKim. "Of Microperception and Micropolitics: An Interview with Brian Massumi." *Micropolitics: Exploring Ethico-Aesthetics. Inflexions: A Journal for Research-Creation* 3 (Oct. 2009): 1–20.

M'Baye, Babacar. "Radical and Nationalist Resistance in David Walker's and Frederick Douglass's Antislavery Narratives." In *Literature of Protest,* edited by Kimberly Drake, 113–43. Ipswich, MA: Salem, 2013.

Mbembe, Achille. *Necropolitics.* Durham, NC: Duke University Press, 2019.

McBride, Dwight A. *Impossible Witnesses: Truth, Abolitionism, and Slave Testimony.* New York: New York University Press, 2001.

McClish, Glen. "Frederick Douglass and the Consequences of Rhetoric: The Interpretive Framing and Publication History of the 2 January 1893 Haiti Speeches." *Rhetorica: A Journal of the History of Rhetoric* 30, no. 1 (2012): 37–73.

McDaniel, W. Caleb. *The Problem of Democracy in the Age of Slavery: Garrisonian Abolitionists and Transatlantic Reform.* Baton Rouge: Louisiana State University Press, 2013.

McDowell, Deborah. "In the First Place: Making Frederick Douglass and the Afro-American Narrative Tradition." In *Frederick Douglass, Narrative of the Life of Frederick Douglass, an American Slave, Written by Himself.* Edited by William L. Andrews and William S. McFeely, 172–83. New York: Norton, 1997.

McFeeley, William. *Frederick Douglass.* New York: W. W. Norton, 1991.

McKivigan, John R., and Stanley Harrold. *Antislavery Violence: Sectional, Racial,* and Cultural Conflict in Antebellum America. Knoxville: University of Tennessee Press, 1999.

McQuillan, Jennifer. "Parsing the Body: Frederick Douglass and the Recorporealization of Self." *Proteus: A Journal of Ideas* 28, no. 1 (2012): 23–28.

Melish, Joanne Pope. *Disowning Slavery: Gradual Emancipation and "Race" in New England, 1780–1860*. Ithaca, NY: Cornell University Press, 1998.

Mills, Charles W. *Blackness Visible: Essays on Philosophy and Race*. Ithaca, NY: Cornell University Press, 1998.

Mills, Charles W. *The Racial Contract*. Ithaca, NY: Cornell University Press, 1997.

Moses, Wilson Jeremiah. *Creative Conflict in African American Thought*. Cambridge: Cambridge University Press, 2009.

Moses, Wilson Jeremiah. "'The Ever-Present Now': Frederick Douglass's Pragmatic Constitutionalism." *Journal of African American History* 99, nos. 1–2 (Winter–Spring 2014): 71–88.

Moten, Fred. *In the Break: The Aesthetics of the Black Radical Tradition*. Minneapolis: University of Minnesota Press, 2003.

Myers, Peter C. *Frederick Douglass: Race and the Rebirth of American Liberalism*. Lawrence: University Press of Kansas, 2008.

Nelson, Dana D. *National Manhood: Capitalist Citizenship and the Imagined Fraternity of White Men*. Durham, NC: Duke University Press, 1998.

Newman, Lance. "Free Soil and the Abolitionist Forests of Frederick Douglass's 'The Heroic Slave.'" *American Literature* 81, no. 1 (March 2009): 127–52

Nielsen, Cynthia R. "Resistance Is Not Futile: Frederick Douglass on Panoptic Plantations and the Un-making of Docile Bodies and Enslaved Souls." *Philosophy and Literature* 35, no. 2 (2011): 251–68.

Noble, Marianne. "Sympathetic Listening in Frederick Douglass's 'The Heroic Slave' and *My Bondage and My Freedom*." *Studies in American Fiction* 34, no. 1 (Spring 2006): 53–68.

Nwanko, Ifeoma C. K. *Black Cosmopolitanism: Racial Consciousness and Transnational Identity in the Nineteenth-Century Americas*. Philadelphia: University of Pennsylvania Press, 2005.

Nwankwo, Ifeoma C. K. "Douglass's Black Atlantic: The Caribbean." In *The Cambridge Companion to Frederick Douglass*, edited by Maurice S. Lee, 146–59. Cambridge: Cambridge University Press, 2009.

Olney, James. "The Founding Fathers—Frederick Douglass and Booker T. Washington; or, The Idea of Democracy and a Tradition of African-American Autobiography." *Amerikastudies/American Studies* 35 (1990): 281–96.

Patterson, Orlando. *Slavery and Social Death: A Comparative Study*. Cambridge, MA: Harvard University Press, 1982.

Pease, William H., and Jane H. Pease. *The Antislavery Argument*. Indianapolis: Bobbs-Merrill, 1965.

Peterson, Carla L. *Doers of the Word: African-American Women Speakers and Writers in the North (1830–1860)*. New York: Oxford University Press, 1995.

Polyné, Millery. *From Douglass to Duvalier: U.S. African Americans, Haiti, and Pan Americanism, 1870–1964*. Gainesville: University Press of Florida, 2010.

Pratt, Lloyd Presley. *Archives of American Time: Literature and Modernity in the Nineteenth Century*. Philadelphia: University of Pennsylvania Press, 2010.

Pratt, Lloyd Presley. "Progress, Labor, Revolution: The Modern Times of Antebellum African American Life Writing." *Novel: A Forum on Fiction* 34, no. 1 (2000): 56–76.

Pratt, Lloyd Presley. *The Strangers Book: The Human of African-American Literature*. Philadelphia: University of Pennsylvania Press, 2016.

Preston, Dickson J. *Young Frederick Douglass: The Maryland Years*. Baltimore: Johns Hopkins University Press, 2018.

Quarles, Benjamin. *Frederick Douglass*. Washington, DC: Associated Publishers, 1948.

Quashie, Kevin E. *The Sovereignty of Quiet: Beyond Resistance in Black Culture*. New Brunswick, NJ: Rutgers University Press, 2012.

Rancière, Jacques. *The Aesthetic Unconscious*. Translated by Debra Keates and James Swenson. Cambridge, UK: Polity, 2009.

Rancière, Jacques. *Dis-agreement: Politics and Philosophy*. Translated by Julie Rose. Minneapolis: University of Minnesota Press, 1999.

Rancière, Jacques. "Ten Theses on Politics." Translated by R. Bowlby and D. Panagia. *Theory and Event* 5, no. 3 (2001): 1–33.

Rankine, Claudia. *Citizen: An American Lyric*. Minneapolis: Graywolf Press, 2014.

Rawls, John. "Justice as Fairness: Political Not Metaphysical." *Philosophy and Public Affairs* 14, no. 3 (1985): 223–51.

Reynolds, Larry J. *European Revolutions and the American Literary Renaissance*. New Haven, CT: Yale University Press, 1988.

Riss, Arthur. *Race, Slavery, and Liberalism in Nineteenth-Century American Literature*. New York: Cambridge University Press, 2006.

Riss, Arthur. "Sentimental Douglass." In *The Cambridge Companion to Frederick Douglass*, edited by Maurice S. Lee, 103–17. Cambridge: Cambridge University Press, 2009.

Roberts, Neil. *Freedom as Marronage*. Chicago: University of Chicago Press, 2015.

Roberts, Neil, ed. *A Political Companion to Frederick Douglass*. Lexington: University Press of Kentucky, 2018.

Roberts, Neil. "Recognition, Power, and Agency: The Recent Contributions of Axel Honneth to Critical Theory." *Political Theory* 37, no. 2 (2009): 296–309.

Robinson, Cedric J. *Black Marxism: The Making of the Black Radical Tradition*. Chapel Hill: University of North Carolina Press, 1983.

Roediger, David R. *The Wages of Whiteness: Race and the Making of the American Working Class*. London: Verso, 1991.

Rogers, Melvin L. "David Walker and the Political Power of Appeal." *Political Theory* 43, no. 2 (April 2015): 208–33.

Rogers, Melvin L. "Running ahead of the Evidence: A Meditation on Delany's Pessimism and Douglass's Faith." Paper presented at the conference on Rethinking the Black Intellectual Tradition: Pessimism as an Interpretative Frame, Amherst College, Amherst, MA, March 30, 2019.

Rosanvallon, Pierre. *Democracy Past and Future*. Edited and translated by Samuel Moyne. New York: Columbia University Press, 2006.

Rosen, Michael. *Dignity: Its History and Meaning*. Cambridge, MA: Harvard University Press, 2012.

Rowe, John Carlos. "Between Politics and Poetics: Frederick Douglass and Postmodernity." In *Reconstructing American Literary and Historical Studies*, edited by Günter H. Lenz, 192–210. Frankfurt: Campus Verlag, 1990.

Rusert, Britt. *Fugitive Science: Empiricism and Freedom in Early African American Culture*. New York: New York University Press, 2017.

Ryan, Susan M. *The Grammar of Good Intentions: Race and the Antebellum Culture of Benevolence*. Ithaca, NY: Cornell University Press, 2003.

Sale, Maggie Montesinos. *The Slumbering Volcano: American Slave Ship Revolts and the Production of Rebellious Masculinity*. Durham, NC: Duke University Press, 1997.

Sandel, Michael. *Democracy's Discontent: America in Search of a Public Philosophy*. Cambridge, MA: Harvard University Press, 1996.

Schiff, Jade Larissa. *Burdens of Political Responsibility: Narrative and the Cultivation of Responsiveness*. Cambridge: Cambridge University Press, 2014.

Schrader, David E. "Natural Law in the Constitutional Thought of Fredrick Douglass." In *Frederick Douglass: A Critical Reader*, edited by Bill E. Lawson and Frank M. Kirkland, 85–99. Oxford: Blackwell, 1999.

Schudson, Michael. *The Good Citizen: A History of American Civic Life*. New York: Free Press, 1998.

Scott, Jacqueline, and A. Todd Franklin. *Critical Affinities: Nietzsche and African American Thought*. Albany: State University of New York Press, 2006.

Sekora, John. "'Mr. Editor, If You Please': Frederick Douglass, *My Bondage and My Freedom*, and the End of the Abolitionist Imprint." *Callaloo: A Journal of African American and African Arts and Letters* 17, no. 2 (1994): 608–26.

Shelby, Tommie, and Brandon M. Terry, eds. *To Shape a New World: Essays on the Political Philosophy of Martin Luther King, Jr.* Cambridge, MA: Harvard University Press, 2018.

Shulman, George. *American Prophecy: Race and Redemption in American Political Culture*. Minneapolis: University of Minnesota Press, 2008.

Shulman, George. "Thinking Authority Democratically: Prophetic Practices, White Supremacy, and Democratic Politics." *Political Theory* 36, no. 5 (2008): 708–34.

Sinha, Manisha. *The Slave's Cause: A History of Abolition*. New Haven, CT: Yale University Press, 2016.

Smith, Kimberly K. "Black Agrarianism and the Foundations of Black Environmental Thought." *Environmental Ethics* 26, no. 3 (Fall 2004): 267–86.

Smith, Kimberly K. *The Dominion of Voice: Riot, Reason, and Romance in Antebellum Politics*. Lawrence: University of Kansas Press, 1999.

Smith, Rogers M. *Civic Ideals: Conflicting Visions of Citizenship in U.S. History*. New Haven, CT: Yale University Press, 1997.

Smith, Stephanie A. "Heart Attacks: Frederick Douglass's Strategic Sentimentality." *Criticism* 34, no. 2 (1992): 193–216.

Sokoloff, William W. "Frederick Douglass and the Politics of Rage." *New Political Science* 36, no. 3 (2014): 330–45.

Spires, Derrick R. *The Practice of Citizenship: Black Politics and Early Print Culture in the Early United States*. Philadelphia: University of Pennsylvania Press, 2019.

Stauffer, John. *The Black Hearts of Men: Radical Abolitionists and the Transformation of Race*. Cambridge, MA: Harvard University Press, 2002.

Stauffer, John. "Douglass's Self-Making and the Culture of Abolitionism." In *The Cambridge Companion to Frederick Douglass*, edited by Maurice S. Lee, 13–30. Cambridge: Cambridge University Press, 2009.

Stauffer, John. "Frederick Douglass and the Aesthetics of Freedom." *Raritan* 25, no. 1 (2005): 114–36.

Stauffer, John. *Giants: The Parallel Lives of Frederick Douglass and Abraham Lincoln*. New York: Twelve, 2008.

Stephens, Gregory. "Arguing with a Monument: Frederick Douglass' Resolution of the 'White Man Problem' in His 'Oration in Memory of Lincoln.'" *Comparative American Studies: An International Journal* 13, no. 3 (2015): 129–45.

Stepto, Robert B. *From behind the Veil: A Study of Afro-American Narrative*. Urbana: University of Illinois Press, 1979.

Stepto, Robert B. "Storytelling in Afro-American Fiction: Frederick Douglass's 'The Heroic Slave.'" In *Critical Essays on Frederick Douglass*, edited by William L. Andrews, 108–21. Boston: G. K. Hall, 1991.

Stewart, Maria W. *Maria Stewart, America's First Black Woman Political Writer: Speeches and Essays*. Edited by Marilyn Richardson. Bloomington: Indiana University Press, 1987.

Story, Joseph. *The Constitutional Class Book: Being a Brief Exposition of the Constitution of the United States Designed for the Use of the Higher Classes in Common Schools*. Boston: Hilliard, Gray and Company, 1834.

Stuckey, P. Sterling. "Afterword: Frederick Douglass and W. E. B. Du Bois on the Consciousness of the Enslaved Author(s)." *Journal of African American History* 91, no. 4 (Autumn 2006): 451–58.

Stuckey, P. Sterling. "'Ironic Tenacity': Frederick Douglass's Seizure of the Dialectic." In *Frederick Douglass: New Literary and Historical Essays*, edited by Eric J. Sundquist, 23–41. New York: Cambridge University Press, 1993

Sullivan, William. *The Political Class Book: Intended to Instruct the Higher Classes in Schools in the Origin, Nature, and Use of Political Power.* Boston: Carter, Hendee, 1832.

Sundquist, Eric J. *Frederick Douglass: New Literary and Historical Essays.* New York: Cambridge University Press, 1993.

Sundquist, Eric J. *To Wake the Nations: Race in the Making of American Literature.* Cambridge, MA: Harvard University Press, 1993.

Sundstrom, Ronald. "Frederick Douglass's Longing for the End of Race." *Philosophia Africana: Analysis of Philosophy and Issues in Africa and the Black Diaspora* 8, no. 2 (2005): 143–70.

Sweeney, Fionnghuala. *Frederick Douglass and the Atlantic World.* Liverpool: Liverpool University Press, 2007.

Takaki, Ronald. *Violence in the Black Imagination: Essays and Documents.* New York: Oxford University Press, 1993.

Tamarkin, Elisa. "Black Anglophilia; or, The Sociability of Antislavery." *American Literary History* 14, no. 3 (2002): 444–78.

Tang, Edward. "Rebirth of a Nation: Frederick Douglass as Postwar Founder in Life and Times." *Journal of American Studies* 39, no. 1 (2005): 19–39.

Thomas, Helen. *Romanticism and Slave Narratives: Transatlantic Testimonies.* Cambridge: Cambridge University Press, 2000.

Tocqueville, Alexis de. *Democracy in America.* Translated by Harvey C. Mansfield and Delba Winthrop. Chicago: University of Chicago Press, 2000.

Trodd, Zoe. "A Hole Story: The Space of Historical Memory in the Abolitionist Imagination." In *Agency in the Margins: Stories of Outsider Rhetoric*, edited by Anne Meade Stockdell-Giesler, 68–90. Madison, NJ: Fairleigh Dickinson University Press, 2010.

Ture, Kwame, and Charles V. Hamilton. *Black Power: The Politics of Liberation.* New York: Vintage Books, 1992.

Turner, Jack. *Awakening to Race: Individualism and Social Consciousness in America.* Chicago: University of Chicago Press, 2012.

Turner, Jack. "Douglass and Political Judgment: The Post-Reconstruction Years." In *A Political Companion to Frederick Douglass*, edited by Neil Roberts, 203–35. Lexington: University Press of Kentucky, 2018.

Vogel, Todd, ed. *The Black Press: New Literary and Historical Essays.* New Brunswick, NJ: Rutgers University Press, 2001.

Vogel, Todd. *Rewriting White: Race, Class, and Cultural Capital in Nineteenth-Century America.* New Brunswick, NJ: Rutgers University Press, 2004.

Wagner, Bryan. *Disturbing the Peace: Black Culture and the Police Power after Slavery.* Cambridge, MA: Harvard University Press, 2009.

Waldron, Jeremy. *Dignity, Rank, and Rights*. Oxford: Oxford University Press, 2012.

Walker, David. *Appeal to the Coloured Citizens of the World*. Edited by Peter P. Hinks. University Park: Pennsylvania State University Press, 2000.

Walker, Peter F. *Moral Choices: Memory, Desire, and Imagination in Nineteenth-Century American Abolition*. Baton Rouge: Louisiana State University Press, 1978.

Wallace, Maurice O. "Violence, Manhood, and War in Douglass." In *The Cambridge Companion to Frederick Douglass*, edited by Maurice S. Lee, 73–88. Cambridge: Cambridge University Press, 2009.

Weil, Simone. "The Iliad, or The Poem of Force." In *On Violence: A Reader*, edited by Bruce B. Lawrence and Aisha Karim, 377–90. Durham, NC: Duke University Press, 2007.

Weinauer, Ellen. "Writing Revolt in the Wake of Nat Turner: Frederick Douglass and the Construction of Black Domesticity in 'The Heroic Slave.'" *Studies in American Fiction* 33, no. 2 (2005): 193–202.

West, Cornel. *The American Evasion of Philosophy: A Genealogy of Pragmatism*. Madison: University of Wisconsin Press, 1989.

Whitman, Walt. *Democratic Vistas*. Iowa City: University of Iowa Press, 2010.

Wilentz, Sean. *The Rise of American Democracy: Jefferson to Lincoln*. New York: W. W. Norton, 2005.

Wilshire, Bruce, ed. *William James: The Essential Writings*. Albany: State University Press of New York, 1984.

Wilson, Ivy G. "On Native Ground: Transnationalism, Frederick Douglass, and 'The Heroic Slave.'" PMLA: *Publications of the Modern Language Association of America* 121, no. 2 (2006): 453–68.

Wilson, Ivy G. *Specters of Democracy: Blackness and the Aesthetics of Politics in the Antebellum U.S.* New York: Oxford University Press, 2011.

Wolin, Sheldon S. "Fugitive Democracy." In *Democracy and Difference: Contesting the Boundaries of the Political*, edited by Seyla Benhabib, 31–45. Princeton, NJ: Princeton University Press, 1996.

Wood, Mark F. "Crises of Authority: Honor Violence in Nineteenth-Century American Literature." *Dissertation Abstracts International, Section A: The Humanities and Social Sciences* 68, no. 4 (2007): 1465–65.

Wynter, Sylvia. "Unsettling the Coloniality of Being/Power/Truth/Freedom: Toward the Human, after Man—An Argument." CR: *The New Centennial Review* 3, no. 3 (Fall 2003): 257–337.

Yancy, George. "African-American Philosophy: Through the Lens of Socio-existential Struggle." *Philosophy and Social Criticism* 37, no. 5 (2011): 551–74.

Yancy, George. *Black Bodies, White Gazes: The Continuing Significance of Race in America*. Lanham, MD: Rowman and Littlefield, 2016.

Yancy, George. "Through the Crucible of Pain and Suffering: African-American Philosophy as a Gift and the Countering of the Western Philosophical Metanarrative." *Educational Philosophy and Theory* 47, no. 11 (Nov. 2015): 1143–59.

Young, Iris. M. "Asymmetrical Reciprocity: On Moral Respect, Wonder, and En-larged Thought." *Constellations* 3, no. 3 (1997): 340–63.

Young, Iris M. *Responsibility for Justice*. New York: Oxford University Press, 2011.

Zafar, Rafia. "Franklinian Douglass: The Representative Afro-American Man." In *Frederick Douglass: New Literary and Historical Essays*, edited by Eric J. Sundquist, 199–217. New York: Cambridge University Press, 1990.

Zwarg, Christina. "The Work of Trauma: Fuller, Douglass, and Emerson on the Border of Ridicule." *Studies in Romanticism* 41, no. 1 (Spring 2002): 65–88.

INDEX

dehumanization, 220n4

Delany, Martin, 86–87, 98, 150, 223n6, 223n11, 230n5, 234n45

DeLombard, Jeannine, 211n7

democracy: and citizenship, 5, 37, 172; duties of, 15–16, 115, 181, 199; foundations of, 117–23; and fugitivity, 228n30; and relationality, 161–62; as a project, 16, 33, 228n38; theories of, 2, 16, 33–38, 82–83, 159, 177, 179; weaknesses in, 35, 54

Democratic Party, 183

Derrida, Jacques, 221n15, 227n27

Dewey, John, 191, 199

dignity: assertion of, 92, 162–63, 167, 175, 224n19; consciousness of, 12, 24, 32–33; denial of, 88, 96; Douglass's descriptions of, 12, 40–42, 56, 63, 75, 82, 134–35, 159, 210n28, 212n8, 212n18, 237n20; and humanness, 10, 29, 52–53, 77–81, 90, 93–94, 112, 132, 150, 157–58, 209–10n24, 222n30; and labor, 19–23, 54, 113; and politics, 95; and power, 43–45; recognition of, 19–24, 40–46, 90, 93–95, 133, 154, 166, 173, 179, 212n18; threats to, 21, 119; and worth, 4, 11–12, 19–20, 42–44, 82–83, 94–96, 129–35, 139–41, 148–50, 157–58. See also equality; freedom; liberty; manhood; worth

Dignity, Rank, and Rights (Waldron), 212n18

double consciousness, 188. See also consciousness

Douglass, Frederick: as an abolitionist, 17, 35–36, 39; and Black emigration, 15, 85–90; and Black nationalism, 186–97; childhood of, 47, 126–36, 139–40, 144–45, 149, 218n29, 230n3; and the Constitution, 228n38; and democracy, 82, 119; and emigration, 222–23n2; and ethic of care, 127, 132; as a feminist, 9–10, 131–32, 161–62; 179; fugitive rhetoric of, 8, 12, 22, 41, 56–57, 60, 65, 70–78, 107–9, 120, 180, 191–92, 201–5, 220n3; and humanness, 10–12, 15, 33, 82, 88, 115, 145, 172, 184–87, 203–4, 215nn3–4,

219n37; and inductive reasoning, 194; legacy of, 71, 90–91, 188–205, 220n10, 221n23, 236n12; perceived inconsistency of, 13, 102, 106, 110–11, 188, 212n8, 226n2, 229n1; perceptions of, 10, 40, 166, 170; and political awakening, 10, 13–14, 124–26, 131, 137, 139–51, 157–58, 224n19, 233n34; political philosophy of, 3–5, 34, 50, 62, 80, 134–35, 161–62, 189, 196–99, 207n3, 209n21, 212n18, 240n6; as a public figure, 1–2, 7, 12, 18, 124–25, 131; and race pride, 165; and reconciliation, 239n50; and slavery, 56, 63, 173–78; and social norms, 56; and visit to Britain, 18–19, 63. See also consciousness; dignity; faculties and powers; fugitive rhetoric; humanness; liberalism; power; public philosophy; racism; republicanism; resistance; Scottish philosophy; specific works

"Douglass Against the Emigrationists" (Boxill), 44

Drake, Kimberly, 231n13

Dred Scott decision, 200

Du Bois, W. E. B., 94, 188, 236n12

Durham, James, 87

duty, 113, 115, 118, 122, 166, 181

economics, 21–23, 170

education, 2, 85–86, 132, 193

Eliot, George, 218n32

Ellis, Cristin, 38, 215n2

Emancipation Proclamation, 202

Emerson, Ralph Waldo, 3, 47, 84, 192, 207–8n5, 216n8, 229n1

emigration, 31, 85, 89, 124, 159, 214n36, 222–23n2, 222n30, 230n5

energy, 26, 51, 85, 123, 150

enfranchisement, 25, 36, 159. See also women's suffrage

enslavement. See slavery

epistemology. See standpoint epistemology

equality, 35, 38, 56, 74, 84–87, 138, 165, 235n51, 242n32. *See also* dignity; freedom; liberty; power
Ernest, John, 170
Essence of Christianity, The (Feurbach), 52, 216n9, 234n42
ethic of care, 127, 132
ethics of intersubjectivity, 109
ethnology, 38, 41
Eurocentrism, 198
European revolutions, 25–27, 51, 123, 213n28

factory system, 20
faculties and powers: consciousness of, 73, 114–16, 144–46, 147, 156, 163, 235n56; and Douglass's philosophy, 12, 29, 41–44, 77, 82, 203, 213n22, 216n12, 216–17n14, 218n27; threats to, 96–98, 152. *See also* aesthetic power; humanness
Fagan, Benjamin, 208n6
family, 127–29, 133
Fanon, Frantz, 96, 198, 225n27
feminism, 9–10, 179, 221n15, 231n13. *See also* gender
Ferguson, Jeffery, 233n41
Feuerbach, Ludwig, 52, 216n9, 218n32, 234n42. *See also* humanness
Finseth, Ian, 148, 150
Fish, Stanley, 11
Foner, Philip, 3
Foucault, Michel, 219n36, 231–32n19
Frank, Jason, 228n35
"Frederick Douglass and the Aesthetics of Freedom" (Stauffer), 233n36
Free Black community, 14, 18–20, 23, 27–28, 51, 81, 85–90, 101. *See also* Blackness
freedom, 2–4, 40, 56, 62–64, 83–84, 105, 115, 120–22, 160, 166, 209n24, 217n17, 223–24n18. *See also* dignity; equality; liberty; power
Freeland, William, 114

free will, 114, 122
fugitive democracy, 177, 228n30
fugitive philosophy, 10, 97, 119
fugitive rhetoric, 12, 56–57, 60, 78
Fugitive Slave Act, 31, 74, 92, 124, 200
Fuller, Margaret, 47

Gaines, Kevin K., 213n25
game of strangerhood, 70
Gandhi, Mohandas K., 90–91
Garrison, William Lloyd, 1–2, 17–19, 61, 71, 86–87, 101–10, 189, 218n27, 229–30n1
Garrisonian abolitionism, 61, 71, 102, 227n27
Gates, Henry Louis, Jr., 59, 62, 70
gender, 6, 25, 31, 34, 42–43, 159, 209n21, 231n13, 235n56. *See also* feminism; manhood; women's suffrage
Gikandi, Simon, 59, 141, 144, 233n34
Gilroy, Paul, 209n22
Glidden, George, 41
"God's Law Outlawed" (Douglass), 40–41
Goldstein, Leslie F., 97, 223n11
Goodell, William, 37, 103, 214–15n50
Gooding-Williams, Robert, 3, 12, 164, 210n32, 222n30, 224n2, 236n12, 236–37n17
guilt, 47, 185, 218n30, 227n19

Hahn, Steven, 133
Hamilton, Charles, 76, 222n38
Harlan, Marshall, 237n20
Harper, Robert Goodloe, 19
Harrold, Stanley, 223n11
Hartman, Saidiya, 153, 231n15, 235n51
Hegel, 223–24n18, 236n57
Heroic Slave, The (Douglass), 95, 229–30n1
Hirsch, Alexander, 177
Hooker, Juliet, 5, 89, 119–20, 214n36, 228n30
Horseman, Reginald, 214n44
"'Human Heart, The'" (Buccola), 226n16
human interdependence, 75
humanism, 53, 196–98, 219n37, 222n30
humanness: and Douglass's philoso-

politics: and awakening to, 128, 144–55, 157; and black communities, 222n30; communities of, 6, 176, 179; definition of, 210n34; and dignity, 95; and parties, 202, 226n2; philosophy of, 12, 71, 178, 189, 215–16n5; and struggle, 242n32; and subjectification, 210n34; theories of, 3, 11, 124

politics of recognition, 224n23

power, 3–5, 9, 15, 24–33, 37–56, 76, 84, 91–96, 117, 144–57, 180–81, 202–4, 217n17, 219n36, 229n1, 235n51, 240n3. See also equality; freedom; liberty

pragmatism, 116, 191–93, 227n27, 240n5

Pratt, Lloyd, 70, 220n1

Preamble to the Constitution, 32, 121, 227n27

prejudice, 68, 169. See also racism

"Present Condition and Future Prospects of the Negro People, The" (Douglass), 89

prison-industrial complex, 15

progress, 26, 30, 58, 94, 128, 144–45, 199, 202–5, 213n25, 223–24n18, 241n15

prophetic mode, 192

public philosophy, 5–12, 33–37, 54, 166, 208n18, 209n24, 214n40, 219–20n37. See also liberalism; republicanism; Scottish philosophy

Publius, 35

Quashie, Kevin E., 149

race: understandings of, 6, 124, 161; visibility of, 36

"Race and the Rhetoric of Resistance" (Ferguson), 233n41

race pride, 88, 165, 183, 196

racism: by abolitionists, 1–2, 8–9, 68; as a cultural construct, 18–23, 30; as a form of oppression, 14; opposition to, 219n35, 219–20n37; persistence of, 14, 31, 55; responses to, 12, 159; and slavery, 5; as a structural issue, 170; and vio-

lence, 70–77; whites' responsibility for, 2, 5–12, 14–15, 18, 31–32, 74, 85–90, 161, 168, 175, 236–37n17, 241n12. See also anti-Blackness; microaggression; oppression; prejudice; segregation

Radical Abolitionists, 226n2. See also abolitionists

radical pastoral mode, 150

Rancière, Jacques, 13, 210n34, 226n9

Rankine, Claudia, 181

recognition (of dignity), 19–24, 40–46, 90, 93–95, 133, 154, 166, 173, 179, 212n18

Reconstruction, 14, 165–67, 238n36

religion, 77, 192, 204, 214n44, 216n9

Remond, Charles L., 73

republicanism, 3, 7, 15, 34. See also public philosophy

resistance: and dignity, 43, 110–13; forms of, 13–14, 49, 83, 124–26, 149, 151–58, 217–18n25, 233–34n41, 235n52; physical acts of, 79, 92–97, 130, 217n17. See also vulnerability

respectability, 29, 74, 132, 167

responsibility, 113, 115, 118, 122, 166, 181

reversal. See chiasmus

revolutions, 26, 105, 118, 161–62, 166, 199, 225n28

Reynolds, Larry J., 213n28

rhetorical style, 8, 22, 41, 215n2. See also fugitive rhetoric

rhetoric of appeal, 153, 157, 227n19, 235n48, 235n51

rights, 15, 27–33, 40–45, 73, 197, 214n43

Riss, Arthur, 139, 232n31

Roberts, Neil, 4–5, 64, 234n43

Robinson, Cedric, 209n22

Rochester Washington Square, 26

Roediger, David, 20–21, 36, 214n44

Rogers, Melvin, 153, 205, 242n32

Romantic individualism, 125

Romantic irony, 71–72. See also irony

romanticism, 46–47, 216n6, 234n43

Rosen, Michael, 217n20